The Feel of Success IN SELLING

The Feel of Success IN SELLING

JIM SCHNEIDER

PRENTICE HALL, Englewood Cliffs, New Jersey 07632

Prentice-Hall International (UK) Limited, *London*
Prentice-Hall of Australia Pty. Limited, *Sydney*
Prentice-Hall Canada, Inc., *Toronto*
Prentice-Hall Hispanoamericana, S.A., *Mexico*
Prentice-Hall of India Private Limited, *New Delhi*
Prentice-Hall of Japan, Inc., *Tokyo*
Simon & Schuster Asia Pte. Ltd., *Singapore*
Editora Prentice-Hall do Brasil, Ltda., *Rio de Janeiro*

10 9 8 7 6 5 4 3

Library of Congress Cataloging-in-Publication Data

Schneider, Jim, 1945-
    The feel of success in selling/Jim Schneider.
        p.   cm.
    Includes index.
    ISBN 0-13-313461-x
    1. Selling.   I. Title.
HF5438.25.S335   1990
658.8'5—dc20   90-43182
                                                CIP

ISBN 0-13-313461-X

PRENTICE HALL
BUSINESS & PROFESSIONAL DIVISION
A division of Simon & Schuster
Englewood Cliffs, New Jersey 07632

Printed in the United States of America

To my parents,
whose love makes me feel special.
To my children David, Bobbie, and Coral,
who add joy and meaning to my life.
To my wife Tien,
whose partnership in our business and my life gives me
the feel of success.

ACKNOWLEDGMENTS

With great respect, I want to acknowledge the many clients, salespeople, friends, and authors who contributed to this book.

My inspiration grew out of listening to the everyday problems and successes of America's salespeople. They helped me understand the close relationship between success in selling and success in life.

Most of the ideas in this book are based on my own experience in selling, and in consulting with my clients and their employees throughout North America. Others are the result of analyzing the thousands of personal interviews Schneider Sales Management, Inc. has conducted with peak performance sellers to develop our customized sales training programs.

Ideas were also drawn from over ten years of research, using hundreds of books, articles, speeches, studies, and training programs on topics ranging from sales and management to science, psychology, medicine, sports, history, and philosophy.

Writing about selling has forced me to confront hard choices about what I believe. In making these choices, I've learned how much other people have contributed to my thinking and to my success.

I especially want to thank my parents who gave me two of life's greatest gifts: their love, and the feeling I'm capable of achieving what I set out to accomplish.

Special thanks go to Bob Meindl, Russ Nehrig, Jr., Bella Selan, Bernice Bowman, Tom Drogos, and my brother Rick who gave me encouragement and ideas when I needed them most.

Finally, I want to acknowledge my wife Tien, whose love, partnership, ideas, and enthusiasm for life give me energy, motivation, and the feel of success.

To all of you ... thank you.

J.S.

Contents

Introduction

Millions of Americans have a secret wish. They wish they had the feel of success with people. As Chrysler chairman Lee Iacocca writes, "He can't get along with people? Then he's got a real problem, because that's all we've got around here. No dogs, no apes - only people!"

The good news in this book is that you can learn to be more successful with people. If you can become good at selling, you can become better at life. You can strengthen your relationships and get more of what you want.

Whatever you want, getting it requires selling yourself and your ideas. You already know more than you think you do about selling. You can repeat those successes and build on them.

Because everything you'll learn to do in this book is based on the *customer's* viewpoint, you'll find that this book is about *soft*-sell.

Salespeople lose the feel of success the moment they try too hard to sell their ideas, when they try to push their ideas through resistance. Even experienced salespeople sometimes forget selling is problem solving, meeting other people's needs as well as their own.

Sales requires a "double win." They begin with the customer's objectives, not with the product. It's a lesson most salespeople never learn. Selling requires the discipline of always thinking from the customer's viewpoint, of always selling with the purpose to solve problems for the customer.

After years of consulting to professional salespeople, I've found success boils down to three factors: feeling confident, committed, and free of discomfort in selling, selling to the customer's objectives; and selling to the right prospects.

Selling is this simple and this difficult.

Attention to these three factors gives you more resiliency and motivation, more sensitivity to the reactions, objectives, and problems of other people, and more persistence in trying new selling actions until you get the response you want.

I see the frustrations of selling every day in the eyes of the salespeople who attend our corporate sales seminars. They tell me they frequently experience fears about their performance and about rejection.

The tension these fears create blocks their awareness of what works successfully for them in selling. Often, it leads to self-defeating behavior and to "people problems."

These salespeople come to my seminars looking for answers on how to increase sales, how to get their employees to do what they want them to, and how to regain their confidence and motivation.

They leave knowing they had the answers within themselves all along.

WRONG WAY ON A ONE-WAY STREET

Americans love simple solutions to complex problems. But no one book or one sales guru can give you "The Way" to success in selling. No one theory of selling can encompass all the subtleties of human relations.

Most sales theories treat all people and all selling situations as if they were the same. They're not. On set for his movies, producer/director Alfred Hitchcock used to say "No, no. That's the way they do it in the movies. Let's do it the way it is in life."

Hitchcock's philosophy of film-making is also a good way to think about selling. Peak performance sellers respond to people the way they are in real life.

Mental toughness is fifty percent of selling. Salespeople need to create and maintain the right kind of feelings, regardless of the situation or the obstacles they encounter. If you can sustain feelings of confidence and relaxation, you can stay focused on the customer. You'll know what to do, and when to do it.

Some people hold back in selling their ideas because they think selling is "pushy." Product-centered selling is "pushy." Customer-centered selling isn't "pushy," because the *customer's* objectives determine the sale.

You won't be effective for very long in any kind of selling unless you give people what they want. Most salespeople succeed or fail on *repeat* sales, on reputation, and on referrals.

LEARNING HOW TO SELL

This book is for new salespeople who need help in their sales relationships; sales managers and master salespeople who have had success and want to regain or sustain peak performance; and *anyone* who needs the willing cooperation of other people.

We can all use help in learning what works best for us so we can do it again and repeat our feelings of success.

If you were writing a book to help people sell more with less stress, what would you write? After all, everyone has an opinion on sales and human relations.

I answered this question by listening to our clients, and by interviewing peak performance sellers to determine what they do *right*.

These salespeople told me they want to be more prepared for a wide range of selling situations, from sales calls to negotiations, from small talk to group sales presentations. They told me they wanted help with the *personal* issues in selling; building self-confidence, controlling tension, managing their time, developing credibility for themselves, and sustaining their motivation.

They asked me to stick to the issues they would confront every day at every level of success, and that's what I've tried to do.

This book is organized for quick reference to help you get back to the fundamentals.

To really learn from this book, underline the key points and write your thoughts in the margins so the book becomes your book. Refer back to it for solutions to specific sales problems. Discuss what you learn about selling with other successful people.

Most important, *try* these new selling strategies.

By the time you've finished reading the book and tried these new selling strategies, you'll have the feel of success in selling. You'll have more confidence and more success in selling your ideas.

Author's note: The English language contains no satisfactory universal singular pronouns. To avoid the awkwardness of "he or she," "him or her," etc., the masculine pronoun is used in this book to refer to persons of both sexes.

GIVE SOMEONE ELSE
THE FEEL OF SUCCESS ®

For information regarding custom developed sales training,
sales management consulting, personal appearances by
Jim Schneider, or quantity discounts on *The Feel of Success
in Selling*, contact:

Schneider Sales Management, Inc.
1704 Mizzenmast Way
Jupiter, Florida 33477
(407) 743-9894

PART ONE

The Feel of Success

CHAPTER 1

You Can Sell

Jaime was a tennis pro at the Colonnades Beach Hotel on Singer Island, Florida. When we met, I had no idea he would teach me the most important lesson in selling.

Jaime told me he believed the secret to peak performance tennis was developing the *confidence* to relax so a player could focus his thinking on his *successes*.

Later, I watched Jaime work his coaching magic with dozens of tennis players in the hot Florida sun. Again and again, he stressed relaxing to get the "feel" of making good contact with the ball. He directed the players' attention outside themselves to the results of their actions so they could repeat what worked, or try something different when their actions didn't work.

The success traits he was trying to develop were the same success traits I have observed in peak performance salespeople. Peak performance sellers get "the feel of the sale" faster than other salespeople. They're more conscious of their successes and more focused on the customer's response.

Watching Jaime, I realized for the first time that if you can feel your success, you can sell. If you can recognize your successes, you can repeat them. You can use them as a guide to adjust your selling to the customer's viewpoint.

As a professional salesperson, your success is measured by your sales. Reaching your sales goals requires hundreds of small successes in helping other people meet their objectives, solve their problems, and satisfy their relationship needs.

You can actually "feel" these successes in selling. You can see them in the results of your actions. You can hear them in the responses of your customers. You can even *feel* them in your body in your intuitive responses to each selling situation.

3

When success hits, you feel alive, energized, on target. It feels good. For a moment, *the feel of success is success.*

If you can repeat that feeling and the actions that led to it, you can repeat your successes in selling.

In later chapters, you'll learn some of the sophisticated selling techniques used by America's leading salespeople to analyze difficult selling situations and close more sales. But being competent in selling requires a willingness to *use* those selling actions.

The most frequent complaint I hear in our corporate sales seminars is, "it's not that I don't know what to do. I just can't get myself to do it."

THE SECRETS OF SELLING:
Salespeople become peak performers the moment they can consistently repeat their successes.

Most salespeople *think* they understand how they make sales, but even peak performers have difficulty explaining what they do right. As a result, very few salespeople can *repeat* their successes consistently.

Their successful selling behavior is *systematic*, but they don't have a conscious understanding of *how* it's systematic. They may succeed twenty times before they notice *why* they're succeeding.

Even when they know what they're doing right, their discomfort or negative *thinking* may prevent them from doing consistently what they know they should do.

Here's what some of the salespeople in my seminars have said about selling:

> When I first started selling, even the word "sales" turned me off. I wanted people to like me, and I always had this picture in my mind of salespeople being pushy, sort of hard-sell. My negative feelings about selling were so distracting, I lost track of what was working for me with customers and what wasn't.

> It took me almost ten years of selling to realize I was afraid of being rejected, afraid of failing. The reason for my fear was not knowing how the sales process really worked.

These feelings are common among salespeople, even among experienced salespeople. Success in selling doesn't come easy.

Why is it, then, that some salespeople seem to have a "magical touch" for success with people?

They're able to do what they need to do to make a sale *when* they need to do it. They're *consistent*.

If you can capture this same "feel of success" in your relations with people, you can have more of what you want, including more sales, more successful relationships, and more feeling of success.

In later chapters we'll look at a six-step selling process that builds success one step at a time. I will help you organize your selling and improve your consistency, so you can repeat what works best for you.

Once the selling actions that lead to peak performance are more visible to you, it will be easier for you to repeat them.

Acquiring a "feel" for success with people has been a pursuit for centuries. Virtually every religion, every sales course, and every self-help guru has tried to define it and "bottle" it for the rest of us.

Sales managers would pay dearly for it.

What is it that salespeople who have the feel of success *do*? If you could find it, then maybe you could do it and feel it, too.

The difference between success and failure in making a sale is often as small as listening when others don't, making a slight adjustment in your selling style, or getting to the right prospect at the right time.

When these small differences in selling are repeated consistently, they add up to peak performance selling.

Researchers who have studied peak performers at the U.S. Olympic Training Center, and at major universities such as the University of Chicago, have proven that success requires both a belief that you can be successful and a mind/body sense for recalling and repeating successful behaviors to fit new situations.

Peak performers from different disciplines describe their feelings during peak performance in similar ways—a sense of relaxed calm combined with high energy and intense concentration.

Think again of learning to play tennis.

As you learn to play tennis, you first have to believe you can become a good player. As you learn to make good contact with the ball, you begin to relax and get the "feel" of it. You learn to repeat those actions and the feelings they produce again and again in new situations.

This ability to relax and imagine yourself being successful, and to recognize and repeat your successful actions, is the *feel of success*.

Aside from personality, most of what separates peak performance sellers from other salespeople is *learnable*. Even if you have never experienced the feel of success in selling, you can start today to know better what's working for you with people, and what's not working.

If you can be successful once, you can be successful again.

If what you usually do isn't working in a certain situation, you can try something else, and if that works, you can file that new information away for future use.

YOU CAN SEE, HEAR, AND FEEL YOUR
WAY TO SUCCESS

You already have a feel for success with people. In a sense, you're walking around with a "success coach" in your head based on what you've learned about people throughout your life.

Most salespeople can discriminate between the desirable and undesirable *results* of what they *do* in a sales situation. But they also need the *sense* of being right when they're right. That's what they act on in deciding whether or not to *repeat* their behavior.

Salespeople need confidence that what seems to work *does* work. Once you learn to identify your successes as success, you can motivate yourself to repeat them.

Unfortunately, most people don't know good selling, good friendship, or the feeling of success in a way that helps them recreate these things. They haven't recognized success when they were having it.

Research in neurophysiology has proven that some people are better than others in using various senses to recognize their successes. But all people can learn to be *better* at recognizing their successes by feeling, seeing, or hearing the results of their actions.

When the peak performance seller tries something new in a selling situation, he analyzes his objectives as being met, or as not being met. He then attaches a positive or negative assessment to that action, and that's what is stored in memory for future sales situations.

Even if a salesperson hasn't had the selling experience he needs as a resource, he can use another salesperson's behavior as his frame of reference.

You can use the behavior of other peak performance salespeople as a model to help you recognize your own successful behavior. Watching them can help you know what to look for in the results of your own selling actions.

You can do what they do if you learn to pay attention to what you feel, what you hear, and what you see as you observe them.

I can still remember how I learned to dance as a teenager.

I would go to parties with my friends, watch the movements of the best dancers, and try those movements myself until I could "feel" in my body how to repeat them, and picture myself making those movements.

I could *see* how I was doing by the expressions on the faces of my friends, and I could *hear* what worked best for me by the comments thrown my way by my friends.

It was amazing how fast I learned those hundreds of intricate movements within hours, while at the same time it took me weeks to learn my math!

I learned fast because I identified my successful behaviors, and I practiced them until I got the "feel" of what worked best for me in dancing. Since I knew what peak performance was for me, I could practice against that norm.

You can learn to sell the same way.

The human brain has a wonderful capacity for making sense out of information so complicated and incomplete it would paralyze a computer.

Thank God. Because that's the kind of information you work with in selling—confused and incomplete. Each time you interact with a customer or plan a sales strategy, you react to hundreds of bits of information, many of them conflicting.

Like basketball superstars Larry Bird and Michael Jordan, the superstars of selling see the game several moves ahead of everyone else. They know where the customer is right now in his thinking, and where his thinking is moving. When they've completed the sale, you wonder whether they knew where the customer was headed or whether their actions led the customer there.

These master salespeople take shortcuts to making sense of each new selling situation.

Peak performance salespeople rely on "the feel of the sale" to provide cues to use the sales behaviors that have worked best for them in the past. They call on a ready reserve of successful responses that gives explosiveness to their selling.

One peak performance seller describes how she recognizes these changing patterns:

> I'd be lost without the information I get by constantly checking out the customer's responses to my selling. That's what gives me the feel of the sale. If I'm not getting my point across, I want to know *now* so I can try something different.

In a sense, getting the feel of success in selling is learning to sell the *easy* way, using the successful responses you've used before.

The problem salespeople have in knowing how they operate best in selling is the distraction of *thinking too much* about themselves, about what they're doing, about their failures, or about the fears they've learned in selling. They should be thinking about the *customer* and his responses.

These distractions keep them from recognizing and repeating what has been successful for them in the past.

Salespeople get in the way of their own success. Peak performers aren't people with something extra, they're people who use what they have.

You don't have to learn many *new* skills to be a better salesperson. You already know something about selling and success no one else knows. You know what works for *you*.

In learning to swim, you might first read about how to balance yourself in the water a certain way for a certain stroke. When you actually jump into the water and go under a few times, you still know the same thing, but you know it in a new way.

At that moment when swimming finally "clicks" for you, when you can both float in the water and *breathe* while you move in the direction you want, you haven't really learned anything new. You know what you knew before, but now you have the *feel* of it. You understand how to use what you know.

Selling is part street smarts; learning to *apply* your people sense.

The specific skills described in later chapters are organized to help you learn them so you can *use* them. They're described so you can feel, see, or hear, when you're using them successfully.

BELIEVE IT: YOU CAN BE SUCCESSFUL

The first step toward the feel of success in selling is a genuine belief you can be a peak performance seller.

If you've just heard "no" on six straight deals, it's easy for negative thinking to set in. You may begin to believe you won't ever be successful.

THE SECRETS OF SELLING:
You won't be successful until you can imagine yourself as being successful.

If you believe you couldn't possibly sell your toughest prospect, negotiate a higher price with a key customer, make an effective group sales presentation, or meet new prospects in their environment without tension, you're probably right. You couldn't do those things well now.

To develop the habit of using an effective sales behavior, you first have to see yourself as having the potential to do it well. Most salespeople won't even *try* new selling behaviors until they feel they have a good chance of being successful.

If you believe your odds for success are at least 50/50, you're likely to try harder. For example, when salespeople believe they have at least a 50/50 chance for a sale they persist longer and do better.

If you can change your *thinking* about your probable success in trying new selling actions, you can improve your success rate in selling—instantly.

You'll find a lot of information in this book about the right attitudes to sustain you in difficult sales situations. Your thinking *does* make a difference.

There's a lot of truth in Henry Ford's statement, "If you think you can or you can't, you're always right."

The *expectation* of success leads to success. Doubt will cause you to give in too soon or to try too hard. And customers won't believe in you until you believe in yourself.

To sell at peak performance, you have to believe in your probable success. You have to feel it in your bones.

Self-confidence and the desire to excel are the critical issues in selling.

They lead to higher expectations and to the relaxation you need, both to avoid negative thinking and to recognize and repeat your successful selling actions.

You make the sale *before* you leave for the sales call.

Red Motley, former *Parade* editor, says, "Nothing happens until somebody sells something." But no one sells anything until he's sold himself on trying and succeeding.

When I first read books by the early proponents of positive thinking, I thought their ideas amounted to wishful thinking. At that time there was little research to back their claims.

Now such heroes of positive thinking as Dale Carnegie, W. Clement Stone, and Norman Vincent Peale have turned out to be better neurochemists than any of us knew. Modern psychology has proven that controlling your thinking is a springboard to success in selling.

SELLING "RIGHT" CONSISTENTLY

Belief alone isn't enough for the feel of success in selling.

You also need to be able to *repeat* your successful selling actions consistently, to *do* what you're telling yourself you *can* do.

Fortunately, once you know a successful action exists, you can recall it when you need it.

Steven DeVore and Mike Michaelson, researchers in sports psychology, write,

> If you have ever served the tennis ball correctly, or driven the golf ball solidly and straight, then your brain and your muscles already know how to perform the action... the memory of that action is etched indelibly in your brain. If you have thrown the perfect pitch, hit the perfect line drive or skied the perfect run, then it is within your ability to do it over and over again, unerringly and consistently. And it is consistency that spells the difference between the winning and losing athlete.

Consistency also spells the difference between the winning and losing salesperson.

Every person has a blueprint of electronic codes in his nervous system that represent his moments of success from the past. And he can transfer his responses in those previous successes to new sales situations.

This means: if you can identify your successful selling actions, you can program them for future use and repeat them. You can increase the odds for your selling "right" *consistently.*

The stronger these neutral patterns are for a specific sales behavior, the easier it is to recall and repeat that behavior. That's how practice burns success into your mind and your body with a tattooing effect.

The new forms of sales training emerging today are based on learning to recognize patterns for "the feel of the sale." These pattern-recognition techniques are covered throughout this book, in combination with traditional analytical approaches to identifying customer objectives and developing "nuts and bolts" sales strategies.

There are times in selling when you know more than you think you know.

Knowing the appropriate thing to do in selling, yet not knowing *how* you know it, is sales intuition. The subtle skills of sales intuition are now regarded as a sophisticated way of thinking, a short-cut used by peak performers and given credence by sociologists such as Dr. Dane Archer of the University of California at Santa Cruz:

> When you dismiss intuition as a sort of magical perception, you sell yourself short. If you sense that a friend is unhappy but don't know what gives you the feeling, you may call it ESP or luck, but in fact you're reading subtle clues; a tremor in her voice, the way she spoke, *too* cheerfully.

In the average salesperson's mind there are many possibilities for making a sale, but in the peak performer's mind there are usually only a few serious possibilities emerging in the pattern of the sale.

Successful salespeople often choose a sales strategy because it "feels right."

I've known sales managers who have "killed" sale after sale for their salespeople on joint sales calls by forcing their salespeople into mechanical sales presentations "by the book." In doing that, they lost the benefit of the intuitive "feel" for the sale their salespeople have developed on previous sales calls.

Tapping into these intuitive insights is an important selling skill. It requires a little focusing of your feelings.

In *Focusing*, University of Chicago psychologist Eugene T. Gendlin writes that when a flash of intuitive insight occurs, "there is a distinct physical sensation of change—a body shift."

Gendlin says when this sense of change comes, it's complicated, murky and unclear. You have to focus it a little. You're saying to your nervous system, "What's going on here? Look for anything that supports my goal."

These feelings allow emotional connections to take place, and provide the vehicle for carrying thoughts and analyzing situations at incredible speed.

Testing and trusting these intuitive insights in selling leads you back to the natural success mechanism you've programmed into your nervous system. To stay close to these intuitions, peak performance sellers lose themselves in "the feel of the sale," focusing their attention on the *customer* and on the *results* of their actions.

As you try to make the selling skills in this book work for you, you may find they feel "wrong," that you don't feel the way you think you should in using them.

Whenever you're uncomfortable in using something new in your selling, refocus your attention from your discomfort to the *results* of your actions. The more you repeat the actions that produce your successes, the more comfortable you'll be.

I can teach you which of the things you do with customers that are likely to work. But you have to teach yourself to recognize your successful selling actions. You have to motivate yourself to stay focused on the *customer* and the *results* of your actions and to repeat what works.

To give yourself a quick assessment of your selling the way it is now, take a few minutes to complete the Feel of Success® in Selling Profile below. Over the years, we've had hundreds of requests from major corporations to reproduce this simple profile for sales meetings and other uses because it quickly focuses attention on the fundamentals of good selling. The picture of your selling that emerges from completing the profile will help you set learning goals for what you want to learn from this book.

THE FEEL OF SUCCESS®
IN SELLING PROFILE

INSTRUCTIONS: Read each statement and mark the box by each statement with the rating below that best describes your selling.

(4)	Almost Always
(3)	Usually
(2)	Seldom
(1)	Almost Never

1. I ask questions and listen much more than I talk in selling.

2. I feel relaxed, confident, and full of energy during difficult sales conversations.

3. I spend time analyzing the customer's probable objectives and problems as a **person** before I decide how to sell the product.

4. I'm able to spend my time with the **right** prospects who represent both high potential and high probability of buying from me soon.

5. I anticipate serious sales objections and prevent them with my presentation so I sell without much price resistance.

6. I'm able to gain a customer's trust for my selling in the first 60 seconds with my first impression.

7. I'm effective in selling **results** as my customer's define them, not just the product details that describe our product.

8. I continually **add** new, qualified prospects so my sales results are consistent, with few peaks and valleys.

9. I'm able to identify the customer's dominant objectives, problems, and buying concept quickly and accurately with questions.

10. I'm able to ask customers directly for sensitive financial information or for a next step commitment without hesitation or fear of the customer's reaction.

11. I'm able to position our products as **clearly different** than the products offered by our competitors.

12. I make sales my competitors miss because of my persistent, organized follow-up.

13. I check customer reaction to my selling by observing the customer's behavior and frequently adjust my selling style to fit the person or the situation.

14. I'm able to prospect for new business aggressively without experiencing much reluctance, discomfort, or fear of intruding on others.

15. I'm able to identify *all* the people who will influence the decision in each sale and adapt my selling to their different objectives.

16. I'm effective in building a referral network that continually produces new leads for me.

17. I notice and repeat what works in my selling, and when what I'm doing isn't working, I try something else.

18. While I'm selling, I'm thinking about solving problems for the customer, not about my presentation, my sales goals, or what might go wrong.

19. I'm able to substantially increase the size of my sales at the time of the sale by asking for more.

20. I know my position relative to competition with my top few customers, and I have a specific strategy planned for getting more of their business. ☐

21. I'm able to control conversations so they stay focused on the customer's objectives and our products' strengths. ☐

22. I'm able to tell a customer "no" without stress, and without increasing the customer's anger. ☐

23. I can give proof and at least three reasons why each product I present is better than other products offered by competitors. ☐

24. I have clear goals that drive me and sustain me when I'm feeling "burned out." ☐

25. I ask questions specifically to get customers to tell me the possible benefits of our products rather than explain all the benefits myself. ☐

26. I'm able to sell my ideas effectively without losing motivation even after people say they're not interested. ☐

27. I'm effective in gaining the cooperation of other co-workers on behalf of my customers. ☐

28. For my most important sales contacts, I sell with specific next step objectives and at least a few preplanned questions and sales points. ☐

Add the numbers you have circled
to determine your total score.   **TOTAL** ☐

HERE'S WHAT YOUR SCORE MEANS

105-112 You have the **feel of success**
 91-104 You're fast on your way to successful selling
 61- 90 You're still in the middle of the pack
 28- 60 It's time to learn more about advanced selling skills

To identify specific areas for improvement in your selling, total your score for each of the four categories of selling. To find out how your sales **technique** rates, total questions 1, 5, 9, 13,17, 21, and 25. Your level of **confidence** is indicated by the sum of questions 2, 6, 10, 14, 18, 22, and 26. Add up questions 3, 7, 11, 15, 19, 23, and 27 to determine how well you're able to **apply your product** and skills to meet customer objectives. For your **sales planning** capabilities, count up the totals from questions 4, 8, 12, 16, 20, 24, and 28. A score of 25 or higher on any of these selling factors is a sign of selling strength, and a score of 14 or lower is a red flag that this aspect of your selling needs improvement.

THE LAM FACTOR

One factor drives success in selling more than any other. I call it the LAM Factor. LAM represents Schneider's Law of Accumulative Momentum.

THE SECRETS OF SELLING:
Success builds on success. Master one skill before you try another.

The most direct road to success in selling is to repeat and build on what works.

The effect of the LAM factor is like an elephant placing one foot forward and gradually shifting his weight onto that foot, then not moving the next foot forward until he's sure the ground will hold him.

Peak performers determine what they do well and they do it again, and again, and again. They also determine quickly what doesn't work in a specific situation, and try something else—*anything* else.

Former Harvard President Charles Eliot urged his teachers to arrange work so students would be more likely to experience success. He said these small successes would give students the "feel of success" for the rest of their lives.

Small successes give you the feeling you've succeeded at something, so maybe you can succeed at other things too.

If you've had limited success in the past, recognizing your success is even more important to your future. The most difficult part of selling is getting your success feelings started, especially from a dead stop.

Developing inertia is the most difficult step in reaching a new level of performance. Once a behavior pattern had been established, it actually takes more energy to stop it than to maintain it.

When salespeople achieve something, they usually want to achieve something else. They know what success feels like, and they don't want to lose that feeling. Meeting their goals becomes a psychological hot spot.

To get your success feelings started again, approach your sales goals, your learning goals, and each sale one step at a time, building one success on top of another.

Work on the selling skills in this book step by step, reaching a comfort level with the first strategies you try before you move on to the others. If you soak in your success each step of the way, your confidence will grow with your success.

Once you have a little success, other people want to share in that success. Peak performance sellers are able to draw some customers to them on the basis of their aura of success alone.

The impact of the LAM Factor on your success in selling is very similar to the laws of chance in mathematics.

Chance is ruled by a condition called "sensitive dependence on initial conditions." This principle says one initial effect, such as a minor movement of your hand in spinning a roulette wheel, can compound exponentially into a colossal effect on the outcome.

The key initial effects every salesperson starts with in selling are his *self-confidence* and his *prior successes.*

Your stored memories of success give you an inventory of success feelings and effective strategies that increase your probability of success in new situations.

What experiences can you build on to become more effective in selling?

You already have the "right stuff" for success in selling. You only need to recognize the stepping stones already in place in your prior experience and to add more stepping stones.

Popular author and lecturer Leo Buscaglia says, "You can only give away what you have, so you better work at getting something. Get everything you can so you can give it away. Having something will give you the feel of success."

I've always been amazed at how often a successful entertainer, say a comedian, has a foundation of talent in acting, dance, music, or some other discipline in addition to the skill he's best known for.

Peak performance sellers also tend to have *multiple* skills. In selling, lack of one important talent, such as group presentation skills or negotiating skills, can hold you back, and the addition of a special knowledge, such as an in-depth knowledge of your industry, can give you an edge.

The secret is to spotlight one strength that makes you stand out, and to add to that as many skills as you can, that when combined make you *clearly different* and *better* than other salespeople.

We'll cover a wide range of skills in this book to give you as many stepping stones as possible for success in selling.

After you've read about these selling skills, take some risks in *trying* them. The earlier you discover a new strength, the more time you'll have to develop it.

One success leads to another.

In the next chapter, we'll explore the most important factor in selling—*self-confidence*. You'll learn why you can't lead a calvary charge if you think you look funny sitting on a horse.

CHAPTER 2

You Can't Lead a Cavalry Charge if You Think You look Funny Sitting on a Horse

It takes *confidence* to sell. You can't lead a cavalry charge if you think you look funny sitting on a horse.

The first step in selling is *feeling* successful.

To become a peak performance seller you have to believe in your probable success, and have the confidence to do what has to be done to strengthen relationships and to close sales.

Self-confidence is the one selling force you carry with you every moment of the day. Sales motivator Zig Ziglar writes, "Selling is essentially a transference of feeling ... to transfer a feeling, you have to have that feeling."

A salesperson who feels successful helps everyone around him share his feelings of success. And that develops *trust*, a key factor in selling.

Even experienced salespeople go through periods when they lose their success feelings. But peak performance sellers develop ways to recharge those feelings before each new sales contact.

In this chapter, you'll learn how they do it.

Mental toughness is the ability to create and maintain positive feelings no matter how difficult the situation.

Here is what some of the salespeople in our corporate seminars have said about self-confidence in selling:

> There's no magic to selling. I can sell as well as anyone else. I just wish I had learned that earlier, when I was so concerned about being young and being a woman. I could have saved myself a lot of unnecessary tension and made a lot more money.

> When I call on a company for the first time I still get a few butterflies in my stomach. I never know exactly what I'm walking into. The toughest part of the sales call is convincing myself I can help the customer and make the sale. I have to fight off feelings that I'm intruding on someone else's time.

17

Many of the salespeople I meet have never felt comfortable in their role. They see themselves as "pushers" of their products, not as problem solvers.

It's your *beliefs* about selling or how other people will react to you that cause your discomfort, not the actions of selling. *Selling is helping.*

Selling isn't a profession until you think of yourself as a professional.

Can you think of any judgment more essential to your success in selling than whether or not you can overcome your discomfort and be successful?

Every salesperson goes through life carrying an imaginary stack of poker chips, each chip representing a good feeling about himself. Some salespeople have a high stack and some are on their last chips.

The number of success chips you have affects your goals, your assertiveness, and your risk-taking. It affects your ability to sell, to learn, and to change.

In my research, I've found that many salespeople believe they have little control over what happens between themselves and a customer.

Self-confidence is particularly important for women in sales. Despite research that proves there is no correlation between gender and success in sales, many women have a lower opinion of their performance and ability to influence situations than men.

It's their *thinking*, not their ability, that holds these salespeople back.

If you believe you have no control over sales situations and are likely to fail, you probably will. You might not even try. If you're distracted by negative thinking or by tension, your customers will know it intuitively, and they'll strengthen their resistance.

Everything you choose for yourself in selling, from your choice of prospects to your choice of how assertive to be in closing sales, is affected by how successful you feel as a person.

Dr. David Burns, prominent author on psychology, writes,

> Almost all negative emotional reactions inflict their damage *only* as a result of low self-esteem. A poor self-image is the magnifying glass that can transform a trivial mistake or an imperfection into an overwhelming symbol of personal defeat.

Popular motivational speaker Rev. Robert Schuller writes, "The really tough person is the one who knows who he is and where his strength is coming from."

SELLING FROM STRENGTH

There's always something unique to you that gives you your strength in dealing with other people. If you know the strategies and personal attributes that contribute most to your success, you can use them as a springboard to success in selling. But how can you identify what these things are?

THE SECRETS OF SUCCESS:
Focus on what you do *right*, and
you'll do it more often.

You've had success with people before. Use that success to help you identify
your strengths.

Search back through your life to find the things you've done, and the
moments you've experienced, that gave you satisfaction. Think of the peak
experiences in your life, the moments you associate most with success and with
doing things well.

Maybe you were recognized for your sales achievement, absorbed in an
activity you loved, surrounded by talented people, committed to a goal—whatever was satisfying to you.

Write down three experiences that gave you strong feelings of success
before you were eighteen and three experiences that gave you strong feelings of
success after you were eighteen. These successes might have been in selling,
sports, work, a hobby, a relationship ...whatever was important to you at the
time.

Evaluate your experiences on what you knew and how you felt then. And
don't be surprised if there isn't much correlation between your strengths and
what you like to do. Success is the result of giving other people what they need,
not doing what you like.

What personal strengths were most responsible for your successes? How
could you build on these strengths for success in your selling today? What's
keeping you from feeling successful in the same way now?

Rediscovering your forgotten stepping stones for success can be like re-
uniting with old friends.

By re-examining their pasts, some salespeople are able to recognize specific strengths or skills they've forgotten, or that they've failed to use in their
selling because they haven't thought of them as being related to success in
selling.

Some salespeople are able to recharge their success feelings simply by
reminding themselves that they've been successful in the past, or by transfer-
ring their success feelings from the past to new situations.

One sales manager, who had been struggling to regain the confidence she
had as a district salesperson, was able to recall the success she had in college
politics. With that picture in mind, she immediately regained her peak performance selling attitude. She began using, as her primary selling strategies, the
networking and speaking abilities she developed in college.

Salespeople frequently try so hard to "improve" themselves, they lose sight of their selling strengths. As a result, they stop feeling successful.

They may achieve peak performance from time to time. But they're not able to sustain success. They deviate from what made them successful in the first place.

When a salesperson begins to lose his success feelings, he's likely to change his strategy or to try to improve his selling technique.

These adjustments may be good strategies to correct something technical, but they're not likely to do much to restore his confidence or his relaxation, and those are the factors that will help him most.

THE SECRETS OF SELLING:
The top performing salesperson spends as much time fine-tuning his *thinking* as he does fine-tuning his sales strategy.

The more time you devote to studying your mistakes in selling, the more likely you are to make mistakes.

Think about it. You would find it much easier to walk a narrow plank on your living room floor than to walk a plank ten stories up between two buildings. High in the air, your worry over falling distracts you.

Lewis Carroll explains the error in most salespeople's thinking in Alice in Wonderland when Alice says to the Mad Hatter,

> Where I come from, people study what they are not good at in order to be able to do what they are good at in order to be able to do what they are good at ...grown-ups tell us to find out what we did wrong, and never do it again... Nobody ever tells us to study the right things we do. We're only supposed to learn from the wrong things... It seems like I have to do something wrong first, in order to learn from what not to do. And then, by not doing what I'm not supposed to do, perhaps I'll be right. But I'd rather be right the first time, wouldn't you?

How do you develop self-confidence in selling?

You build self-confidence by succeeding often and by feeling your successes as they occur. You'll feel and be more successful if you focus on what you do right.

Self-confidence is a special problem for salespeople who are in the midst of a transition period in their life. They may be moving from one industry, one sales position, or one territory in which they have proven their success and are at ease, to one in which success has yet to be established.

They worry that in this new situation they may not prove to be as successful as they thought they were.

Whenever you're feeling down on yourself, refocus your thinking on your strengths as a person, on your successes, and on your goals for future successes.

The impact of not building your self-confidence is demonstrated in the experience of tennis pro Vic Braden.

Braden says,

> I once conducted a survey in which I asked 100 people to name an incident in some kind of sports activity in which they were deeply hurt, had lost their pride or self-respect, and which continues to bother them as adults. Every one of them, 100 out of 100, named an incident almost immediately.

I see the same negative thinking in our corporate sales seminars. When I ask salespeople to recall their best and worst experiences in selling, they invariably dwell on their *worst* experiences.

Success builds on *success*.

Salespeople want to believe they can accomplish *anything*, but the truth is, unrealistic goals give them a sense of *failure*, not the feel of success.

Charles Atlas is the famous body-builder whose muscle-building ads feature his transformation from a 97-lb. weakling to a muscle man after a sand-kicking incident at Coney Island Beach.

His friend Angelo Sicilian says Atlas developed his exercise system of "dynamic tension" at Prospect Zoo in New Jersey. Atlas was watching a lion stretch and came to the conclusion the animal was pitting one muscle against another and strengthening both.

You can build your muscle in peak performance selling the same way.

The "dynamic tension" involved in selling is between what you think you can accomplish, and what you *can* accomplish. The tension between these two success factors strengthens them both. In other words, the more you accomplish, the more you think you can accomplish and vice versa. If you try to do too much too soon, you'll strain your self-confidence by over-streching your limits.

Don't call on your toughest prospect first. Instead, build a series of small successes. Stop to enjoy your successes. Really let them sink in.

A real estate saleswomen in one of our seminars explained how she uses this technique to strengthen her selling confidence and momentum:

> Selling can be frustrating at times, but when I finally make a sale, I celebrate. I reward myself with a nice lunch or something else that makes me feel good about what I've done. Closing a sale is probably the most exciting part of my job, and it motivates me to work harder

for the next sale. I start thinking that if I can make one sale, I can make another one. I usually call every one of my pending prospects so I can use my enthusiasm over the last sale to sell them too.

These are simple ideas. But they work in building the confidence and relaxation necessary to reach peak performance.

RELAX—FOR THE FEEL OF SUCCESS

Most salespeople are as concerned about selling with less stress as they are about making more sales.

Relaxation helps you avoid the negative thinking and nervous physical responses that distract you from the customer and from your successes.

Salespeople frequently experience fear of rejection which often stops them from being as assertive as they need to be, or leads them to overly aggressive behavior or other self-defeating behavior.

Whether you're feeling successful or you're feeling tense, you transfer these feelings to other people.

Peak performers often find they're at their best when they feel as if they're not even trying hard.

THE SECRETS OF SELLING:
Relaxation opens the seller's mind and body to the feel of success in selling.

When salespeople are tense, they tend to be more interested in themselves than in their customers. If you can avoid excess tension, you can get in touch with the feel of the sale and move communication along fast. You're less likely to feel pressure to go all out against maximum resistance, a mistake which is self-defeating in selling.

As sports psychology researchers DeVore and Michaelson write,

> ... when you are in a completely relaxed state, your body will react to your mind and your mind will react to your body ... If the muscles are not relaxed (oxygenated), or if they are in a state of tension (lack of oxygen), the codes you are putting into your brain will not have the opportunity to work effectively. Tension creates roadblocks to physical performance; relaxation enhances performance.

Actually, you can improve relaxation and make *every* sales contact a success by changing the way you *think* about your selling.

What you *say* to yourself about selling has a powerful impact on the way you *feel* about selling, and the way you feel about selling has a powerful impact on what you *do* in selling.

You can start by separating your success as a person from your success in any one selling situation.

If you think of success as a combination of your *results*, your *experience* (was it fun, interesting, or challenging?), and your *learning*, you can find success in any sales experience.

In fact, peak performance authority Charles Garfield says if you can find success in any one of these three factors, you also improve the quality of the other two. You'll feel more successful, and that will relax you.

It's more important to keep from losing touch with what you're doing *right* than it is to find new techniques for closing sales.

Listen to Olympic Champion sprinter Carl Lewis:

> The reason I'm so powerful the last forty or fifty meters is because I can relax very well and when you relax you don't decelerate as much... When you get to the point when you can't accelerate any longer, you just settle into trying to just maintain. Relaxation is basically maintaining—just trying to keep running the way you are instead of running faster. It's just something people have to feel out—when do I hit this speed? Is it when I get *this* feeling? Or is it when I get *that* feeling?

Lewis knows *why* he's successful and he knows how to relax. It's no wonder he can repeat his successes consistently.

You can try *too* hard in selling, in the same way you can try too hard in sports. When you do, you make it more difficult for yourself to relax.

When salespeople are facing a major sales presentation, they often make the mistake of concentrating on it for days ahead. By the time they face the real situation their mental energies are worn down to the point that small distractions from their customers can break their concentration and keep them from doing what needs to be done.

At this point, relaxation is more important to their performance than any sales strategy could ever be.

Much of the skill of selling is learning to relax in crisis situations. Instead of trying to perform under pressure, peak performers take the pressure off. They concentrate on what they *can* do to influence the outcome of their selling, instead of thinking too much about the outcome itself, which only the customer can control.

Just *thinking* about relaxing is a good start.

You can train yourself to relax *before* a sales contact by mentally rehearsing your success.

SNAPSHOTS OF YOUR FUTURE SUCCESS

Mental rehearsal is a simple technique for building confidence and programming your brain for success. It's a way to get the feel of success before you encounter a real sales situation.

Your visualization gives you a mental picture of how your response will look, and kinesthetic awareness in your nervous system gives you a sense of how it will feel. Using mental rehearsal, you can try alternate approaches and redo what doesn't seem to feel right.

Even watching someone else sell effectively and imagining yourself doing the same thing successfully can improve your performance.

The nervous system can't tell the difference between an actual experience and a vividly imagined experience.

Psychologist Richard Restak says, "Imagery exerts a measurable physical effect on the brain ... Merely imagining that we are doing something can bring about brain activation similar to what happens when we are actually doing it."

In *The Breaks of the Game*, David Halberstam describes how basketball superstar Bill Walton fine-tuned his confidence for peak performance during his NBA championship season with the Portland Trail Blazers by mentally rehearsing his success on the day of a game.

Halberstam writes,

> This was the time in which he felt the rhythm and tempo of the game, almost like feeling a dance of his own... He would sit in his home or hotel room in those hours and actually see the game and feel the movement of it. Sometimes he did it with such accuracy that a few hours later when he was on the court and the same players made the same moves, it was easy for him because he had already seen it all, had make that move or blocked that shot ... He was amazed in those moments at how clearly he could see the game, see the spin of the ball and the angle from which different players were coming. Moment by moment in that time he became more confident, until when he arrived at the locker room he knew he was absolutely ready.

He had the feel of success.

You can use the same mental rehearsal techniques that Bill Walton used to develop your confidence in a selling situation. Mental rehearsals help you replace negative thinking with positive, realistic thinking. They strengthen your confidence and relax you. Most salespeople spend their entire sales preparation time working out how to present the facts of their product persuasively. Peak performance sellers also spend time preparing their thinking.

FILL YOUR SENSES WITH SUCCESS

You can learn to translate your immediate sales goals into sights, sounds, and feelings that will relax you and program your body to execute the selling responses you want.

Before you meet with someone in a stressful encounter such as a difficult sales call or a negotiation, pause for a few minutes to get control of your thinking.

Remember, you make the sale before you make the sales call. Think to yourself, "I can influence the results of this meeting" and "How can I help this person?"

When your mind says, "There's no way I can sell these people," or "This guy knows more than I do," think "I'm prepared. I can handle this. Relax."

Now picture yourself with the customer.

Imagine how you're going to help the customer solve his problem. Picture a happy ending, with the customer using your product, benefiting from it, and feeling good about it.

Pay attention to small details—all the sights, sounds, and objects you see in your imagined environment. Add as much color, dimension, feeling, and other detail as you can to make the image seem real.

Rehearse the successful execution of your plan again and again, particularly your success in handling resistance and adapting to the customer's objectives.

When you make a mistake, do the scene over in your mind until it seems right. Once you've made the sale in your mind ten times, the eleventh time is easy.

Even 30 seconds of mental rehearsal before a sales contact can strengthen your confidence and improve your success.

The positive feedback you give yourself after each real sales contact is also important as a rehearsal. It serves as the first rehearsal for your *next* sale.

If you can feel the probability of success in your bones, really *believe* in it, you create the possibility of having it.

REACHING YOUR OPTIMUM
PERFORMANCE STATE

Every salesperson wants to reach his optimum performance state in selling, in which he operates at peak mental and physical performance.

Peak performance sellers often rely on a success cue, or psychological anchor, as they enter a sales contact, to increase their confidence and serve as a cue to use the behaviors that work best for them.

Like peak performance athletes, they develop small habits or routines they can rely on to trigger their relaxation.

A success cue is a consciously-invoked word, image, or behavior that triggers a positive frame of mind or a memory of a successful experience. The thought these cues produce improve sales performance by triggering feelings and actions that the salesperson has found effective in previous situations.

Peak performers use these success cues to recall the thoughts they associate with their previous successes and to transfer them to new situations.

Sometimes the cue is as simple as picking up a favorite briefcase on the way out—something that means, "I'm ready to sell."

For other salespeople, these cues may involve creating a mental picture or story of themselves at their best, dedicating themselves to a routine in their preparation, or concentrating on the feelings or images they had as they observed another successful salesperson sell.

Sometimes the success cue is what they wear. Successful salespeople dress to meet the customer's expectations, but they also dress to bring out their own feelings of success so they gain a mental edge.

Your success cue may even be another person. As a rule, walk with winners. Spend your time in the hours before an important sales contact with other positive thinkers who have similar goals and who encourage you to pursue your goals.

You can learn one more thing about relaxation from peak performers: as you approach the customer, forget your presentation and focus entirely on the *customer* and his responses.

This change in your thinking will do more than anything else to relax you and get you feeling successful.

In selling, success requires *persistence*, the positive attitude to sustain your energy for one more follow-up call, for one more response to an objection, for the first step out of a slump.

The most important success factor of all is the sheer *will* to achieve.

Remember, there are people out there who *need* you. You're selling with purpose, solving customer problems.

Mary Kay Ash built one of the most successful sales organizations ever on the "go give" principle: "What can I do so these women will leave here today feeling better about themselves?" Reminding yourself of what you can do for your customers will put the edge back in your selling motivation.

Hitting a slump or a plateau in your selling usually means you're pressing, and that's mental. Probably the best thing you could do to improve your selling if you're in a slump is take a vacation.

To sell your way out of a slump, or learn what you need to move to the next plateau in your selling, the most important prescription is *relax*.

Too much coaching can overload your circuits or make you feel less confident. If you're relaxed enough to recognize your successes, you can repeat them. And that's what it takes to break a slump.

When you try too hard to improve, you're likely to tense up so badly you'll actual impede your ability to recall the selling responses which have worked best for you in the past.

One of the best ways to feel lots of disappointment is to construct a picture of how your selling should be, and then try to make all your selling go that way. Work your way out of slumps and plateaus step by step, building on one small improvement after another. Concentrate on *improving*, not on a complete recovery.

Drop back a notch in the difficulty of the sales contacts you're making. Set aside a few days specifically for the purpose of regaining your touch. Get into the pleasure of improving. If you try to compete at peak performance level before you've regained your form, you'll immediately revert to bad habits.

Avoid comparing your results to the results of other salespeople. Instead, step up your concentration on the *fundamentals* of selling. There's no selling activity too simple to apply total concentration to. You'll reduce stress by moving your focus away from your slump.

Timothy Gallwey, sports psychologist, writes,

> We introduced the concept of the Zen Buddhist who chops carrots real straight and real fast not because they taste better straight in the soup but because he's working on his own concentration. He's working on himself, and the carrots are the medium for working on himself.

To chance a fast breakthrough, watch what other peak performance sellers do. Watch for how their customers respond and for what seems to work. By concentrating on the customer's *response* to selling actions, you can recognize how your own selling may have gotten off-track.

Make each sales contact a learning experience. If you learn from each sales contact, you'll never have a failure, and you'll find the motivation you need to climb back to peak performance.

When you have a major success, use the surge of energy that comes with it to push yourself to contact as many prospects with pending commitments as possible. Prospects seem to sense your feel of success. It's amazing how frequently you can bust out of a selling slump by building one success into a run of successes.

Feeling successful is the first, and most important, step in selling. You can't lead a cavalry charge if you think you look funny sitting on a horse.

At the 1968 Poor People's Demonstration at Resurrection City in Washington, D.C., the Rev. Jesse Jackson urged the crowd to say, "I am somebody. I *am* somebody."

It was a lesson in self-respect every salesperson should learn.

In the next four chapters, you'll learn how to think from the *customer's* viewpoint, beginning with the greatest secret in selling.

PART TWO

The Customer's Viewpoint

CHAPTER 3

The Greatest Secret in Selling

What's the greatest secret in selling? You're about to find out. Many of the great secrets of selling have been recorded by history's most successful people and passed on to succeeding generations.

The Golden Rule, "Do unto others as you would have them do unto you," is probably the best-known secret of human relations used in selling. But it doesn't tell the whole story.

People also have needs and motivations that are *different* from yours. The great persuaders of history have always considered the thinking of other people as well as their own.

Salespeople have difficulty when they base their selling exclusively on what *they* want or on what *they* think their customers want.

This chapter is about finding the excitement in your ideas for *other* people, about selling to *their* objectives. In sales jargon, this chapter is about *benefit selling*.

The concept of benefit selling is so important that it's taught in every sales training course in America, but it's seldom taught in ways salespeople will use. You're going to learn to sell benefits *every* time you sell.

The concept of benefit selling is so powerful you can change your life with it.

I've seen benefit selling work for thousands of salespeople. And I've seen it work after our seminars for people such as flavorists and technical researchers who don't even think of themselves as salespeople. After all, *everyone* is a salesperson.

To be effective in life, you need to learn how to get people to do what you want them to do. Success in making change is largely salesmanship. To solve a problem, it will help if you realize that part of the problem is persuading people to do what you want them to.

Author Jesse Nirenberg writes, "You need to sell your ideas to get ahead. Your talent can't be known unless your good ideas are tried. Their successes mean your success."

Finding solutions for problems is only half the job in life. The other half is building *support* for them, gaining the *willing* cooperation of other people. As President Harry Truman used to say, it takes skill to get people "to do what they ought to do without persuasion."

THE SECRETS OF SELLING:
The greatest secret in selling is that people do things for *their* reasons, not yours.

Peak performance sellers have discovered what successful people in every field have known for centuries: you can't talk people into anything they're not willing to do. Being persuasive is finding what people want and helping them get it.

Learning to sell from the *customer's* viewpoint is a lesson most salespeople never learn.

Successful sales trainer Larry Wilson says the best way for salespeople to reduce their stress is to stop trying to get people to do what they don't want to do. Yet every day I hear salespeople talking about their frustration in getting people to do something, without any concern for the *other* person's viewpoint.

I hear, "It's easier for me," or "I'd like you to do this for me." I don't hear, "Here's a way *you* could save some time."

These salespeople focus too much on their own objectives and not enough on the *other* person's viewpoint. As a result, they encounter *sales resistance*.

The salesperson who doesn't sell from the *customer's* viewpoint won't make many sales.

The frustrated father who can't help his son find his *own* reasons for wanting to learn in school will feel the pain of seeing him struggle.

The female executive who asserts herself without letting other managers know what *they'll* gain will eventually feel the pressures of prejudice.

The attorney who isn't able to create an atmosphere of trust in negotiations by convincing the other side that *their* needs are being met will *lose* the important deals.

The brilliant Ph.D. graduate who doesn't sell what he can do for a prospective employer—from the *employer's* point of view—won't get the job he really wants. Neither will the hard-working foreman.

A job interview requires the same sales skills as a sales call. You won't get the job you want unless you can translate your work experience and your skills into *benefits* to your employer. You've got to sell what you can *do* for the employer, not what you've done.

The *habit* of benefit selling would be new to most salespeople, but not to the great persuaders in history. From religion to politics, the great persuaders have always been benefit sellers.

Focusing on the needs of other people is doctrine in every major religion, although you might not recognize it in that context as a *sales* concept.

Evangelist Billy Graham is one of the world's great salespeople. Rev. Graham learned to sell as a sales "drummer" for Fuller Brushes. Now he's been seen in person by more people that anyone in history.

Graham excites audiences all over the world by speaking about Christ this way: "*He* can bring light to the city, light to your heart, give you new motivation, give you a *reason* for motivation."

Graham knows how to sell the end results of his religion, the *benefits* from the *believer's* viewpoint.

The Rev. Jesse Jackson carried what he learned about benefit selling as a preacher to his pursuit of the presidency:

> If you want someone to *feed the hungry*, here am I. Send me! If you want someone to *clothe the naked*, here am I. Send me! If you want someone who can *pull this nation together* —black, white, brown, old, young—here am I. Send me!

The Bible itself is rich in promise, rich in benefits.

The *New English Bible*, John, XI, vs. 25-26, reads, "I am the resurrection and I am life. If a man has faith in me, even though he die, he shall come to life: and no one who is alive and has faith shall ever die ...".

Can you think of a stronger benefit than that?

On the dark side, Adolph Hitler used benefit selling in his rise to such incredible personal power that he could motivate people to commit some of the greatest atrocities of history against mankind.

According to author B.F. Smith, Hitler developed at least some of his legendary power of influence by selling his paintings in beer halls, and in door-to-door canvassing.

Thinking benefits, Hitler wrote, "It (the new Reich) shall help people find an *easier road in this world. It shall help them in *making their lot a happier one.*"

In response to Hitler, Sir Winston Churchill used benefit selling in the House of Commons, June 18, 1940: "If we stand up to him, *all Europe may be freed*, and *the life of the world may move forward into broad sunlit lands.*"

Those were strong benefits, but Churchill didn't stop there. He spoke of the losses his ideas would prevent:

> But if we fail, the whole world, including the United States and all that we have known and cared for, will *sink into the abyss* of a new Dark Age made more sinister and perhaps more prolonged by the lights of a perverted science.

Finally, Churchill appealed to one last *emotional* benefit for his country-men, the pride they would *feel* in victory: "If the British Commonwealth and Empire last for a thousand years, men will still say this was our finest hour."

Ronald Reagan, considered one of the greatest sales communicators ever among world leaders, used these techniques when he was a candidate, debating with President Carter.

Reagan made voters think about the losses he believed they were incurring under the Carter Administration. "Are you better off today than you were four years ago?"

He promised to *free people from bureaucrats and taxes* so we could again *feel good about ourselves and our country*, benefits that many Americans wanted after years of government spending, inflation, and the recent nightmare of the hostage crisis in Iran.

Reagan consistently simplifies his message in easily understood stories that drive home the benefits of his programs. He's one of the most effective leaders ever in reducing complex issues to such understandable benefits as *more money per family, more control over your life, or feeling better about yourself and your country.*

Whether you agree with him or not, Reagan is a peak performance salesman, a benefit seller.

In contrast, Reagan's opponent for the Presidency in 1980 was the bright, but detail conscious, Jimmy Carter. Andrew Young said that Carter had an "engineer's view of the world," with the result that "every detail of the bridge was in place, but he didn't tell the American people where it was going."

Carter didn't tap into our motivation with any compelling vision of the *benefits* of his ideas.

That's where most salespeople go wrong. They talk too much about the *details* of their product. Research has proven that salespeople who dwell on the details of their ideas encounter substantially more questions and objections, sidetracking them from conversation about the positive impact of their ideas.

As sales pioneer Elmer Wheeler said in the 1930's, "Sell the sizzle, not the steak." Sell the *results* customers can expect from your product when they use it.

The same benefit-selling techniques that have worked for the great persuaders of history will work for you.

YOU'RE SELLING CONCEPTS, NOT PRODUCTS

Everything you do in selling must be done with the *customer's* viewpoint in mind.

Customers buy *concepts*, their unique idea of what our products will do for them. The real products are always the *results* customers want from the products.

The reasons for buying are so personal that two people seldom buy the same product for the same reason. Each customer wants different results based on how he'll *apply* the product to his situation. The ability to provide these expected results become his criteria for selecting one product over another.

What the customer wants from using the product is always more than what the product is or does. It goes beyond the normal boundaries of how we define our product so that effective sellers are almost always working "outside the product."

When you meet a customer, the customer's basic concept of the results he wants is *already in place*. It's easier to use the customer's thinking *as it is* to influence him than it is to change his concept of results.

Since the customer's situation and feelings are always changing, and he's exposed to new information, the results he wants are also always changing.

The one critical skill in selling is the ability to think from the *customer's* viewpoint so you can customize the application of your product to the customer's objectives and way of thinking about his situation. No one can describe how a customer thinks about results better than the customer himself, so one of your first goals in selling is to get the customer to *verbalize* his concept of results.

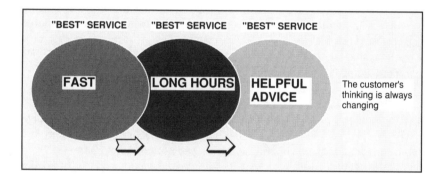

WHAT'S IN IT FOR ME?

One of the advertising slogans for Wendy's Restaurants raised the critical issue in benefit selling as well as anything I've seen: "Where's the beef?"

Are your customers still asking, "Where's the beef?" when it comes time to buy? Maybe you're not putting enough beef into your products, enough *reason* to buy.

Think of the most difficult person you know to sell—your boss, your toughest prospect, maybe even your spouse or a parent. Down deep, even this person has a *hot button*, a motivation lever that can be your yes button if you can trigger it. If you can link your ideas to that lever, you can drive him to action.

THE SECRETS OF SELLING:
No matter what your product is, every customer wants you to answer one question: *"What's in it for me?"*

"What's in it for me?" The answers to this question are the *benefits* of your idea from the customer's viewpoint.

Benefits are usually results such as *feel better, have more money*, or *save time* that represent a *gain*, something the customer can have more of or do better. They cut through to what your product really means to your customer in plain language.

Benefits can also be solutions to *problems*. They may be results that resolve troubles or *prevent* potential losses that may occur from what a customer is doing now.

Soviet leader Mikhail Gorbachev spoke bluntly of losses when he said, "To exercise self-determination through secession is to blow apart the union, to pit people against one another and to sow discord, bloodshed, and death."

Research in decision making has proven that saving your customer from a sure loss is frequently more persuasive than promising him an even larger gain.

Trouble takes precedence over gain in creating urgency for a sale. The threat of *losing* is tangible, immediate, and motivating.

Think what excites you about other people's ideas.

You're probably willing to pay money to *have more money*, to *make life easier*, to be *free of stress*, or to have *more fun*. As a business owner, you might pay more for *faster profits*, or for *profits that are more certain*. From your viewpoint, any of these benefits could be good reasons to take action.

World renowned advertising executive David Ogilvy writes, "Consumers still buy products whose advertising promises them value for money, beauty, nutrition, relief from suffering, social status and so on. All over the world."

The famous human relations trainer Dale Carnegie demonstrates how well he knew how to win friends and influence people:

> Personally, I am very fond of strawberries and cream; but I find that for some strange reason fish prefer worms. So, when I go fishing, I don't think about what I want. I think about what they want. I don't bait the hook with strawberries and cream. Rather, I dangle a worm or a grasshopper in front of the fish and say, 'Wouldn't you like to have that?'

Nothing is a benefit unless the customer *thinks* of it as a benefit. You can sell a refrigerator to an Eskimo if you can show him it will help keep things *cool*, instead of frozen.

A customer's evaluation of your product is always distorted by his fear of change, and by his not *thinking* of all the benefits. He's likely to ask himself if it's worth the price and the hassle of changing what he's doing, and worth the risk of feeling less secure. He may ask himself if it's worth the extra effort now.

Normally, you won't be able to change your product much to meet the customer's objectives, but you can change how he views the *value* of your product by mentioning its benefits. Unless *you* establish the value of your product, the customer will create his *own* idea of the value.

All too often, salespeople stop short of giving their customers *reasons* to buy.

Businessman Leo McGinneva is remembered by salespeople for his classic line about why people buy drill bits: "They don't want quarter-inch bits. They want quarter-inch holes." The *results* of your product are what drive a customer to action.

THE SECRETS OF SELLING:
The customer doesn't care about what your product *is*; he cares about what it *does*.

Promise is the soul of selling. To learn how the sales professionals sell the promise of results, watch for the benefits in television ads and in those direct mail letters you receive at home.

The next time you're in a bookstore, look at the nonfiction titles. *How to Win Friends and Influence People* and *Learning to Love Forever* are typical of the many benefit-promising book titles that catch your eye and your money.

These sales professionals know it takes strong benefits to make their products stand out and be noticed among hundreds of other products.

If I could teach new salespeople just *one* skill, it would be benefit selling. Legendary automaker Henry Ford wrote, "If there is one secret of success, it is the ability to get the other person's point of view and see things from *his angle* as well as your own.

Think of your customer as if you were him, and you'll get "the feel of the sale."

STRETCHING THE BENEFITS

There's an easy way to identify the results in your products that will drive people to action. We call it *Stretch Benefit Selling,* in our Feel of Success® Sales Seminars.

Every product or idea is comprised of FEATURES which are the attributes that describe what it is, how it's made, how it works and how it's different from other products, whether or not it's used. Features are the facts and characteristics that make a product what it is.

A product's features may include such things as size, color, shape, price, location, or the material it is made of. Features are usually tangible. You can see them or touch them.

In a sense, features *cause* the results your product provides. The key to benefit selling is to translate these details into *benefits*, *stretch benefits*, and *custom stretch benefits*.

Most salespeople allow themselves to be trapped into talking about details and never get around to talking about *results*. Compared to benefit sellers, these salespeople encounter substantially more sales resistance, have to answer more questions, and take longer to make a sale.

Here's what an industrial salesman in one of my seminars said about using benefit selling to sell a technical product:

> My business is a technical business. It can take 45 minutes to explain even the basics of some of our products properly to a buyer. That makes it tough when the buyer has only given me twenty minutes to sell him. If I didn't stick to stretch benefit selling, I couldn't do it.

And here's what a sales manager for an electronics firm had to say:

> Since I've returned from your seminar I haven't let a sales letter go out of my office until it has answered, "What's in it for me?" for the prospect. That's what makes the world go around.

The features of your products are only important because they function in some way to solve problems or provide benefits for the customer when the product is used.

BENEFITS are the positive results of your product from the *customer's* viewpoint: what the features do or how they function to solve a problem. Product benefits are typically things such as *works faster, costs less*, or *lasts longer*.

Most salespeople *stop* at features in their selling. Some mention the benefits. But very few salespeople stretch their thinking to show customers the positive end results of their products, the one thing guaranteed to excite your customers.

Features and benefits are only important to customers because they lead to STRETCH BENEFITS, the positive end results of your products from the customer's point of view. Stretch benefits are usually benefits stretched to the end result for the customer such as *save time, save money*, or *feel better*.

But don't stop there! Stretch again!

To really communicate with people, describe the CUSTOM STRETCH BENEFITS that tailor the product to the customer's objectives the way the customer talks about them. For example, the most motivating result of saving time on the job might be that a buyer could be *home in time to have dinner with his family more often.* To stretch this far, you need to think through how a customer might apply your product.

Some of the most powerful stretch benefits are *emotional benefits* such as *feeling important, having a sense of accomplishment, being free of worry, feeling good,* or *having fun.*

Marketing Professor Theodore Levitt of the Harvard Business School writes, "People buy hopeful expectations, not actual things ... How we feel about a car is more important than how the car feels."

Selling is a transference of feeling, of conviction. If you can help other people get the feelings they want, you can get what you want. Motivation begins with feelings.

With custom stretch benefits you're talking the customer's language. No jargon. No details to sort through to find the beef in your ideas.

THE SECRETS OF SELLING:
Stretch the benefits of your ideas until you're sure you've speaking from the *customer's* viewpoint.

To be sure you always stretch the benefits of your products, keep saying to yourself, "which means" or "that means" after each description of your product until you reach the last possible positive end result from the customer's point of view.

For example, a retail salesperson might sell a product with an extra-strength lock by saying,

> This product comes with an extra-strength lock (feature) which means you'll have more protection than you would have with other locks (benefit). That means you'll save money on your insurance (stretch benefit) and your valuables will always be there when you need them (stretch benefit). Ultimately, that means you'll have less worry (stretch benefit) and feel better in your new home (a custom stretch benefit).

As you keep moving toward that last answer to what your product means to the customer, the persuasive impact is higher for each successive answer.

Some salespeople actually discipline themselves to stretch the benefits of their products by using the words "features," "benefits," and "which means" in their conversation with customers until they lock in their new behavior.

This same stretching process works in driving home the losses a buyer might incur by continuing to do what he's doing. Stretch them out to the logical end result.

Let's say you wanted to sell someone a tax-deferred retirement investment product. The customer may now be relying on social security to meet his needs for retirement. By not having your product, he's paying more taxes than he needs to pay *(a loss)*, which means he'll be faced with lifelong worry *(a stretch loss)*.

As you mention the benefits and stretch benefits of your products to the customer, use the words "you" or "your" to drive them home as personally as you can (e.g. "you will save"). When you mention the losses the customer is incurring without your product, stay in the third person to minimize his defensiveness (e.g. "when a *company* uses second hand parts").

For customer service employees in high-traffic sales situations such as airline, hotel, and car rental service agents, bank counselors, and food service employees, one sentence benefit selling is the only way they can sell. They don't have time for extensive sales presentations when they have a long line of customers waiting for service.

With stretch benefit selling, these front-line salespeople can make their sales points fast and powerfully.

Stretch benefit selling *works*.

You can practice stretch benefit selling by picking up a common object you see every day, such as a clothespin or a toothbrush, and describing each of its distinguishing features. Mention as many benefits as you can, and stretch the benefits to the point of being ridiculous to burn that thinking process into your mind.

Once you have the feel of selling stretch benefits, make a Stretch Benefit Selling Chart on a piece of paper to plan a real presentation of a product or an idea that you want to sell.

Begin by describing what you want the person to do in one sentence. It's very important you keep your objective to one sentence because once you've completed your conversation with this person, you want him to walk away knowing exactly what you want him to do.

Next, describe your product or idea as you might describe it to another person by listing the features, benefits, and stretch benefits in separate columns on the chart, and then by stretching the stretch benefits one more time to customize them for the customer. Any one feature may have several benefits or stretch benefits.

Most sales training courses teach only features and benefits, without the stretch benefit and custom stretch benefit columns. We include the two extra columns because we've found that without them most salespeople stop short of *stretching* the benefits. They end up selling features.

Knowing the fine difference between the four columns isn't as important as developing the *habit* of thinking and talking end results from the *customer's* viewpoint.

As you look at your Stretch Benefit Chart, which column do you think customers buy from? The custom stretch benefit column, of course.

But which column do most salespeople sell from? The features column, by a landslide. It's no wonder so many salespeople don't sell more than they do!

COVER YOUR BASES WITH ALL THE BUYING INFLUENCES

Whether you're selling to an organization or a family, you may have to identify different stretch benefits for each of several people making or influencing the buying decision. *One sales strategy won't fit all.*

In a business or a family, you will find people playing the following roles in the buying process: signer to the financial decision, user of the product, screener of potential suppliers based on criteria such as cost, legal considerations, or engineering requirements, and the champion or antagonist who can either help you make the sale or stop you.

THE SECRETS OF SELLING:
Cover your bases with the *signer*,
the *users*, the *screeners*, and your
champion or *antagonist*.

For any particular sale, there's only one signer. The signer gives final approval to release the dollars to buy. The larger the purchase, or the more unfamiliar the seller is to the buyer, the higher this role is performed in the organization, or the more members of the family are likely to be involved.

While each signer's personal style is different, in general the signer is most interested in five things: return on investment, the seller's knowledge of his company or situation, how the product concept fits with the business, the seller's credibility, and how the purchase will affect the organization's future.

Users either use the product or personally supervise its use. They're problem-centered. They're most interested in technical issues and how your product will help them solve a problem *now*; do their work faster, easier, or more efficiently on a daily basis; or enjoy themselves as they use it. They want to know how it will save them hassles and work for them personally.

The role of screeners is to eliminate suppliers, to screen out those products from consideration that don't meet specifications. They can say "no," but they can't say "yes."

The screener is more interested than other buyers in minimizing risk and in features such as price, delivery, and technical specifications. Even in a family, one person often shops many suppliers to select the ones that will receive final consideration.

People in a position to play the role of champion or antagonist for your idea are usually interested in looking good by association or disassociation with your idea. It often helps to develop a champion relationship before you meet with the signer so you have access to information that will help you make the sale.

Most salespeople sell only to the buying influence with whom they are most comfortable, the one who seems most interested in their product.

To be a peak performance seller, you have to discipline yourself to cover your bases with the people playing all these roles in each sale. Remind yourself to develop a strategy of stretch benefit selling to the different objectives of each buying influence.

By now, you know why product knowledge and customer knowledge are so important in selling. Without them, you'll have trouble thinking of the right custom stretch benefits to use to satisfy each of these different interests.

When you know and believe in the many stretch benefits of your products, you're almost always more motivated to sell the product so others can enjoy it.

SELLING TO THE RIGHT OBJECTIVE

Your product will explode in the customer's mind if you can link it to his most important objective *at this moment*, the dominant objective that serves as his motivation lever. The dominant objective is the customer's hot spot of motivational impact.

The stretch benefits of your product won't grab real attention until you've linked them to the customer's immediate objectives. Keep in mind that your customer's top priorities may change from day to day, as his needs and feelings change.

The dominant objective that makes the sale may even change between sales calls. It's unrealistic to assume that a buyer's objectives won't change from one sales contact to another.

The application of stretch benefit selling requires discipline. You can't afford to confuse the customer's viewpoint with your own viewpoint, or with the viewpoint of other customers.

What is accepted as a stretch benefit of your product by one customer may not be seen as a stretch benefit at all by another customer. The hot spots that sell in the heartland of the U.S. may not sell well on Wall Street.

The key to stretch benefit selling is selling to the right customer objectives, the ones most important to the customer at this moment in time.

The most effective way I've found to think clearly about a sales problem and to organize my selling is to complete The Feel of Success Sales Planner in chapter Nine.

The first step in completing the sales planner is to think of the person you're trying to sell. List as many of his objectives as you can think of, even objectives that don't seem to relate directly to your product.

Some of these objectives will be personal objectives such as "be promoted to marketing manager" or "have more time with my family." Some will be job-result objectives such as "stay within budget" or "increase sales."

Think of the customer's objectives as though he were not even considering your product. This way of thinking usually leads you to new insight into how your product might benefit the customer. It may even lead you to think of a different product that would meet his needs better.

This is one of the creative sides of selling: looking for the key objective to sell to.

THE SECRETS OF SELLING:
Sales strategy begins with the *customer's* objectives.

Starting your analysis with the customer's objectives forces you to be customer-centered rather than product-centered.

You can identify these objectives by thinking of your experience with similar customers, by asking the customer questions about his objectives, by making a preliminary call to learn more about the customer, by asking other people what they know about the customer, or by simply imagining what your objectives might be if you were in his position.

Really empathize with the customer. What would your problems and objectives be if you were in his shoes? Think of what his customers want from him. Think of his goals with regard to finances, customers, employees, sales, inventory, suppliers, seasonality, promotion, competitors, anything that will give a clue to his objectives at this moment.

Second, define in one positive sentence what the customer is doing now that you would like him to change (e.g., buying from many suppliers).

Third, describe what the customer is losing by continuing to do what he is doing. List as many losses as you can. Stretch the losses by describing them the way the customer might talk about them. Make them "hurt."

Fourth, in one positive sentence, describe what you want the customer to do, when you expect him to do it, and, if your objective is an order, what quantity you want him to order. "Buy 1,000 units from me by April 1" is better than "Stop buying from my competitor." When your customer walks away from your conversation he should be able to tell himself in one sentence exactly what it is you want him to do.

Sixth, stretch the benefits.

Seventh, list the objections you expect to encounter as sales resistance. Many times, just listing them next to the stretch benefits of your product will help you identify possible answers to those objections.

Finally, select and circle the one customer objective or one problem you think is most motivating to the customer at this moment in time. If it matches the benefits and stretch benefits your product can provide, this is the dominant objective on which to build your sales strategy.

If you're not able to match any of the benefits and stretch benefits of your product to the customer's dominant objective, move to his second most important objective, then to his third most important objective, and so on until you find a match.

If none of the benefits and stretch benefits you can offer match any of the customer's key objectives, start over with a different product or with a different customer. You're not likely to make the sale.

The sales planner provides a good framework for talking about your product. You can create a smooth sales presentation by moving back and forth across the chart, from what the customer is doing now to his losses, and from his objectives to the stretch benefits of your product.

This simple analysis is the heart of selling. It rivets your attention to the *customer's* viewpoint.

If you can discipline yourself to think this way consistently in approaching customers, you can be more persuasive every time.

You don't have to write this analysis out for each prospect, only think this way. Remember, to get a customer excited about your product, you have to answer one question for him: "What's in it for me?"

Selling becomes difficult the moment you lose sight of this simple idea.

When my father and I started our first training business, we received an inquiry I'll never forget from the training director of one of the world's largest corporations. In the space "number of employees" on the reply card, he had marked 750,000.

The prospect wanted the programs immediately, and they weren't even completed. And he wanted them in *Spanish*!

We weren't about to lose an opportunity this large over an issue as "small" as not having a product. We gave a presentation armed with nothing more than ideas, workbook covers, and the promise of helping our prospect meet his objectives. The promise was backed by the proof of our past successes in our respective careers.

You know what? He didn't want to see *training programs*. He wanted to know what results we could achieve for him, and we showed him by selling benefits.

That sales presentation was one of the most effective I've ever made. I was forced to concentrate on building trust, on listening for the prospect's objectives, and on selling the benefits and stretch benefits that met his needs.

We made our sale.

KNOWING BENEFITS ISN'T ENOUGH

Most salespeople, especially experienced salespeople, know they should sell from the customer's viewpoint. They just don't do it.

The most frequent reason salespeople don't use benefit selling is the false assumption that the customer knows the benefits of their products, and that he is *thinking* of them when he makes his decision to buy.

I call this breakdown in thinking "seller's trap:" the tendency of salespeople to stop short of talking about benefits because they *assume* the customer knows them, or because they think they would be talking *down* to the customer to mention them.

Real estate selling is one of the best examples of how salespeople fall into a trap of *assuming* too much.

I can think of few professions that offer more opportunity for benefit selling than real estate. Everywhere you turn in a house there are dozens of features, ranging from the home's location to the layout of the kitchen—which produce benefits that make life easier or more enjoyable for potential buyers.

Yet, listening to most real estate salespeople, you would think houses were nothing more than price, square feet, and number of rooms, without an ounce of emotion involved in their purchase. You would think no one intended to live in the house.

Most real estate salespeople assume too much. They assume their buyers are thinking of the conveniences and good feelings they would have living in the home so they don't sell benefits.

Salespeople worry they're talking down to customers by mentioning the obvious benefits of their products. They're even more concerned if they're suggesting a product which has ten features that all lead to the same stretch benefit, such as save money.

If you could show a customer ten ways he could save money, do you really think he'd mind if you mentioned them all? He would love it!

THE SECRETS OF SELLING:
The peak performance seller "hits his customer over the head" with the stretch benefits of his product until they register. If the customer isn't *thinking* of the benefits, those benefits are not part of the sale.

As actress Mae West said, "Too much of a good thing can be wonderful."

No benefit is too simple, or can be mentioned too often, if it's important to the customer. The big ideas in selling are simple ideas, simple solutions to problems.

Some salespeople complain they can't sell because their product is the same as other products.

Your competitors may offer the same benefits, but if you're the only salesperson who mentions those benefits, the only salesperson who forces the customer to think about them, those benefits are all yours.

Joel Raphaelson, of Ogilvy & Mather Advertising, writes,

> In the past, just about every advertiser has assumed that in order to sell his goods he has to convince consumers that his product is superior to his competitor's. This may not be necessary. It may be sufficient to convince consumers that your product is positively good. If the consumer feels certain that your product is good and feels uncertain about your competitors, he will buy yours.

An insurance salesman in one of my seminars has this to say about benefit selling:

> I learned benefit selling in a sales class years ago, but I never used it much until I realized that my customers didn't know the benefits of my products as well as I thought they did. I had always thought everyone knew what insurance was all about. Now I can't imagine making a sales call without mentioning the benefits of my products.

In *In Search of Excellence,* consultants Thomas Peters and Robert Waterman cite an example of a friend of theirs who bought an IBM computer system, even though IBM'S price was twenty-five percent higher than the competition. Their friend explained his thinking this way:

> IBM alone took the trouble to get to know us. They interviewed extensively up and down the line. They talked our language, no mumbo jumbo on computer innards... their presentations were to the point. Everything about them smacked of assurance and success.

The IBM salespeople sold benefits, not details.

In today's selling environment, if you don't make your points about your product fast, you won't make them at all. Your prospects will tune you out.

During many sales presentations, the prospect is thinking, "Faster, faster. Get to the point." Don't let this happen to you. Get right to the results of your ideas.

This same rule applies to letter writing. A letter of 50 words that includes three strong benefits linked to the customer's objectives will be far more powerful than a letter of 250 words with lots of detail but no "beef." The details water down the impact of the benefits. The extra features mentioned in the longer letter may even raise questions and concerns unnecessarily. And confused customers won't buy.

If you can't be persuasive in 30 to 60 seconds of describing your product, you probably won't be persuasive in an hour. You haven't thought through your idea well enough to know the custom stretch benefits for the customer.

WHY YOUR PRODUCT IS BETTER

The complaint I hear from salespeople in every industry is, "I can't sell my product when our price is so much higher than the competition."

Sometimes it may seem as if every competitor has the edge over you on every product. But if that were true, you wouldn't have any customers.

There will always be someone with a lower price or some other important selling edge. What are you going to do, give up every day?

Professor Theodore Levitt of the Harvard University Business School writes, "The fact that price differences are measurable becomes the usual, and usually false, basis for asserting their powerful primacy."

Products are worth what they *do*, not what they cost. If you can sell the *value* of your product, you can maintain a higher price and make more money.

Sales consultant Zig Ziglar writes, "People buy what they want when they want it more than they want the money it costs." Every price is too high until the customer sees the stretch benefits in the product for himself.

Know your products well enough, so that you can say, "My company can do something for you that no one else can do." And it had better be something other than price.

I conducted personal interviews with the salespeople of a major financial services corporation in Florida. One of the questions I asked them was, "Why should I come to you for your checking product, rather than go to your competitor down the street?"

Of the 60 experienced salespeople participating in the interviews, only thirteen could give us one reason! Only seven could give us as many as three reasons.

There's always at least one reason, even if it's only, "I'm here, and I'm not down the street. I'm going to see that you get the service you want from us."

No matter what you're selling, you should know at least three good reasons why your product is a better value than what your competitor offers.

Most salespeople are too "down-in-the-mouth" about their products. They focus on their product's weaknesses, and they think they can't sell their product if their price is higher than the competition.

One customer has said product A is better than their product in some way. Another customer has said product B is better. So when a third customer says product C is better, a salesperson may start feeling as if everybody's product is better in every respect, that he has no advantage, nothing to offer.

Remember, your customers are comparing your product one on one against the competition, not one against the world.

Every product doesn't have the same total value your product does. The uniqueness of your product goes beyond the details to the promise of satisfaction.

The key to benefit selling is to know what has value to each customer.

It's not your product, but what you put into your product, the way you link it to what customers want, that gives you the edge. And those few customers for whom you can't offer enough value aren't the prospects to be spending your time with.

THE SECRETS OF SELLING:
Sell the satisfaction in your product that gives it value, not the product or it's price.

When I think of selling value, I think of the computer consultant who pressed a few keys on a computer terminal for his client and solved his problem. When he was questioned by his client later about his invoice for $1,000, he explained, "That's $ .50 for my time, and $999.50 for knowing what keys to press!" It's difficult to put a value on twenty years of experience.

Your competitive edge is the total value you create for your product, the whole package of expectations.

David Ogilvy writes, "It pays to give most products an image of quality—a first class ticket."

Think of your own experience as a shopper. Do you always buy the least expensive car or the least expensive clothing? Probably not.

For most products, market research demonstrates that factors other than price rank highest in importance to buyers. Many grocery shoppers will pay almost twice as much for hydroponically grown spinach as for dirt-grown, because they don't have to wash it and pull out the stems!

In the long run, IBM's Peanut computer was a mixed success because the industry overestimated consumer demand for home computers.

But the Peanut computer received instant short term market acceptance, not because of its price or its representing anything genuinely new, but because buyers were presold on the intangible benefits of buying from IBM. They bought "hassle free" maintenance and service, the security of knowing that IBM is likely to be around a while, and the ease they felt in recommending IBM to their management—or their families.

IBM sells *total value*.

As a rule, sell results, not price. You can negotiate a sale when competitors have ten advantages over your product, if you can offer the one result that's most important to your customer.

The Profit Impact of Market Strategy team of The Strategic Planning Institute in Cambridge, Massachusetts concludes, "the variable most closely associated with long-term financial performance... is relative perceived quality." If you can sell quality, you can sell at a higher price.

To identify exactly where your product strengths are, select the product you're most interested in selling more of, and compare it directly to your competitors' products using the value categories below. Analyze your product by identifying at least one advantage you have over the competition, and one stretch benefit this advantage provides the customer.

KEY VALUE CATEGORIES

1. *Dollar differences* such as price, rates, charges, or incentives to buy.

2. *Conveniences* such as location, hours, time savings, self-service, toll-free service lines, or sales staff who go to the buyer.

3. *Personal attention* such as frequent contact, counseling, relationship management, or you as a salesperson.

4. *Information* such as easy access to account data, product specialists, or experts; financial information for counseling, statements, or reports; or newsletters, and seminars.

5. *Service quality* such as speed or accuracy, responsiveness, waiting time, cleanlinessness, or "little" things done better.

6. *Protections* such as insurance, security against risk, guarantees, warranties, or privacy.

7. *Emotional satisfactions* such as simplicity, prestige, sense of belonging, account manager relationship, familiarity, recognition, or office environment.

8. *Product selection* such as availability of related products, innovation, or special products for selected customer groups or new customers.

9. *Service policies* on decision making, "fixing" problems, approvals, contract release, or flexibility.

10. *Customer support* such as education, local contacts, co-op advertising, warehousing, or product servicing.

11. *Contract terms* such as payment plans or product minimums.

12. *Technical superiority* such as systems, automation, product durability, or hassle-free operation.

13. *Financial impact* such as cost savings, productivity gains, or return on investment.

These factors and others make up the total value of your product. Every plus factor on your list helps to make your product seem *worth* more. Any one factor on the list could be the most important factor to one customer at any moment in time.

Author and sports agent Mark McCormack writes that the value of your product can also include how unique it is, how badly the customer needs it, what it would cost the customer to replace it, precedents that are testimony to its higher value, and the presence of a "passion factor" with the customer. If the customer has a significant problem, the value of your product increases substantially.

Selling from the *customer's* viewpoint is the building block of motivation for all the great secrets of selling. In the next chapter, you'll learn how to apply this greatest secret in making favorable first impressions.

CHAPTER 4

First Impressions

Every sale begins with a contact moment, a first impression that is part personal chemistry. Your success in first impressions is always measured from the customer's viewpoint.

I've listened to thousands of salespeople share frustrations like these:

She's the key buyer for my best prospect, but after our first meeting she won't even see me, much less buy from me.

There are some prospects I just can't seem to get close to. I feel like we're on totally different wavelengths.

In my business I've got about two minutes to get a customer interested, or it's all over. Prospects just don't take me as seriously as I'd like them to, unless they take the time to get to know me.

These salespeople, many of them *experienced* salespeople, still have trouble getting appointments, building rapport, establishing their credibility, and getting a fair hearing or overcoming resistance in their first meetings with prospects. Their *first impressions* are holding them back.

Success in selling is built on success with *people*, and people care about first impressions.

In selling, first impressions are an integral part of developing trust. Given roughly equal products, the salesperson who meets the personal needs of his prospects in first impressions is more likely to get the sale.

Before you develop strategies for selling to one of your best prospects, you need strategies for establishing solid contact with him as a person.

Every salesperson wants to get close to more people in order to increase sales. Even if you are good at attracting people to you, you may want help in attracting the *right people*.

This chapter is about how to get the attention of these people, connect with them psychologically, and make a favorable first impression. Mastering these basic relationship and social networking skills is critical in building a successful sales career. Without them, your ideas won't be heard.

Executive research consultant James Challenger says of looking for a job, "how well you are liked, not how competent you are, will determine if you get hired."

When Henry Ford II fired Lee Iacocca from Ford Motor Co., his entire explanation to Iacocca was four words: "I don't like you." Fair, or unfair, first impressions and personal rapport matter.

In your selling, you can act in ways that make people feel better about themselves and draw them to you, or you can act in ways that make them feel rejected, unimportant, or threatened, and push them away. Fortunately, you can *learn* to make yourself more easily liked, respected, and trusted by people so you can connect with them quickly.

The more people you connect with, the more you increase the possibility of meeting someone who can add something to your sales.

Here's what a realtor in Florida told me about why he views every prospect as a potential buyer:

> When people walk into our office, I never know at first if they're
> really serious about buying a home or not. In either case, that may be
> my only opportunity to sell them on doing business with me rather
> than with some other realtor. If I can connect with them as someone
> who cares about them, at least they might mention my name to some-
> one who *will* buy.

Every salesperson wants to be *remembered*. Think of the thousands of people who pass through your life like speeding bullets. How many of them do *you* actually remember?

You can't possibly relate closely to everyone you encounter. Your mind would be swamped with information about them. Your time would be fragmented into hundreds of hopelessly scattered contacts.

Instead, you *choose* who to relate to. So do your prospects and other people you want to influence. They also carefully select the people with whom they spend their time.

THE SECRETS OF SELLING:
Sell yourself before you sell your ideas.

If people resist you or withdraw from you in the first moments of a sales contact, you may be giving off negative cues and *creating* resistance.

People like people who help them to like themselves. That's what first impressions are really about.

THE CONTACT MOMENT

If you don't connect during your *first impressions* in selling, you may never connect.

Research by Dr. Leonard Zunin and others has shown that you have an average of four minutes to connect with a stranger in a social situation before he decides to continue or not continue the contact.

On a sales call, that figure may be as little as *fifteen* seconds. These first seconds should be devoted totally to the other person. This is the *contact moment*, and it affects everything that follows. And doesn't your customer deserve a few seconds of one-to-one, "It's you and me only," human contact before you get down to business?

Putting customers at ease is essential in developing *trust*, yet salespeople who have excessive customer contact often find themselves trapped in a routine-like "sales trance" in which they focus inward on themselves. As a result, they may fail to take even simple actions to make their customers feel important, such as standing to greet them.

Breaking this trance is the first step toward a strong first impression.

Most of the impressions you make in these first seconds are made before you say a word. Some impressions are actually made before you meet your prospect, as you're walking into the building or talking with other customers or employees in a service area. In selling, you're *always* on stage. And like it or not, these first impressions *last*.

People tend to make judgments about you long before all the information is complete. Very often, a person can't even explain why he has an instant bad impression of a salesperson. The salesperson may have reminded him of someone with whom he once had a bad experience. Or the salesperson may have somehow made him feel less important.

Through a psychological phenomenon called *closure*, people tend to "lock on" to these first impressions and to "lock out" later information. The customer closes his mind to new information as his mind jumps ahead, fitting in the missing pieces.

In other words, it's actually possible to burn your bridges *before* you.

THE SECRETS OF SELLING:
First impressions *last*, so make them count.

Ronald Reagan's success in building a "teflon presidency" prior to the Iranian arms scandal is a good example of the power of first impressions in selling.

Once the public made up its mind to trust Reagan, it became very difficult to make the nation's problems "stick" to him. As Reagan himself said, "Maybe the people have a way of sensing that I like them."

Think of the time you spend with the people closest to you—your life partner, your best friend, your children, maybe even someone at work.

The most important moments of the day between you are the first moments that you're together, and the first moments when you get together again at the end of the day. You wouldn't want to greet these people by complaining or by putting them on the defensive. How much positive attention would you get for the rest of the day?

If you walk into your first sales call with a frown or a frazzled look on your face, aren't you likely to get tension and resistance in return? You've already set the tone and created the expectations for everything that follows.

These first moments are especially important in your relations with people you're meeting for the *first* time. First impressions are the only basis they have for judging you. And in the contact moment, perceptions are more important than reality.

Most of us *care* about the people we meet, but not everyone can get those feelings across.

Good intentions aren't enough. If other people don't *feel* your caring, it's not there as far as they're concerned. You may be very professional and interested in your customer, but if he interprets your behavior as evidence you *lack* professionalism or you're *not* interested in his needs, you're destined to have trouble gaining his trust.

Behaviors such as seeming nervous, talking too much, or projecting a negative attitude are *trustbusting*. They could cost you a sale or a relationship that might have worked had it been given a chance to develop.

In *Four Minute Sell*, author Janet G. Elsea urges everyone to ask themselves, "What do I look like?," What do I sound like?," What do I say?," and "How well do I listen?"

How do you think others interpret *your* behavior in the first seconds of contact? Are your first seconds working *for* you, or against you?

MAKE ME FEEL IMPORTANT

Everyone wants good feelings about himself. That's really what you're selling in the first moments of contact.

Dr. Leonard Zunin writes, "In general, the ability to make another human being feel better about himself in the first four minutes of communication is synonymous with the ability to make that person feel good about you.

This means you can sell yourself best by creating the expectation for customers that they'll feel good being around you, that you can be trusted to treat them as though they're important.

THE SECRETS OF SELLING:
The most important rule for strong first impressions is *help people feel important*.

Whenever you meet someone new, think, "Make him feel important."

Sales Analysis Institute sales consultant James Foster used to make up signs for his executive sales classes that read, "Make me feel important." He said those signs were the only training materials that consistently disappeared after his classes. It was a concept *every* student identified with.

Banesh Hoffman, professor emeritus of physics at Queens College in New York, still recalls his first encounter with the great thinker, Albert Einstein.

> I had been working on something in relativity at Princeton when my friends told me, 'Why don't you go show this to Einstein?' I said, 'What, me?' They almost had to push me into his office. I knocked on the door timidly, and Einstein said, 'Come'—that was the European way—with a rising inflection. I went in, and there was Einstein. He was sloppily dressed and his hair was in its usual untidy array. He was sitting in the chair and he had a pad in his lap. He was evidently calculating something—that's the way he did it. He saw I was nervous, and said 'Put the equations on the board.' Then he added, 'Please go slowly—I don't understand things very quickly.'

One of the greatest thinkers in the history of science had the good human relations sense to help another human being feel comfortable and important.

The warm feelings people have when they're attracted to people are something they would like to repeat and develop further. They "lock in" to expectations of feeling good in the future.

It's this glow of feeling good about ourselves that explains the power of *sales charisma*. Charisma is really a promise we'll feel good when we're around a person who has a certain "presence."

The combination of feeling successful and helping other people feel positive about themselves leads to the good feeling, "I'm OK. You're OK." It's that feeling that gives you sales charisma. And, once you're perceived as having charisma, customers are more likely to overlook occasional "out of character" behavior.

Author and sports agent Mark H. McCormack writes, "One of life's biggest frustrations is that people don't do what you want them to do. But if you can control their impressions of you, you can make them *want* to do what you want them to do."

It's human nature to think of your own needs, but it's better human relations to think of your customer's needs.

Your first impression strengths may be your appearance, your credentials, your contacts, your conversation skills, your self-confidence, your energy, or one of a hundred other things. Even old fashioned, often-forgotten, *courtesy* plays a key role in selling.

Courtesy is simply doing or saying things that reinforce a person's self-esteem.

No one is too important not to have to think of the impact of courtesy. If you observe powerful people closely, you'll find they go out of their way to make gestures that put people at ease and show respect.

President Harry S. Truman's daughter, Margaret Truman writes,

> My father hated to use the buzzers on his desk to summon a man peremptorily. Nine times out of ten, he preferred to go to the aide's office. When he did summon a man, he would usually greet him at the door of the Oval Room office ... This constant consideration for others, the total lack of egotism with which Dad conducted the day-to-day affairs of the White House, was the real source of the enormous loyalty he generated in those around him.

When customers come to you, the minimum courtesy is to put aside what you're doing and stand to greet them.

Some salespeople who sell to walk-in customers from a desk tell me they'd feel like a piece of toast if they popped up and down all day to introduce themselves to each new customer. And they probably would. But they'd also break free from their sales *trance*, have fewer human relations problems, save themselves time because of less resistance, and make more sales.

THE SECRETS OF SELLING:
The golden rule of selling is, "Treat people the way *they* want to be treated."

The Golden Rule, "Do unto to others as you would have them do unto you" is probably the most frequently mentioned guideline for human relations.

But people may also want to be treated *differently* from you. Different people want different things from you, and what any one person wants changes every day.

APPEARANCE

Your appearance is your first impression. Appearances count. They buy you time until your customer gets to know you.

In selling, the limits of your relationship are sometimes established *before* you begin to sell.

The question most frequently asked by prospects before they meet a salesperson is probably, "What does he look like?" In fact, many first encounters are *entirely* superficial.

Looks count a lot. Gestures, dress, physical attributes, grooming, gender, age, facial expressions, posture, and style have importance far out of proportion to other issues in the first seconds of contact.

For example, psychological research has proven that people consistently attribute virtues to attractive people that they may *not* possess, such as conceit.

Also, based on a customer's prior experience with other people who look or act like you, some part of your appearance may stand out and distract him from seeing you as you really are.

Surprisingly, there is almost universal agreement on what is considered attractive; for example, we tend to be drawn to people who look confident because we respect competence, and confident people look like they could do things well.

While many key attributes in attractiveness are genetically determined, most are attributes you can influence.

The tendency of people to make quick judgments based on your appearance is an *opportunity* for you. By paying a little attention to your first impression, you can be seen as more confident, more intelligent, more likable, more interesting, and more credible.

To some extent, the way a person looks *is* him. When somebody says his name and you think of him, it's the way he *looks* that's in your mind.

Your appearance projects your attitude and your goals. Most salespeople look as though they don't know where they want to go.

Think of what you're saying without saying anything in the first seconds of contact! At a minimum, prospects judge how you feel about yourself, how professional you are, how intelligent you are, how organized you are, how much authority you have, how self-confident you are, how much they can trust you, how much respect and concern you have for them, and how you're different from or similar to other salespeople.

Remember, they're deciding many of these things *before* you've said a word.

Even if you're *thinking* positively, you'll create *negative* expectations for your selling if you project a negative impression. Why put yourself at a disadvantage?

The way you relate to other people includes both what and how you feel, and how you tell and show other people what you feel.

Do *you* look in charge of yourself? Will other people feel better about themselves when they're around you? Does your appearance *strengthen* their trust in you?

THE SECRETS OF SELLING:
If you *look* like a professional salesperson, you're more likely to act like one and to be treated like one.

Research on the way people dress and present themselves has proven that some people actually *choose* to put themselves at a disadvantage in human relations with their appearance.

Of course, everyone has the right to choose an appearance that builds walls between himself and other people. Exercising that choice may even give a sense of independence that temporarily makes you feel better about yourself. This choice is OK, as long as you can accept that it may increase the resistance you get from other people every minute of every day.

It may prevent you from having *other* things you want *more.*

It doesn't matter whether the expectations of other people are "fair" or "unfair." You're not going to change those expectations.

What matters are the *results* of your appearance, the impact of your appearance on what you can accomplish and on your feelings of success.

How you dress is the first thing people notice about you when they meet you for the first time, particularly when you're meeting someone of the same sex. Peak performance sellers view dressing to meet the expectations of their customers as one of the small trade-offs they're willing to make for success.

If you're uptight when people suggest changes in your appearance, ask yourself why it's so important to hold onto a part of your style that may not be effective. Whenever you tell yourself, "I don't care what *they* think," there are people you won't be able to sell.

The way you dress tells customers how you feel about yourself and how you're likely to treat them. Dressing professionally says you care about yourself and you care about them.

If you want to be taken seriously in your selling, *dress for your objectives.*

IBM and most other successful corporations require trust-building conservative dress from their sales staff to save their salespeople unnecessary resistance and to increase the probability of their success.

IBM's founder, Thomas Watson, demanded IBM salespeople wear dark suits and white shirts to instill self-respect, and to build respect among the public.

When I started in sales, I invested in five high-quality business suits, one for each day of the week. I wanted to increase my chances for success, and I know it paid off.

But I've known hundreds of salespeople who use the way they dress to increase their feelings of independence, to act out self-defeating thoughts about themselves, or to make some "statement" about themselves that no one else understands.

They've misread the impact of their appearance on other people. Dealing with a salesperson who looks professional helps customers feel more important, and increases their trust in him.

Some salespeople want to dress better, but believe they don't have the money. Improving your appearance doesn't have to mean spending a lot of money. It means choosing the *right* look to meet the expectations of your customers.

It doesn't take a lot of money to wear clothes that fit, that are neat, that look professional, and that bring out the best in you regardless of fashion. It may cost more than you're spending now, but dressing professionally will *make* you money.

Get organized. Throw out clothes that don't work, and get some that do. When you buy clothes, figure the cost per wearing. Good clothes will last longer, as well as look better.

There's no reason why a saleswoman can't be feminine as well as professional, or why a salesman can't add a touch of "himself" to even the most conservative look. Just remember that distractions in your appearance such as flashy jewelry, sexy clothing, or sloppiness can send the wrong signals and *distract* customers from your message and natural strengths.

Dress to bring out the best in *you*, not to mirror the latest trend in high fashion (unless your business is fashion-sensitive). Your goal is to have people notice *you*, not what you're wearing.

Your choice of clothing can even be used to compensate for weaknesses in your first impression. For example, if you come across as too stern and threatening, you might choose to soften your look. If you look younger and less experienced than you want to look, you might choose a "high authority" look with a dark pin striped suit.

Confidence in your appearance helps; you're more likely to imagine yourself selling successfully. Executive clothing consultant John T. Molloy writes, "The proper clothing can give you authority, presence, and the look of success..." He adds, "Dressing well just makes life easier."

Your appearance should also be *appropriate* for the setting. Whenever your appearance is much different from what people *expect*, you risk losing trust. For example, wearing a dark pin-striped suit to speak to a group of farmers in their environment would probably create *more* resistance, not less.

Most experts agree that the clothing that's a hit for you socially will probably weaken your credibility in a business setting by making you appear less serious. Molloy writes, "Dressing to succeed in business and dressing to be sexually attractive are almost mutually exclusive."

Young, first-time workers in the service industries who dress to be noticed for a date instead of a promotion often don't realize the impact that mistake has on their career, and perhaps on their ability to meet the "right" person.

Of course, the way you dress and your natural features are only part of your sales appearance. The image you project is the net result of a variety of choices, from your clothing, your grooming, and the way you wear your hair, to the energy, confidence, and interest you show with your movement, your manner, your eye contact and your smile.

EASY BEGINNINGS THAT MAKE POWERFUL FIRST IMPRESSIONS

It doesn't take much to make a strong first impression and get people interested in you.

For starters, you can *smile*. On most lists of what attracts people to each other, a nice smile ranks near the top.

THE SECRETS OF SELLING:
The simplest behaviors make the greatest difference in selling.

Describing General Dwight Eisenhower, author James Salter writes,

> He possessed, like his boss, an invincible smile. Their era had two of them. Roosevelt's was the hail of a champion. Ike's they say, was worth twenty divisions. Generals never smile. That was only one of the rules he broke.

Smiling builds trust. Throughout history, smiling has served as a signal of friendly intent. In selling, a smile says you have positive expectations for your contact with the customer.

In *Death of a Salesman*, Arthur Miller captures this expectation with his famous description of a salesman: "He's a man out there in the blue, ridin' on a smile and a shoeshine... a salesman has got to dream, boys."

Throughout the world, smiling is recognized as the *one* universally- accepted symbol of interest in another person. Think about it. What do two people who speak different languages *do* when they get together? They smile and nod a lot, right?

We shouldn't have to devote space in this book to something as basic as smiling, but I regularly see experienced salespeople lose sales because they come across as too stern and uncaring.

Many senior sales executives have problems they're not even aware of because of their stern demeanor. When they do smile, it looks like the smile of a witch doctor at a human sacrifice, not something spontaneous and fresh.

Despite the obvious effectiveness of this simple social skill, it's surprising how infrequently salespeople smile. In one service quality audit involving 1200 business transactions with customer service employees in commercial banks, over 40 percent of the employees did not smile once at their customers over an average transaction time of eighteen minutes.

Some salespeople are afraid to smile because they feel it might come across as insincere. And often it *is* over-done by the "goody-goodies" of selling who try to be "up" *every* minute of every day.

To smile sincerely, you have to smile out of *real* interest in the customer. You have to find the *fun* in meeting new people.

You can understand better the impact of smiling on first impressions by thinking of the experience of shy salespeople. They try to *avoid* social contact. They don't smile and they give little or no eye contact. To no one's surprise, it *works*! That's exactly what closes off the possibility of really connecting with other people.

In our culture, eye contact conveys intense interest, a sense you're willing to put aside other interests to connect one to one with another person. If you *don't* look at a customer eye-to-eye as you meet, he may assume you're nervous, dishonest, or more interested in what's going on where ever you *are* looking.

Another way to recognize a person for his value as a human being is to *touch* him. Touch conveys immediate recognition and acceptance.

Many salespeople are afraid to touch, even to shake hands. Touch *can* be misinterpreted. But as a general rule, touch, especially *shaking hands*, is a way to *break down* barriers, to say you want real contact with another person. Between races or cultures, it's an especially powerful symbolic act.

The importance of touching can be seen in the words of Zhou En-Lai, former Premier of the Republic of China, to President Richard Nixon on his historic first trip to China. In his greeting, Zhou said, "Your handshake came over the vastest ocean in the world—25 years of no communication."

The handshake is doubly important in *first* encounters because it's normally the *only* touching contact you have in the first moments.

There are several myths about shaking hands that need to be shattered.

The first myth is that shaking hands isn't proper for everyone, or will be seen as too forward. Today, it's proper for *every* salesperson to introduce himself to a client and to extend a handshake.

I've noticed many saleswomen still resist hand shaking on the grounds that only a man should initiate a touching contact, that taking this initiative is too "forward."

Get rid of this type of thinking. Use what *works*. Shaking hands is a good way for *any* salesperson to develop trust and head off possible questions about his professionalism and experience.

The second myth is that a handshake must be bone crushing. It is true that charismatic salespeople almost always have a firm, solid handshake. A confident handshake that pulls the prospect slightly closer to you builds trust and shows your enthusiasm for meeting the customer. President Lyndon Johnson even used to put his left hand over the other person's right hand, to give an extra feeling of warmth.

Too many people release their grip so quickly that the handshake seems like a meaningless, routine gesture instead of a true *contact moment.*

However, remember a handshake is *two*-sided. It should be stronger or weaker depending on how the *other* person responds. With frail or elderly people, it may be appropriate to combine a soft grasp on their hand with a reinforcing touch to their arm or shoulder with your other hand.

When a customer is under stress, he may have an even greater need for physical contact. A recently widowed customer evaluating a major financial decision alone for the first time might appreciate a gentle touch on the shoulder to know you understand what she's going through. And if you're uncertain about touching, remember that customers will often signal you that touching is OK by lightly touching *you.*

How you move also says a lot about your self-confidence in first impressions. Some salespeople can make even *walking* look like a struggle. Peak performance sellers convey a feeling of ease and confidence.

Describing Ronald Reagan, author Gerhard Gschwandtner writes, "Before he says his first word, he has begun a successful sale. His relaxed appearance, his sparkling eyes, the sincere simile and open body language show his belief in himself and his ability to sell."

Too much formality and coolness by a salesperson may turn customers off by implying he thinks he's better than they are and a salesperson who walks and talks in a monotone, afraid to put life into his selling, will bore them.

Send out a feeling of *energy* and *enthusiasm* for what you do! Peak performers, like millionaire broadcasting executive Ted Turner, often get visibly excited over their ideas.

Watch other salespeople who have good success with first impressions, and imitate them until you get the feel of their success. Then adapt what they do to a comfortable manner of your own.

If you're not sure how you come across to your customers, ask your sales manger, a friend, or even a customer with whom you're close to give you some feedback on your first impression.

Together, all of these easy beginnings in first impressions refocus your selling on your customer. Most customers would rather have five minutes of intense, undivided attention from you than an hour of divided attention.

In the April 11, 1983, issue of *Time Magazine*, Hugh Sidey describes the secret behind President Reagan's personal popularity even among those who disagreed with his policies:

West Germany's Helmut Schmidt and Canada's Pierre Trudeau both came to meetings with Reagan ready to eat him for breakfast. They ended up proclaiming their good feeling for him. India's granite lady, Indira Gandhi, actually seemed coquettish with Reagan. 'He looks straight at you, gives you an eager handshake, always smiles, and it's obviously an honest expression,' says a diplomat. 'For the time he is with you,' claims one of Reagan's closest friends, 'he really is interested in you.' Simple but powerful.

MORE THAN A NAME

In the Camp David negotiations with Egyptian Premier Sadat and Israeli prime Minister Begin, President Carter was able to jar Begin loose from an inflexible position at a crucial period by giving Begin autographed photos of the three men for his grandchildren.

The photos were especially moving to Begin because they were personalized with the *names* of his grandchildren.

There's something irresistible in knowing that another person recognizes you by name. Using a person's name in your conversation is one of the quickest ways to make him feel important, to show your interest in connecting.

Everyone loves the look and sound of his own name. That's why direct mail companies slap your name all over those credit card and sweepstakes mailings you receive at home.

Use the customer's name *every* time you're with a customer, and use it throughout the conversation. You probably can't *overuse* a customer's name.

The first step in building the habit of using names is to begin offering *your* name to the customers. I'm amazed how few retail salespeople introduce themselves to me when I'm shopping.

When you introduce yourself to someone, it gives him confidence you'll take responsibility for your actions, that he can *trust* you.

At Ireland's Restaurant in Chicago, the parking attendant has a sign outside that reads, "Valet parking by Hubert." I don't know Hubert from Adam. There may not even be a Hubert, but I have the feeling my car will be safe with Hubert because he knows I know his name!

Don't expect yourself to instantly remember the names of every prospect you meet. That's too big a goal for most salespeople. You'll only frustrate your self into not using names at all.

Instead, introduce yourself to get another person's name when it's appropriate. Concentrate on each customer as a *person*. Try to see something in the physical appearance of each customer that makes him unique.

Famous memory expert Harry Lorayne says not getting names is simply a matter of not really hearing them in the first place. To improve your *memory* of names, write or repeat the name *immediately* when you get it, and use it *several* times. Eventually, you'll remember names consistently.

TALK TO ME, STRANGER

First impressions boil down to one key issue. In the first moments of contact you're judged on your *spirit* of connecting. This spirit is an aura about you that says, "I'm open to people."

Unfortunately, thousands of salespeople suffer from chronic shyness. They've learned how to be successful at not connecting. The signals shy salespeople send out, such as lowered eyes, hesitation in speaking, or even an over-compensating cockiness, act as *stop* signs to other people.

Peak performance sellers can't afford to *create* resistance to themselves.

Shyness is a good way to stay nervous in selling, to fail to expand your prospect base, and to fall short in achieving your sales goals.

I was shy myself when I entered high school. I know what it's like for your heart to pound out of control before an important social contact. But I did something about it. And so can you. Successful salespeople are *always* on the lookout for new people to connect with. Each new contact has the possibility of leading to another.

Pope Paul II is a good model of this spirit. His willingness to go out among his church's members, even learning the language of almost every nation he visits, tells Catholics their church is reaching out to them, that the church wants them as active members.

Tell yourself you *want* to be involved with people.

THE SECRETS OF SELLING:
What is human relations all about but connecting with people? Talk. For God's sake *talk*.

One of the most important rules in expanding your contacts is: *talk*. Say almost anything to get people involved with you.

It's unrealistic to expect strangers to care about you if you don't seem interested in them. Prospects don't *know* you're interested in them unless you show them. As the seller, it's up to *you* to take the initiative to connect.

Salespeople who take the initiative to introduce themselves to strangers reduce these people's risk in returning that openness. They've taken the first step. The easier you make it for another person to talk to you without fear of rejection, the more likely it is he will.

In *Leaders*, Richard Nixon writes, "Virtually all of the major leaders I have known were exceptionally skilled in the vanishing art of face-to-face conversation."

If you talk, you can be certain other people *know* you're interested in them. Looking back over my life, I can think of hundreds of times when I felt like kicking myself for missing an opportunity to meet someone who seemed interesting, or potentially helpful to my selling, because I didn't open my mouth and talk.

This story of lost romance by author Alan Garner could just as easily be a story of lost sales.

> I decided to marry her. Courtship would be a mere formality. But what to say to begin the courtship? 'Would you like some of my...?' seemed too low-class. 'Hello' was too trite a greeting for my future bride. 'I love you! I am hot with passion!' was too forward. 'I want to make you the mother of my children,' seemed a bit premature. Nothing, That's right, I said nothing. And after awhile, the bus reached her stop, she got off, and I never saw her again. End of story.

Talk to people. Rejection won't make you a loser. Only *you* can make yourself a loser. And if you don't talk, you're already losing.

"OK," you say, "but *what* do I say? The words never seem to be there when I need them."

Many salespeople who consider themselves shy say the most difficult time for them on a sales call or at a social event with business implications is the first few minutes of small talk with their prospects.

Connecting on a sales call, at an exhibit booth, or in a retail store is different than connecting at a party, but the principles are the same. Talk about what interests the prospect, usually *him*.

People spend most of their waking hours thinking about themselves. After all, that's what they know best! Dale Carnegie writes, "You can make more friends in two months by being interested in other people than you can in two years by trying to get people interested in you."

I've always enjoyed the story of the man talking to a lady at a cocktail party who says, "Enough of all this talking about me. Let's talk about you. What do *you* think of me?"

Experienced salespeople know the best way to get through to a tough prospect is to ask him about his business or about himself, to ask him how or why he got to where he is. There may even be signs of his interests in his office or in his home.

To connect with people, get involved in *their* topics. You can talk about yourself later, when they show interest in you.

Surprisingly, when you concentrate on the prospect instead of yourself, it's even *easier* to think of things to say. Certainly, it's more effective to say *something* than to wait for the "perfect' words. If you concentrate on learning about the customer, the words will come.

All you're trying to do in the contact moments is to get across your spirit of openness and to close the gap between what you and the prospect *don't* know about each other. You're trying to find some common ground to build on, even if it's only experience *everyone* has in common, like the weather.

Don't be afraid to start with simple conversation. It's only a springboard to other topics of mutual interest.

Psychologists say the most successful opening lines are straightforward invitations to talk, or questions that show your interest in a person. For example, you might say, "Hi, I've noticed you in our store several times and I'd like to meet you. I'm George Duncan."

This approach builds more trust and opens the customer more to you than any manipulative sales pitch ever will.

Thinking *too much* about what you're going to say robs you of the spontaneous things you're likely to say if you're relaxed and thinking about your customer's viewpoint.

To really connect, get the *customer* talking. Nothing strengthens first impressions better than *listening*. Once you've asked a question, the ice is broken. You only need to keep the conversation rolling.

Asking questions helps you uncover the topics which will be of most interest to your customer. It also relaxes you by shining the spotlight somewhere else.

In most retail sales organizations, such as retail stores, banks, car dealerships, and even real estate offices, there are times when unattended customers need to be approached. Have you ever noticed how often you can shop in retail outlets for thirty minutes without a salesperson *approaching* you? They're talking to each other!

Customers should receive *contact, contact, contact.* Contact leads to *sales.* Some of our retail clients have substantially increased their sales by training their staff to capitalize on these quick moments of opportunity.

In a retail setting, greet the customer with a simple welcome such as, "Good morning, *how* can I help you?" It's more difficult for the customer to say, "Just looking," to this question than to the question, "*Can* I help you?."

Next, stalling for a few seconds is usually appropriate, since most of your customers will tell you what they want. If the customer is looking at a product or a display, say something about it: "How do you like that?" Try to focus his attention on *one* idea.

Get the customer talking about what *he* wants, instead of you talking about what you have.

With "lookers," approach them from a "safe" social distance of about ten feet and say something. Never just follow a customer without talking. Customers worry they'll get stuck with a pushy salesperson they won't like.

Let the customer wander until he finds something of interest. Then say something positive about the product. "That's really a good way to keep your costs down, isn't it?"

Small favors, such as offering a seat, getting a customer a cup of coffee, or complimenting him are also effective ways to help people feel a little better about themselves in first meetings.

Everyone likes a sincere compliment. But be *specific*. Tell customers why you like what you're complimenting. Anyone can say, "This is a beautiful office," but not everyone shows enough interest to say why the office is especially nice compared to most offices.

THE SECRETS OF SELLING:
Talk *positively* if you want to make a positive first impression.

Most salespeople are overly hesitant to say positive things about themselves and their products.

Why not put your best foot forward? Customers feel better about themselves when they're around a positive person. If you connect, there's plenty of time to discover the "charm" of your differences.

When someone calls me to ask if we do sales training I tell them they've called the *one* firm in the country that can give their sales staff the *feel of success*. We believe we're the best at what we do, and we're not afraid to tell people we are. Customers like that.

Think about the way you qualify yourself to new people you meet. You only weaken your first impression by saying, "I'm just a trainee," or "I'm *new* in this territory."

Henry Ford once said, "It's all one to me if a man came from Sing Sing or Harvard. We hire a man, not history."

First impressions are for *new* beginning, not for unfinished business, not for your problems, not for negative talk of any kind.

Leave your problems and your negative thinking at home. Customers are attracted to *positive* salespeople. Try to increase your ratio of positive comments to negative comments in all your relations with people.

A positive, optimistic attitude increases your energy and creates an aura around you that causes other people to respond to you in positive ways.

HOW TO DEVELOP YOUR CONFIDENCE
FOR PROSPECTING

You won't overcome your shyness in prospecting until you've overcome your shyness with people.

Most of us are a little shy in some situations, and not at all shy in others. You can use your success in some social situations to develop your confidence for prospecting.

In social situations that present sales opportunities, such as a business cocktail party, a convention, or a function for a community organization, think of yourself as the *host* of a party.

A good host would introduce himself to people he didn't know and then introduce them to each other. As he introduced people to each other, he would provide a conversation bridge by mentioning something about one person that would be of interest to the other. He would bring over new people to a group that was quiet.

Why not use the same strategy to expand your sales network?

The salespeople who are the best at prospecting are not necessarily the best looking, most talented, or most intelligent salespeople. They're the ones who are best at being themselves—open, willing to talk, and interested in other people.

The key to overcoming shyness is to minimize the uncertainty in new situations.

You can eliminate some uncertainty just by deciding you'll take advantage of the openings other people give you to connect with them. That eliminates the stress of thinking, "Should I, or shouldn't I?"

To increase your chances for success, add structure to encounters that might be stressful to you.

Pick your situation. Start conversations with strangers in situations in which you feel most comfortable. Go places where your best qualities stand out. Learn something in advance about the people you expect to meet so you can think through the type of questions you'd like to ask.

As you build a track record of successes, you can try increasingly less structured ways of connecting.

Set goals for yourself. What results do you want from your social or business encounters? What do you want the people you meet to know about you?

If you know the result you want, you can structure how you look and what you say to meet your goals for that situation.

Set achievable short-term goals for yourself that you can increase gradually as you build your confidence. For example, you might set a goal of introducing yourself to one new person each day.

The rewards of a little planning for strong first impressions are more prospects, less resistance, less stress, and more *sales*. People will like you better.

In the next chapter you'll learn how you can strengthen your first impressions and expand the *range* of prospects you can sell by adjusting your selling style to treat people the way *they* want to be treated.

CHAPTER 5

Selling Styles: Champions and Chameleons

Some people are more memorable than others. Actor Cary Grant occasionally received phone calls from President John F. Kennedy in which the President began, "Say anything. I just want to hear you talk."

Cary Grant had *style*.

The leaders in any field always have their own style. They're so relaxed and natural that their style shines through in first impressions.

Style has been described as what's *memorable*, what's left of first impressions after you've left a room.

Your selling style is *your* way of doing things, your central selling tendencies and consistent ways of dealing with people across different situations. Your selling style is *you* to your customers.

Mae West one said, "It's not what I do, but how I do it. It ain't what I say, but how I look when I do it and say it."

Your selling style can be an important tool for developing trust in first impressions, but most salespeople don't fully use it, because they sell to their own style, not to their *customer's*.

In the first moments of contact, you're trying to find common ground with your customer, implying, "You'll feel good around me," and "I'm like you. You can trust me."

In those first moments, customers judge you both by your *similarity* to them and by what's *different* about you.

Peak performance sellers adjust their selling styles to the needs of their customers. They *create* the similarities that build trust and minimize sales resistance.

The differences you establish with your selling style create interest.

Sometimes an attribute you see as a weakness may make you unique and memorable.

If you're not going to be yourself in selling, who are you going to be, and still be unique?

THE CHEMISTRY OF STYLE

You have a unique selling style. Each of your customers also has his own unique style.

If you're a driving, fast-paced, goal-centered seller, and you're selling to an easy-going, relationship-centered buyer, there is likely to be tension unless one or both of you adjust your style.

When a salesperson and a customer get together, the ways they can react to each other are almost limitless. The combinations would tax even the most sophisticated computer.

Edward Teller of TRW describes these selling possibilities with a chess analogy:

> Suppose a chess-playing computer not only had to take account the rules of the game, the positions of the players, and the outcome of possible moves, but also had to deal with uncertainty. Imagine the computer confronting an opposing piece and not knowing for sure whether the piece were a rook or a pawn.

No two people and no two selling situations are exactly the same. The behavior customers prefer for themselves or expect from you may change from one meeting to another.

To meet these changing needs you may want to supplement your basic selling style with a variety of others.

To be successful with certain prospects, or in selected sales situations, you may have to *stretch* your natural style to change the behavior you prefer most of the time.

Ask a computer salesperson with a problem-solving, soft-sell style to sell encyclopedias door to door, where he would have twenty seconds before his prospects said "yes" or "no" to hearing more, and he would probably have to become more assertive.

A saleswoman in one of my seminars sold office equipment to one of her best prospects for two years without success. She had *proven* in dollars and cents that her product would save the buyer $1,800 per month, and still hadn't made a sale.

After the seminar, she followed my suggestion to change her approach. She built her approach around his *feelings* and the impact of her equipment on *people*, and made the sale in fifteen minutes. His style was different than most of her regular buyers.

Each extra selling response you have in your portfolio increases your probability of success by increasing your odds of finding common ground with your customer.

Having more styles to use in the first moments of contact gives you more choices in selling.

Some salespeople use the *same* strategies in every situation. Sometimes they work, sometimes they don't.

Once a peak performance seller gets the feel of a customer's style, he varies his presentation style to support the customer's needs in problem solving, decision making, atmosphere, pace, and the way he wants information.

When you enter the land of the opposite thinker, everything can seem upside down. Whenever there's relationship tension with a customer that doesn't seem to make sense, always think first of possible style differences. People walk away from people they find difficult, don't understand, or don't get along with.

THE SECRETS OF SELLING:
If what you're doing with a customer isn't working, try something else until you get the response you want—*anything* else.

When you recognize tension, defensiveness or disinterest, stop what you're doing and try something else.

The champions of first impressions are the salespeople who are confident and comfortable enough to temporarily *adjust* their natural communication style to meet the expectations of their customers.

These sales champions know customers will be more receptive if they feel comfortable with the way their styles mesh. If you can determine *how* a customer wants to buy, you can package your sales information in a way he'll find irresistible.

Selling style is closely related to *timing*, knowing when to back away from your natural tendencies.

Stretching your selling style for short intervals will help some customers become more comfortable with you while you build rapport. At the very least, you'll increase the comfort between you by reducing pressure for the customer to adapt to your needs.

Once a customer has accepted you as a comfortable person to be with, you can often stop concentrating so hard on adjusting, and return to *your* basic selling style.

After you've built a base of trust, the other person is usually less likely to form impressions of you based on style alone.

Adjustments in your selling style are especially important when you're establishing trust in your *first* contacts with prospects.

Flying to Jacksonville, Florida, I met a salesman from a telecommunications firm. He had just been moved from his company's fast-paced San Franciso office to a more laid-back sales region in the south, and he told me a story that illustrates the impact selling style has on closing sales.

On his *first* sales call on a major account, midway through his usual fast-paced presentation, he was stopped short. The prospect said, "Son, I've heard about every other word you've said. Slow down a little and relax. Get yourself a cup of coffee and tell me how you like Florida. We're going to do some business. Don't you worry."

He said when he slowed down, he found that even *he* became more comfortable. He made the sale.

Changes in style can help you adapt to fit the specific needs of people, situations, and organizations.

In *The Big Time*, Kaplan writes,

> If there is any such thing as the 'secret of success,' it is this: One must know specifically how things work in a given business and what will be expected... Behavior that might rocket a person to the top in one will ruin him in another.

Selling requires understanding what customers want, including how they want to be treated. How responsive you are to other people's expectations will have a lot to do with your success.

THERE'S NO BEST SELLING STYLE

One professional woman I know has a sign in her office that reads, "Now is the time to drop the lines that divide things neatly."

Contrary to what some sales gurus would have you believe, there is no best selling style that works for every salesperson, or with every customer. If you have only one selling style, you may as well be a robot. It will be easy for another person to outmaneuver you by playing to your weakness.

The challenge for you in selling is to match the right selling style to the right job at the right time.

Research in salesperson selection by industrial psychologists has disproved the idea that one personality style of a high-performance salesperson is best at selling anything to anybody, or that one best-selling style is necessary for success with all customers. Each style of customer and each type of selling requires different talents and different styles.

Thomas Watson, founder of IBM and one of the world's most successful salesmen, is an excellent example of how even someone with a reserved personality can become a peak performance seller by choosing a type of selling that fits his style, and by adopting his selling to the needs of his customers.

Cultural differences also make the "one best style" theory unfeasible. What will work in one culture, even a corporate culture, may not work in another. What will work today with one prospect may not work tomorrow with the same person.

The consensus of most management authorities is that your selling style should change as situations change, as the needs of those around you change, and as different objectives are sought.

Vary your selling style, but don't change what really counts—your ideas, your values, and your basic identity of who you are as person.

The selling styles you take on have to be consistent with your personality in order for you to use them successfully.

The dangers of sacrificing who you are to be liked was described well in Woody Allen's movie *Zelig*.

Allen played the role of a fictitious character named Leonard Zelig who was called "the human chameleon" because he was able to change his personality and his physical appearance to resemble anyone around him.

Zelig changed personality because he wanted to be liked, but in the end he lost both his friends and his identity.

Don't lose sight of what makes you successful. Over the long run, you want to be you because that's when you're at your best.

You can be successful in some form of selling with almost any natural style, if you like the satisfaction of persuading other people, if you're resilient and optimistic enough to handle rejection, and if you're empathetic enough to adapt your selling style to the needs and reactions of others.

STRETCHING IT A LITTLE

Your natural selling style is so much a part of you that you're not likely to make any big shifts even if you try. But with practice, you can *stretch* your style.

Since customers are most comfortable staying within their own communication styles, you can cut the resistance you encounter in any situation if you adapt your style to the customer's needs.

THE SECRETS OF SELLING:
It's much easier for you to go to the *customer's* world than it is to persuade him to come to yours.

Sell your customers the way *they* want to be sold.

When I sell in New York City, I usually have to make my point in five minutes or I'm out the door. In some other areas of the country, I'm expected to share more of myself in small talk over a cup of coffee, as we discuss football or local politics.

If you present yourself and your product differently from what a customer expects, he may feel rejected. And you can bet his feelings of rejection will lead to rejection of your product.

If you make the *customer* the reference for what you're doing, then all you have to do is keep acting differently until you recognize the response you want.

Dr. Donald J. Moine writes,

> The good salesman has a chameleon-like ability to pace the language and thoughts of any customer. With hypnotic effect the agent matches the voice tone, rhythm, volume and speech rate of the customer. He matches the customer's posture, body language and mood. He adapts the characteristic verbal language of the customer ('Sounds good,' 'rings a bell,' 'get a grip on'). If the customer is slightly depressed, the agent shares that feeling and acknowledges that he has been feeling a little down lately ... The best persuaders build trust by mirroring the thoughts, tone of voice, speech tempo, and mood of the customer— literally, the techniques of the clinical hypnotist ... whose initial aim is to create in a subject a state of intensified attention and receptiveness, leading to increased suggestibility. All successful persuaders produce such an effect, probably without understanding the exact nature of the techniques that accomplish it.

Think of the Chinese finger trap you may have played with as a child.

As you put a finger into each end of the woven cylinder, you discovered the harder you pulled your fingers apart to get free, the tighter the cylinder stretched. You could escape the trap only by letting go.

The same principle is true of relationships in selling.

To free yourself of resistance, you may have to let go of your personal style at times to meet the needs of your customers.

The inability of a salesperson to adjust his selling style can lead to rigidity. He may lose the spontaneity, energy, and trust he needs in his selling relationships.

How far does *your* selling style stretch?

Your dominant natural selling style plus your supporting styles make up your selling style range, your ability to *stretch* your selling style.

Your versatility in selling style determines how customers perceive the effort you're willing to make to see the relationship succeed.

A salesperson with a narrow selling style range *can* be effective if he stays in situations in which his style has a high probability of success. For most of us, that's not possible.

Regarding his use of Western-style politicking prior to his summit meeting with Ronald Reagan, U.S.S.R. General Secretary Mikhail Gorbachev was quoted in *Time* as saying, "It is not a question whether I enjoy that style or not. You cannot work otherwise."

To widen your selling style range, practice stretching your selling style way beyond what you actually want it to be. You can do this by experimenting with your own style or by mimicking the movements, manner, pace, and words of other peak performance sellers.

Acting out different selling styles and mimicking successful salespeople will help you identify new styles so you can *repeat* them.

Most salespeople are too inhibited to try anything new.

Give yourself permission to act in the way you need to act. Why label yourself or limit yourself unnecessarily with one selling style?

Stretching your selling style is like stretching a rubber band. Once you stretch you inhibitions, they'll snap back just a little looser than before.

Dr. Alfred Kinsey conducted 8,000 interviews to compile sexual histories for his research on human sexuality. He found that to build the trust he needed, he had to vary his personal style widely. When he didn't adjust his style, people wouldn't talk openly.

The same thing happens to salespeople.

Get the feel of new selling behaviors with a little experimenting. Try more enthusiasm, more movement, more smiling, or more assertiveness in your selling, and see how it works for you. If you're a "talker" try listening more.

In sales training, salespeople who say they *can't* stretch their style almost always *can* when they're asked to mimic themselves selling as they would like to be able to sell, or as top performers sell.

Extend your experimenting to situations away from work. If you're a defensive player in your favorite sport, try playing more aggressively.

If you're certain you're not going to make a sale, why not try something new?

Take a minute right now to think closely about your selling behavior. What do you do to help your customers feel more comfortable? How do you respond when you're faced with strong resistance? How far are you able to stretch your own style in giving information or building rapport?

These are just a few of the factors that make up your selling style as your *customers* know it.

There's likely to be a difference between your perception of your selling style and your customers' perception. some authorities estimate that we are perceived differently than we think we are as much as fifty percent of the time.

To understand the impact of your selling style on your sales results, study the *response* you're getting from your customers in different selling situations and the variance in *results* you're getting from one type of customer to another.

Each of us has different tendencies we need to control most in working with the customers who are different than us. Salespeople who tend toward methodical, analytical selling behavior need to work on demonstrating more emotion, getting to the point faster, and giving less product detail.

Salespeople who tend toward supportive, passive selling behavior need to work on getting down to business faster, socializing less, and demonstrating more assertiveness.

Salespeople who tend toward driving, goal-focused selling behavior need to work on controlling their tendency to overpower customers by investing more time in rapport building and listening to demonstrate their personal concern for customers.

Salespeople who tend toward promoting, sociable selling behavior need to work on toning down their enthusiasm, slowing their pace, giving more detail, and talking less.

THE SECRETS OF SELLING:
The more you can *stretch* your selling style to fit the way different people want to be treated at any one moment, the more prospects you can sell.

With a little practice, most salespeople are able to become comfortable with a wide variety of selling behaviors and expand the number of potential prospects with whom they can be effective.

It's possible to *overreact* to the style of your customers, however.

If you adapt your style too far beyond your comfort zone, you may seem more interested in the sale than in what's right for the customer.

In sales, there's a bottom line of excitation necessary for a sale to occur. If you fail to demonstrate leadership with an overly relaxed or passive customer, *nothing* will happen! Your goal should be to shift your selling style just enough so it doesn't interfere with your relationship.

Once you know you're able to stretch your selling style if necessary, you can work on recognizing the situations when it's necessary.

RECOGNIZING CUSTOMER STYLES

The better you recognize customer styles, the better you can change your behavior until customers respond the way you want them to.

Think of the customers you see regularly. What are some of the ways they differ from each other? Do you respond to them all in the same way?

Reading a customer's style involves knowing his central tendencies, his comfort zone, his responsiveness to what you're doing, the way he likes to give and receive information, the benefits he responds to best, and his relationship needs.

While most people can switch from one thinking or communicating style to another, some can do it better than others. Most have one dominant style they use as home base.

To understand a customer, watch for his central tendencies and the situations that provoke them. What you observe will give you clues about how the customer wants to be treated, how he wants information about your product, and what style he's most comfortable in.

Some people are more likely to think about your ideas by generating visual images; others, by having feelings; yet others, by constructing stories and sounds in their minds.

Even though people think in all three of these styles, each of us is most comfortable in *one* of these styles.

By listening to a customer's choice of words (particularly the adjectives) and observing his eye movements and other nonverbal signals, some highly sensitive salespeople are actually able to change their selling to fit the way a customer is thinking.

Think of the advantage you have if you know whether a customer is trying to get a *feeling* about your ideas, to *picture* the results, or to *tell* himself something about what you're saying. You can match his sense imagery to your information in ways he understands best.

The key point is that all people are different, and they give you a lot of information that goes unnoticed about how they want to be treated. One of the important qualities of *the feel of success in selling* is sensitivity to the customer's responses.

Listen to the language the customer uses. Look at the work environment he selects for himself and the clothing he chooses to wear. Ask him what he's chosen to do for his career and for fun.

Does he seem comfortable with concepts, or does he insist on facts and proof to evaluate your ideas?

Does he like small talk, or does he want to get down to business immediately? ("Whatcha got?") How much listening does he do versus how much talking?

Does he want to be innovative and "first," or does he want to avoid risk?

Does he display his feelings, or control them? Does he primarily talk about *people*, or about tasks and things?

Does he want structure, or flexibility? Does he prefer to have all the details of your ideas step by step, or merely an overview?

Mark McCormack adds another key question to ask yourself,

> How secure is this person? A person's security quotient has a direct bearing on how he will behave in business situations. Will he be stubborn or reasonable? Will form be more important than substance?... Is he likely to say one thing and do another?

A buyer who is insecure may block a sale to protect his own position.

THE SECRETS OF SELLING:
The peak performance seller follows the customer's responses to his selling so he knows in which selling style the sale will be made.

If you aren't able to understand a customer's style by observation, *ask him* directly how he would like to be treated. You might ask, "Would you like me to *diagram* this, or would you rather hear some case history stories of how our clients have used it?" or "Would you like an overview, or would you rather go through this step by step?"

If you seem to be making your point with one person in a group, but not with the others, it may help to shift your approach and draw a picture of your point, tell a story, or find some other way of getting in touch with those people.

You'll also get a sense for a customer's style by observing how he responds to questions like, "How do you *know* when you're having a problem with your operation?" A question like this gives your customer room to display his style.

Ask other people about your prospect's usual tendencies and communication style. There's almost always someone who can give you insight into the person behind the position.

If necessary, duplicate the customer's body language or facial expressions to get the feel of his style.

Examine the response the customer elicits from *you*. How do you *feel* when you're with him?

When I left home for the University of Denver, my friend Dana Weithers, one of the nation's top marketing consultants, urged me to pay as much attention to the communication styles of my professors as to the content of their lectures. It was good advice.

From observing my professors, I learned as much about how to communicate—and how *not* to—as I learned from their courses.

I've certainly learned not to *judge* a customer's style in counseling customers. Knowing that a customer treats me in a certain way because that's his natural style helps me sustain my patience with his sales resistance longer.

Remember, you won't know a customer's style unless you're focused on the customer.

SELECTING THE RIGHT SELLING STYLE

Since it's important to adapt your style to customers, it's also important to form accurate first impressions about them.

All salespeople unconsciously classify and stereotype their customers. These stereotypes provide a framework for *predicting* how they're likely to react. They're useful as a *guide*, but not as absolute predictors of behavior.

As Sherlock Holmes remarked to Dr. Watson, "While the individual man is an insolvable puzzle, in the aggregate, he becomes a mathematical certainty." (Not completely, of course. Some people's behavior does not put them clearly in any box, and knowing a person's style is only the beginning of knowing the person. A salesperson can't allow stereotypes to prevent him from really getting to know a customer.)

Never try to "force fit" a customer into one behavior style. The idea is simply to treat customers the way they seem to want to be treated *at this moment*. Tomorrow they may want to be treated differently.

Stereotypes are merely a first step in understanding a customer's behavior. If you're wrong, you can usually adjust them.

The key to successful stereotyping is to find descriptions that are *useful*.

Research in the behavioral sciences has produced dozens of selling models that stereotype customer behavior styles. As well researched as these theories are, none of them encompasses *all* the dimensions of customer behavior. Still, these selling models are a good place to start learning how customers are likely to interact with you in certain dimensions, such as how people prefer to give or receive information.

You've also created your own customer style stereotypes based on *your* interpretation of the world. You've programmed yourself to repeat certain responses to various customer behaviors because you've had successful experiences.

These are the stereotypes you'll remember and use most naturally. They're based on actual results.

I find very few salespeople who consistently use the analytical style models they've learned in seminars, because it's difficult to learn enough about selling styles in several days to apply the knowledge on a practical basis. They use their own style categories. What those seminars really teach them is to become more sensitive to the differences that exist among people, and to respond to them.

If your first impressions are wrong, you can keep changing your behavior until you get the responses you want.

Remember, it's both the situation and the person that determine the style you should be using.

Below are some common stereotypes of customer styles that I find many salespeople use in their selling. Many categories overlap. Study them carefully. They'll help you understand how widely you may have to vary your style to become a peak performance seller.

For each stereotype shown below, I've listed ways to adapt your selling, based on the way each type of customer is likely to want to be treated.

As you read each description, think of someone you know who fits that style, how the person occasionally displays a different style, and how the recommended strategy might work with that person, on most occasions.

DOMINATOR

(Wants to control situations)

Help him "correct" your plans and feel in control of conversation; fight your negative feelings by reminding yourself of your goals; don't go over his head for a decision; give him options so he feels in control; get right to the point; stress facts rather than feelings; never "win" an argument; refocus conversation by referring to his objectives; make your ideas his ideas; and take a firm stance in negotiation.

ANALYZER

(Organized, evaluates ideas on facts and details, doesn't show emotions)

Stress results rather than relationships; make your points with stories; use "thinker" language such as, "Based on your analysis, what's your evaluation of the facts?;" explain ideas step by step; make a detailed analysis of his needs; be formal and businesslike; demonstrate your preparation, punctuality, and organization; document product benefits but don't overstate what you can do; explain both pros and cons of ideas; offer factual evidence and proof of performance; meet alone; avoid gimmicks; use charts and other statistical sales aids; limit options or he'll consider them all; don't rush him since he'll want to verify your claims; show how to track the results; follow up in writing with letters, proposals, and written agreements; provide details of how your product works; stay in a problem-solving manner; develop timetables; and do what you say you'll do.

PEOPLE PERSON

(More interested in relationships than results)

Sell whom he's dealing with; use first names and an informal manner; socialize to develop trust; don't be too task-oriented; support his ideas and feelings with active listening; develop solutions together; talk about people and the effects of your products on them; ask for his ideas, opinions, and dreams; limit options; continually check for unspoken concerns; mention the names of other people who have used your product; pin agreements down so they aren't left hanging; praise his ideas and accomplishments; offer personal assurances about your product; share your feelings; be spontaneous and enthusiastic; make your points with stories about people; stress your relationship after the sale; define clearly what you'll do so there's less risk of disappointment; and don't bore him with details.

NONRESPONDER

(Nonexpressive, doesn't give feedback)
Check your timing; speak energetically; ask him to talk about himself; wait out inattention or time spent considering your idea; ask him to guess what his problems or objectives are if he's having trouble discussing them; stress potential losses if he doesn't act; ask directly if something about your product concerns him; make a wild guess about his objectives for him to correct; try to close the sale to prompt a response; and meet with other people present.

DRIVING COMPETITOR

(Action-oriented, direct, driven toward specific goals at any cost)
Check his priorities immediately; continually refocus conversation on his objectives; be firm, straightforward and confident; offer and compare alternatives; be organized, get to the point fast; ask questions to help him "discover" your viewpoint; stress action and efficient use of time; sell your credibility; stress results more than relationships; move at an energetic pace; avoid direct disagreement and confrontation; sell quality; emphasize independent action rather than cooperation with others; avoid talking about feelings or giving advice; pace yourself to his agenda; create a businesslike atmosphere; allow room for negotiation; answer expected objections before he raises them; follow up immediately; and stick to "what" questions such as, "What has to get done?"

CRITICIZER

("Know-it-all," thinks nothing other people do is ever right)
Continually refocus attention away from criticism to facts, objectives, and stretch benefits; avoid getting hooked into an *emotional* response; maintain a calm, adult manner; don't interrupt; limit options; help him feel important with positive strokes; avoid reinforcing criticism by giving it undue attention; rephrase criticisms to soften them; and ask questions to help him "discover" your viewpoint.

SLOW DECIDER

(Passive, extremely friendly, likes your ideas but never acts on them)
Show interest in him as a person; continually check his concerns; hold solutions until he's ready to hear them; mention reason after reason to buy; use guarantees and testimonials; confront him over delays directly, but don't pressure him; use questions to force him to tell the truth instead of what he thinks you want to hear; continually report your progress towards a decision; involve others favorable to your idea in the decision making; provide facts to help justify his decision to others; avoid conflict; get commitment in writing; make it

easy and risk-free to start, with a first step or conditional commitment; give your maximum personal assurance that your product is reliable; provide incentives to act now; be clear about what you're going to do so he won't be disillusioned after the sale; and establish mutual goals, timetables, and critical events that lead to the sale.

TOUCHY-FEELER

(Buys intuitively, on the basis of how ideas and relationships feel to him)

Stress the impact of your product on people; focus on how he'll feel using your product; tell him how others have felt about your product; use touch in developing trust; let him touch your product, if possible; give him time to get in touch with what he's feeling; be dramatic and enthusiastic; show support for his intuition; go with the flow of his flexible agenda; and assume an empathetic manner.

PROMOTER

(Excitable, likes people and ideas, wants attention)

Sell concepts and the big picture; stress what's new and different; invest time to develop trust; get him talking about himself, his opinions and goals; stress the opportunity to be first and in the spotlight; minimize detail; take him to lunch; speak at a fast pace; praise his ideas and dreams; use humor; ask him to try the product; sell possibilities, independent action, and quick benefits; close quickly, but keep him from moving ahead too fast; summarize what you agreed upon; add a touch of class to your presentation; sell by phone; demonstrate your willingness to handle the details; don't compete for attention; show what you'll do to put ideas in action.

BARGAIN-HUNTER

(Price-conscious, negotiates everything)

Sell the total value of your product; raise questions about what might be missing in less expensive products; state his possible losses; show confidence your price is fair; show why your product is worth any difference in price; always provide reasons not to shop around; present your product in a way that some features appear free, or throw in "something for nothing;" leave room for negotiating by adding something to the sale that he can negotiate; and give detailed information about product features not available from competitors.

RISK-AVOIDER

(Security-conscious, concerned about losses)

Take time to develop trust, sell your credentials; relate new ideas to his old ways of doing things; stress risk-reduction benefits; provide proof of performance, guarantees, and personal assurance; don't ask for long-term commitments unless they minimize risk; make it easy to become a customer, with a low-risk first step; use tension-relieving statements to reduce fears; provide incentive to act now; speak at a slow, confident pace; and prove that the worst-case scenario isn't as bad as he may think.

OLDER BUYER

(Mature, experienced customer)

Sell to the objectives of the person instead of to senior stereotypes; show extra warmth, respect, and courtesy, but don't over-adust; ask questions to separate wants from actual needs; give reasons to act now, but don't rush decisions; mention referrals from seniors; adjust to the needs of the physically-impaired; avoid overly structured "hard-sell" presentations; be organized; make detailed product comparisons; establish your credentials; use tension-relieving statements to introduce age-related topics; relate new ideas to old ways of doing things; stress quality, brand name, service, and benefits that reduce risk; gain access to other buying influences such as children; sell one product at a time; give personal assurances your product will work, and you will be available after the sale; follow up in writing with personal letters; stress how your product helps him do what younger buyers do; offer a low-risk, first-step way to buy; give reasons not to shop around; sell up to high-quality options; prove he won't pay for features he won't use; and provide chances to touch or experience the product.

There *are* differences in the way customers want to be treated. *Stretch* your style to accommodate those differences in your selling.

One frequent concern I hear from salespeople is, "If I apply what I've learned about selling style and change my usual way of doing things, will customers regard me as a phoney?"

No. They're more likely to say to themselves, "He and I really speak the *same* language. I can *trust* him."

CULTURE SHOCKS

Every salesperson in our diverse culture has to interact with people from a wide variety of cultural sub-groups.

The number of these sub-groups is increasing in America, due to immigration from new areas, and consolidation of life styles around issues of race, religion, age, or ethnic background. More salespeople are also selling overseas or selling to overseas buyers.

There factors increase the pressure on salespeople to understand *cross-cultural* communication to meet the unique style needs of other groups.

Communication between yourself and someone from a different cultural background often requires a more delicate style.

One well-intentioned but misinterpreted move can create barriers you may never break through.

Most of us like to believe "people are people." After all, we're all human beings living with the same emotions, and facing similar struggles with survival, love, fear, self-worth, and a sense of success.

But there *are* differences. Each cultural group has different ways of coping with these universal human feelings and situations.

THE SECRETS OF SELLING:
The key to cross-cultural selling is demonstrating respect for differences in viewpoint by joining customers in *their* space.

Differences among cultures and languages set up roadblocks to sharing understanding and objectives in selling.

Think of the differences that exist among people with different cultural experience.

They're likely to differ in values, perceptions of formality, openness in self-expression, nonverbal cues, distance in conversation, power, time, comfort with uncertainty or structure, male/female roles, concern for individualism versus concern for the common good, religion, or belief in the possibility of determining their own future.

People from some cultures are more likely to negotiate every aspect of a sale, or to resist giving you information about themselves.

These differences are in *addition* to the individual differences in communication style we've already reviewed!

The best example of cultural differences in values is found in research in decision making.

Respondents to one survey were asked, "On a sea voyage, you are traveling with your wife, your child, and your mother. The ship sinks. Of your family, you are the only person who can swim and you can save one other person. Whom do you save? In Western countries, 60 percent of those responding save the child; 40 percent save the wife; and none save the mother. In Eastern countries 100 percent save the mother. The rationale? You can always remarry and have more children, but you cannot have another mother.

These differences in values may affect everything you do in selling, from the way you develop trust to the benefits you emphasize.

Differences in *language* also create obstacles to understanding that require adjustments in style.

There are some languages in which "no" is never used (the salesperson's dream!). How to interpret a yes or a no is an art of its own in many cultures.

The Japanese language may be the best example of style flexing. Much of the Japanese language is geared toward recognition of subtle differences in status that require different behavioral responses.

Anthropologist Masao Kunihiro writes, "English is intended strictly for communication. Japanese is primarily interested in feeling out the other person's mood."

Time Magazine describes the subtlety of the Japanese language this way.

In Japanese, the verb comes at the end of the sentence, rather than in the middle. It is thus possible to state the subject and object of the sentence all the while watching the reaction, and then adjust the verb ... softening it. For example, if the sentence begins to seem too strong or displeasing, the speaker may even change his mind and insert a negative at the end, thereby reversing the entire meaning of the sentence, but preserving the human relationship.

Imagine how all this affects perceptions and expectations in selling!

The daily experience of a senior citizen in rural Appalachia is far different from that of a young black man in Harlem. The communication styles and expectations of people from mainland China are far different from those people of Hispanic origin.

And when a group shares experiences you don't, such as specific types of discrimination, its members are likely to see life through filters you could probably *never* be aware of.

Anthropologist E.T. Hall writes, "the only culture that I'm deeply contexted in is my own, so that regardless of what I know about another culture, I will never really know what is going on."

Many of the problems that occur between people in selling are the result of not understanding what's important to another person.

For example, customers of some cultural backgrounds are more likely to *negotiate* every aspect of a sale. You'll be more patient with them if you know that the negotiation *process* is as important to them as the outcome. Saving face is an *especially* important issue in cross-cultural selling.

Research by E.T. Hall has found that cultures differ significantly in terms of the *context* in which relationships are understood.

Members of "high-context" cultures, e.g. Hispanic or Japanese, place relationships in the longer-term perspective of their entire lives. They have less need for information or written rules, because they weave their relationships into every aspect of their lives. In contrast, members of "low-context" cultures, e.g. American or German, place relationships in the context of a continuing series of events with little attention to the pattern they're weaving.

It's no wonder we have to work harder at cross-cultural communication!

Cultural differences are sometimes so subtle that only other members of a subculture will be able to tune in.

Nonverbal communication is the area in which the most important differences in culture are likely to surface first, and misunderstanding this communication is one of the major sources of inter-cultural conflict.

One of the newer developments in foreign language learning is training in nonverbal language skills, such as the appropriate speaking distance for the culture in which the language is spoken. The jokes we hear about Italians using their hands and Asians showing little outward emotion are based on real cultural differences in style.

Many of the people in cultural subgroups live their lives without things the rest of us take for granted.

Imagine trying to live your life in America without understanding what is said, with a sense of powerlessness, with a sudden loss of the respect or sense of purpose you enjoyed for most of your life, without money or good health, or with customers so different that even an issue such as a greeting creates constant misunderstandings!

Some people are consistently treated almost as nonpersons. You can imagine the layers of resistance this adds to your sales communication in first impressions.

But if you allow yourself to join customers in *their* space by adjusting your selling style, you can break through. You're saying to the customer, "I take you seriously. The way you want to be treated matters to me."

The most important rule of first impressions with people from a different cultural background, or with special needs, is to resist the natural temptation to adapt your style too much.

In selling to the handicapped (the "inconvenienced," as they refer to themselves), to people who don't speak English well, or even to children or the elderly, the first inclination of most salespeople is to try to do more for them than needs to be done.

More than anything, these customers want to be respected as equal partners. Don't talk down to them.

Sometimes a salesperson's actions around customers who are different from him are exaggerated by his anxiety over making them feel comfortable, or by stereotypes he hasn't taken time to update.

Focus on the *person*, not the stereotype. Believe it or not, your customers may think *you* act strange.

I've been fortunate to have many Asian-American friends in my life. It's always amusing to watch people approach them and try to compensate for anticipated language barriers by talking louder—as if that would make a difference!

An Asian might think that if you valued people, you wouldn't cut your time short with someone to conform to an arbitrary appointment calender. A Latin American might be insulted by your wanting a written contract when he has given you his word.

THE SECRETS OF SELLING:
Taking extra time to develop *trust* is
especially important in cross-cultural selling.

In many cultures, people are accustomed to spending more time in developing personal trust in selling than we usually do in the U.S.

There is a dramatic contrast between the way American business people come to the point immediately, and the way Hispanic, Asian, and some European business people take time to develop the right atmosphere for trust.

I learned this difference in style the hard way in my first sales presentation in Europe.

Selling to a major English bank, I adjusted my selling style substantially, but not far enough to overcome the perception that Americans are too straightforward. I lost the sale.

Now I invest whatever time it takes to really connect with people on their terms, even if it means hours of trust-building without mentioning our business objectives.

Mark McCormack writes, "Business situations always come down to people situations. And the more—and the sooner I know about the person I am dealing with, the more effective I'm going to be."

Don't ignore the *courtesies* of cross-cultural communicating. For starters, smile more.

Follow the appropriate courtesies of the culture, such as speaking to the elder male, bowing, or not talking business immediately, to show your respect. Adjust to the customer's speaking pace, and to his touch or space needs.

If you don't know what a specific customer's courtesy needs might be, do some research *before* your sales contact, follow his lead, or ask him.

When *language* is a problem, try to speak more *slowly*, not more loudly.

Take one step at a time, and check to see if the customer understands what you've said to that point.

When customers have experienced memory loss or have poor skills in *your* language, you may have to repeat yourself many times. Patience is a lot easier when you understand what it's like to be on *their* side of the conversation.

Use examples or pictures to clarify what you mean. On many occasions, I've stopped a conversation to draw a simple diagram of the idea I was talking about.

Good communication may come down to something as simple as sitting on the same side of the table as your customer so he can read your sales material while you're talking. Many people can read a second language better than they can speak it.

If you're talking to several customers, give them an opportunity to stop and talk among themselves, until they've gotten the meaning of what you've said. Follow up your meeting with a written summary.

You can often use a third party to sell your point. In many cultures, family members or third-party referrals carry a lot of weight.

If you spot tension or confusion, relax the customer before you continue. You may want to make a tension-relieving statement such as, "It may take us a while, but we'll get it," or "This is what we'll do..."

Customers who are anxious or confused usually *want* assurance and firm direction from you. They want you to set limits on their behavior.

In many cultures, people in authority are *expected* to use their authority. Customers may find it frustrating if you don't take the lead.

Before you make a sales call on someone whose perspective is quite different from yours, learn what you can about his values, and about the gestures that would show your concern for him.

Once you've met him, ask yourself how what he says and does might be based on his prior experience. If he pushes you in negotiation, or resists when you ask him for information, have the patience to explain and sell your position to him with understanding for *his* tradition.

The most important message in this chapter is that differences in style *do* exist. To have the feel of success in selling, you may have to let go of your natural style and meet the needs of other people.

The champions of first impressions are as adaptable as chameleons.

In the next chapter you'll learn how listening for "the feel of the sale" can help you sort out the customer's viewpoint and lead you to peak performance.

CHAPTER 6

Listening for the Feel of the Sale

The one trait shared by *all* peak performance sellers is they *listen*. Good listeners make better first impressions in selling than good talkers. They find out faster what their customers *really* want. And they can adjust their selling to the *customer's* objectives.

Japanese executives call sensitivity to others "Haragei"—the art of getting within the other person.

I call this sense of the customer's thinking, *the feel of the sale*. It means knowing what it takes to make the sale.

People often do business with an organization solely because they believe a salesperson in that organization *understands* their situation. Yet, as much as we talk about communication, how many times each week do you still find yourself asking, "Whey doesn't he *listen?*"

Few things are more frustrating to a customer, or more damaging to first impressions, than for a salesperson not to *listen*, not to understand what he wants. By not listening, the salesperson misses the customer's objectives and his *response* to his selling.

Much of the creativity in selling lies in finding the problem that needs to be solved. To find it, you have to listen.

Sales communication starts with *you*. It's one thing in selling that can't be delegated. You won't be effective in selling unless you accept responsibility for understanding others and for being understood.

Once a gap in understanding opens, it widens every minute. Your relationship is left to chance, to *guesses* about what the customer is thinking. George Bernard Shaw writes, "The greatest problem with communication is the illusion it has been achieved."

Most salespeople *think* they listen, but if you ask them for the information it takes to make the sale, they can't tell you.

Peak performance sellers are much better than average sellers at listening and recognizing selling cues. Here are some comments on listening from salespeople in my seminars:

> I always open my group sales presentations with a few questions to feel out the audience. If I listen carefully, the audience gives me my presentation.

> I've seen some salespeople talk themselves right out of a sale. If you're listening, you know immediately when you've made a sale.

> Most shoppers are afraid they're going to get pounced on by a salesperson. I wouldn't even get a chance to sell if I didn't prove to my customers they could trust me by listening to them.

> In my business it's the add-on sales that give me most of my commissions. I'm always listening for the *second* sale.

People want to be understood. They want you to know what they want so you can help them. It's not easy to get tough prospects to tell you what they want. They may not know themselves. Getting customers to talk, and then *listening*, is the heart of selling.

The respected psychologist Carl Rogers said empathy is "understanding with you, not about you." Selling and *listening* are ways of communicating you do *with* people, not to them.

You can get away with a lot in selling if your first impression to customers is that you're a listener. When a customer senses your basic interest in him, he looks harder for things to be pleased about in your relationship.

SO WHO'S LISTENING?

Who's listening? I'm listening.

As a consultant, I'm in the business of listening. It's the only way I can understand my clients and help them solve their problems.

Employees at Sperry, Ford, IBM, and 3M are also listening. Their organizations have invested thousands of dollars to teach their employees *how to listen.*

In our sales seminars, listening is one of the most popular topics. Every salesperson wants to know more about it. Too few are willing to *do* it.

We spend 80 percent of our waking hours communicating, and at least 60 percent of that time is spent listening. With all that practice, you'd think we'd be good at it.

We're not.

The University of Minnesota has shown that immediately after listening to a ten-minute presentation, the average listener retains only about 25 percent of what was said. That figure drops substantially within the next forty-eight hours.

Think how much information the average salesperson misses by not listening. He may miss the customer's key objective or problem. He may miss "the feel of the sale."

Many salespeople are so concerned about their presentation and what their customer will think of it that they don't listen, and they miss the opportunity to make their first impression a good one.

CUTTING THROUGH THE FOG

The first step toward better listening is to spend less time talking.

The best actors and the best salespeople aren't great talkers. They're great listeners. Actors and salespeople both play off the reactions of other people.

They don't *fake* paying attention. They *are* paying attention.

THE SECRETS OF SELLING:
Listen more than you talk in selling, you have to really *want* to listen.

Listening requires giving up your own thoughts and interests for a while to give attention to someone else. This isn't so hard with someone you like, but it may take a little discipline with a customer you're just getting to know, or in situations in which there are distractions.

Why is it that the times you most want to influence someone are usually the *toughest* times for listening?

It's difficult to fight back "talking tension" the compelling desire to talk before you're ready to listen. It takes real interest to listen effectively despite distractions such as time pressure, noisy surroundings, language barriers, or someone attacking your ideas.

Listening is an *attitude* as well as a skill, an attitude of genuine interest in your customers. Author Truman Capote was a popular party guest because his social philosophy was, "I refuse to be bored." It's a philosophy that works in selling, too.

Nothing is interesting if you're not interested.

Osborne Elliott, former editor-in-chief of *Newsweek*, writes, "I learned that once you get to know something about anything, that anything can be quite interesting. I think this essentially describes a journalist: someone who can be interested in *anything*."

This is also a good description of most peak performance sellers.

One of the most exciting aspects of selling is the opportunity to learn about other people. I could never get bored with selling because I could never get bored with the differences in people.

Interest in people is critical to sales *concentration*.

Dr. Lyman K. Steil of the University of Minnesota, an institution which has pioneered listening research, writes,

> One of the things we continue to find is, when we ask people in our testing to identify the major problems they face as listeners, the things they list continue to be lack of concentration, mental tangencies their thinking goes off on, daydreaming. One thing we work very hard at to improve listening is to suggest ways of focusing, sharpening, and enhancing the ability to concentrate. Many students say that they can only pay attention to a speaker if he says something they are interested in hearing... With listening, the basic problem is that you will never know if you're interested in something until *after* you've listened to it.

To fight off *dis*interest, try to *learn* something new or look for some area of common ground between yourself and your customer, even if it's only guessing how you might feel if you were in his position.

The next time you're listening to a prospect's "boring" story of his problems, revive your interest by asking how he *felt* when he was in that situation, or what he learned from it, or how that experience will affect *your* relationship.

To put yourself into a listening manner, picture yourself as an understanding person. Find an answer to the question, *"What's in it for me* to listen?" The answer may surprise you.

If you're listening, you'll know what it takes to make the sale. You'll know the customer's objectives, his problems, his concerns, and his communication style. You'll know *when* to close the sale.

What your customer wants most from you as a listener is a sense of psychological presence, a sense of *being there*. Listening, even listening without understanding, is often enough to strengthen your relationship with a customer.

You probably know people who are married to someone much less attractive than they are. Obviously, they see something more important than physical beauty in their spouses. Often the compelling attraction of these people is they *listen*, really listen.

Freud may have given salespeople their most important clue to understanding their customers.

Psychiatrist Arnold Mandell writes, "Freud discovered something very profound. When he put a person on a couch in Vienna in 1900, turned out all the lights, and told him to say whatever came into his head, there were only a few basic patterns."

The pattern of communication says what customers don't say.

Following one of President Reagan's meetings with Soviet Foreign Minister Andrei Gromyko, *Time Magazine* gave this account of Reagan's reaction:

> Reagan listened and watched Gromyko as he had rarely scrutinized a man before; looking for clues from words, from eyes, from a touch or a hand-clasp... one signal came through to Reagan loud and clear. It was that Gromyko had no signal to send at all. No message in his eyes. No meaning in his grip. No words that held promise for any kind of agreement.

It was the *pattern* in Gromyko's communication that Reagan read.

Looking past the surface communication helps you see a customer in better perspective.

The challenge of listening is to identify the underlying *theme* of what your customer is saying, and what he's not saying. You can *hear*, *see* and *feel* a customer's tension, interest, or resistance.

If you're sensitive to how a customer is responding to you, you're in a better position to choose whether to stick with what you're doing or try something else.

In selling, you've got to stay in touch with what your customer is thinking *now*. You've got to clear your mind of distraction and *listen*.

THE ACTIVE LISTENER

Think of someone you know who is a good listener in selling. What does this person *do* that makes him a good listener?

Act like an effective listener and you'll become one. Get *active*. Tell your customers with your whole body that you're listening.

Lean forward and nod your encouragement. Repeat what the customer has said. Check what you think you're hearing. Ask questions. Listen with your *eyes*.

Think how you feel when a small child is looking at you as he listens to you. You *know* you have his full attention.

Television personality Art Linkletter writes,

> Most people being interviewed feel insecure, children most of all. Take a five-year-old and put him in front of lights and cameras and a big audience of strangers; what are the chances of getting him to say much? Almost nil. But, I found that by looking him in the eye unwaveringly, never glancing around, never seeming amused or shocked, never demeaning his replies no matter how ridiculous, al-

ways staying on his level—by doing all this I virtually hypnotized him, narrowing his focus of attention to me exclusively so that he talked naturally. I realized that if I could do this with a child I could do this with adults.

If you're not understanding something, take responsibility for not understanding and ask the customer to speak up, to slow down, or to repeat what was said.

President Franklin D. Roosevelt was known for his ability to get people talking about themselves simply by saying, "Tell me more."

You can keep a conversation going with encouraging comments or nonverbal signs, such as nodding, that signal you're listening and you're interested. If you notice the *way* the customer phrased his point was significant, let him know you noticed.

One study by Learning International found that sellers on successful sales calls made more than twice as many acknowledgments of the importance of what the customer said as sellers on failed calls.

Body language shows you're listening. Move with the *customer*, but avoid any distracting motion, or one that mirrors negative body language on his part.

Even *silence* is an active listening strategy.

Your silence enables the customer to take himself deeper into his thinking and to proceed at his own pace. If you interrupt the customer, finish his sentences, try to read his mind, or try to top everything he says, you'll increase his resistance and miss his point.

When a customer becomes silent, he may be processing what you've just said. If you're patient enough to wait him out, he'll probably tell you exactly what it will take to make the sale.

President Lyndon Johnson used to say, "If you're talking, you're not learning." If you listen your way into the sale, you won't have to talk your way out!

At times when a customer is speaking, you may find yourself thinking, "faster, faster, *faster*." Since you *think* faster than the customers speak, use that excess listening time actively to summarize to yourself what the customer is saying.

If you're feeling impatient with the customer's talking, remind yourself that it's probably working in your favor. It generally means he's involved, he's trying to think your ideas through, and he wants to relate to you.

Customers often give information in small chunks and wait for your reaction before they risk telling more. If you can control your emotional reaction, they'll be comfortable in telling you more.

"Yes, but" is one of the worst replies possible for a salesperson, because it says you're more interested in what *you* have to say than in listening. Even worse, salespeople tend to say it when they encounter sales resistance—a time when it's especially important to hear what the customer is saying.

Take notes, but don't take so many notes you lose eye contact or lose track of what the customer is saying. Jot down only key phrases and add to your notes later. If you're making a call with another salesperson, have one person take notes so the other is free to think about the customer's remarks and follow them up with questions.

Separate the customer's main ideas from the supporting details. Use these ideas to form a mental outline of what he's saying, and where he's going with the conversation.

Participants in our seminars always seem surprised when I tell them that asking questions is one of the key active listening skills. Asking good questions *forces* you to listen carefully. You can't ask good questions if you're not listening.

Of course, if you ask *too many* questions, or ask questions in a threatening manner, you can cause customers to *stop* talking. Think of asking questions as problem-solving, not as probing.

The most important active listening technique is *checking* what you think the customer is telling you.

CHECKING OUT THE SALE

Salespeople tend to *assume* too much. They hear what they want to hear or what they *expect* to hear. As a result, they may not hear at all.

Since your expectations distort what you hear, effective listening requires *checking* that you understand what other people are saying.

The closer your selling is to what the customer is actually thinking about his objectives and problems, and the more the customer talks about the losses he's incurring now or the benefits he might gain from your product, the better things will go for you.

THE SECRETS OF SELLING:
Develop the customer's needs fully so he understands the impact of your ideas before you make recommendations.

Resist the urge to talk about your product at the first sign of a sales opportunity. Instead, ask the customer several questions to check what you've heard and to develop the customer's needs fully before you make benefit statements. Introducing benefits before the customer's needs are developed fully, doesn't have much persuasive impact.

One of the checking techniques that has been proven effective in selling

grew out of research by Dr. Carl Rogers. It's called *reflection*—reflecting back
to the customer in your own words the content and feeling of what you understand he's said *without judging it.*

You simply paraphrase what's been said, using the customer's key words
to trigger your recall. It might sound like this, "So this problem is really your
first priority. Is that right?"

Reflective listening can be used to clarify what's been said or to reflect a
nonverbal message ("You *look* discouraged. Would you like to talk about it?")

Most important, it demonstrates that you understand and accept what
your customer is saying.

In my own selling, I've found that I get the best response when I reflect a
customer's comments with a story. By relating a similar situation with another
client, I let the customer know I understand how he's feeling.

Reflection is particularly effective when a customer uses emotionally
charged words, or seems tense, excited, angry, depressed, confused, or defensive or when he's expressing objections or other forms of sales resistance.

Reflection is a good strategy whenever communication seems stuck. For
example, you might say, "Mike, it seems like there's something *else* that still
concerns you that we haven't yet gotten a good handle on."

In especially difficult moments, focus on the customer's *immediate*
feelings. "Right now, you seem frustrated."

Remember, you're *checking*, not agreeing or disagreeing. The idea in
reflective listening is to stay *neutral.*

To identify the feelings behind what the customer is saying, look for the
pattern in his choice of words, in his body language, and in the emotional tone
in his voice. Ask yourself how *you* would be feeling if you were in his position.

Remember to reflect *both* the words and the feelings in the customer's
message.

If a customer has difficulty expressing his reactions to your product, give
him several possible responses to choose from, almost like choosing an answer
on a multiple choice test.

Sometimes you'll pick up red flag messages that signal a hidden meaning
in what people say. One of the most common of these red flags in selling is
projecting feelings on other people with statements such as, "*They* won't like
it." The customer probably means, "*I* don't like it."

Much of this red flag communication takes place on the *edges* of conversations. Often a person will tell you his real feelings ("Oh, by the way...")
when the end of your conversation is in sight.

When you notice these red flags, *check them out.*

Some customers express their feelings best through stories. In fact, when
you notice that a customer isn't able to express himself well, expect him to tell
you his feelings *indirectly* by repetition of the same stories.

Check out the underlying patterns that give these stories their meaning.

Is the story told in an angry way? Is the focus on the past or the future?

Does the customer describe himself as active, or as passive and victim-like in the story? How does he describe his objectives?

You'll actually be able to *sense* when you're doing a good job of listening. You'll *feel* the customer being drawn to you. You'll *see* him open up physically. You'll hear that you're on target as you check out what he means.

Of course, hearing what's said and checking what you hear are only the first steps to peak performance listening.

What people say is important, but the *way* they talk, the *way* they look, and the *way* they move can tell you even more. Surprisingly, most of what you'll learn about customers, you'll learn by observing what they *do*.

SO, READ MY BODY

For years, I've been fascinated by mimes. Without saying a word, they use language so clear we understand them immediately.

In selling, customers speak a silent language, too. What you see, and what you sense in the customer's response is a significant part of the feel of success. And peak performance selling requires checking out the *silent* messages customers send you.

In *Silent Messages: Implicit Communication of Emotions & Attitudes,* Albert Meharabian estimates nonverbal "body language" represents 55 percent of our communication. Customers' bodies will tell you what they're thinking before they say it.

A salesperson might say, "Yes, but the nonverbal clues are so slight they're difficult to interpret." That's a statement about his ability to *detect* them, not about the signals themselves. You can *learn* to be more sensitive to body language.

Chances are, you're blocking out many of these selling cues with your concern about your presentation.

THE SECRETS OF SELLING:
Good Salespeople are like good *lovers*.
They immerse themselves in the needs and
responses *of other people*.

From now on, whenever you feel a hunch, or sense something is wrong during a sale, trust your feelings and pay attention. Those feelings work at supersonic speed—in as little as one twenty-fourth of a second, Harvard researchers found. And that gives you an extra edge.

If you feel angry, pushed, or uneasy—seemingly without cause—ask yourself why. If you feel as though the customer is signaling his readiness to buy, look for opportunities to close the sale.

Unfortunately, some sales gurus portray body language as an *exact* science. The salespeople who read their books think they can identify what product a customer will buy by noticing whether or not he pulls his left ear or crosses his leg! This just isn't true.

You can only rely on *patterns* of nonverbal behavior. Most of the significant cues you need to recognize in selling appear in clusters. Few gestures have specific meaning by themselves—they have to be considered as part of a larger pattern.

For example, if a woman continually gives a man long glances, she may be signaling her interest in him. Or she may not. If she also sits facing him, smiles a lot, and plays with her hair, he could be more certain.

Some indicators are more important than others.

Eye contact and eye movement, in particular, provide important information about a customer's interest in you, and about his communication style. Strong eye contact is usually a sign of interest. The eye contact of participants in a group presentation will even help you identify the decision-maker; the one looking at *you* rather than at other participants at crucial decision points.

The most important features of nonverbal behavior in selling are *when* and *how often* it occurs. Customers often use their most important signals to underscore key points, consistently placing voice or nonverbal emphasis on the points they want you to remember.

You can use this underscoring to judge the response of prospects to your sales presentations, to evaluate the relative importance of the various objectives the customer talks about, or to spot resistance. If you notice *resistance*, you can stop what you're doing and adjust.

Peak performance sellers are continually asking themselves, "Is he signalling he's receptive?" Most authorities in nonverbal communication agree that excessive eye contact, touching, open posture toward you, leaning forward, pupil dilation, and signs of relaxation can usually be interpreted as *positive* indicators. The more the customer imitates your behavior, the more likely it is his response is positive.

The experts also agree unnecessary movements such as foot or finger tapping, touching the face, covering the mouth, placing both hands behind the neck, wringing the hands, or folding the arms are often indicators of tension or resistance. So are a clenched fist, shoulders pointed at an angle to you, tight lips, "cold" eyes, backing away, and short answers.

A customer sitting back in his chair with his arms tight to his body, his feet crossed, and his hands held together is probably expressing resistance.

Read your customers from the *bottom* up. Words and facial expressions are relatively easy to control, and lower body movements are difficult to control. When what a customer is saying seems quite different from what his body is telling you, believe his *body*.

THE SECRETS OF SELLING:
If you have a hunch or you're not sure what a customer's body language means, *check it out*.

Whenever you sense resistance, ask the customer if there's something that concerns him, or tell him he looks concerned. He'll like the fact you're understanding what's he's feeling.

In selling, you're looking for the *feel* of the sale. Getting a grip on it requires a little experimenting with what you hear, what you see, and what you feel.

Sometimes you'll detect a mood to buy *something*, even if it's not what you've set out to sell. With a little imagination, you can change course and sell something else.

The point of listening is to get to the common ground between you and your customer where you operate most successfully.

There are some salespeople who break down the walls customers build, and smooth the way for themselves with their listening and concern. There are others who invade their customers' territory like a bull in a china shop with nonstop talk, and who always seem to remain strangers to the customers they meet.

When it's your turn to listen, which of these salespeople are you?

Peak performance sellers help their customers feel important. They make strong first impressions by their active effort to listen. They get the *sense* of what their customers want, and *do something* with that information to strengthen their sales relationships.

In the next chapter, you'll learn how to organize your selling around the customer's viewpoint and build a strong problem solving partnership with the customer.

PART THREE

*Jim Schneider's Secrets
of Selling*

CHAPTER 7

The Six Steps of Selling: Building the Relationship

Most sales training and books on selling teach either "the *one* right way to sell" or "the 99 ways to *close* a sale." They deal with *techniques*, not with people.

This thinking reminds me of my industry's popular definition of a consultant: a person who knows 99 ways to make love, but doesn't have a partner.

Selling is influencing people by *developing relationships* and by *solving customer problems* so there's a mutual exchange of value. Sometimes even experienced salespeople forget that selling requires meeting other people's needs as well as their own.

In selling, it's the subtlety in the relationship you have to learn, the *feel* of success. What matters most are each customer's objectives, problems, concept of results and style, and your sense of what is working with this person the best.

Forcing one sales approach into every sales situation is *hard*-sell, exactly what most salespeople want to avoid.

Curtis R. Berrien, senior vice president for the Boston based Forum Corporation, says this kind of salesperson has,

> An inability to listen, to care, to get off his agenda and onto the customer's agenda, to be patient. He's pushy, talks all the time, goes in with preconceived notions, shoots down objections, drops a client after he makes a sale.

Ironically, the salespeople who are most afraid of being seen as pushy often revert to hard-sell because some sales guru's selling formula is the only approach they know. They don't have confidence in their own ability to recognize and repeat what has worked for them.

They think of selling as *pushing* their ideas through resistance with the force of these magical sales techniques they've learned. As a result, they're likely to talk about their products monologue-style, without identifying their customer's problems and objectives.

Whenever a salesperson tries to *push* his ideas through sales resistance, he destroys *trust*, the take-off point for success in selling.

Peak performance sellers know that the customer and salesperson move through the sales process *together*, one step at a time. They don't try to make something happen that isn't there yet.

Actually, there's no such thing as "soft-sell" and "hard-sell." There is only smart-sell and stupid-sell, *sell* and *no-sell*.

The Australian proverb, "Softly, softly, catchee monkey," is a good guide for peak performance sellers. Soft-sell sellers know how to adjust.

Whenever two people get together, there have to be some adjustments made if there's going to be trust. Peak performance sellers listen *before* they recommend, they develop trust, and they sell to the *customer's* objectives. That's *soft*-sell.

When we began marketing our Feel of Success® Seminars in 1979, I found the biggest surprise to most participants was the ease with which they got comfortable with a soft-sell style. Once they accepted the premise that selling flows from the *customer's* viewpoint, they found they could build comfortably on their successes in other relationships to be successful in selling.

I've found peak performance sellers are more likely than other salespeople to have developed a feel for the needs of other people.

Selling is a delicious chowder of relationship-building, problem-solving, and responsiveness to the customer.

All success in selling takes is relaxation, a little knowledge of how the sales process operates, concern for the customer, the confidence to close sales, and the courage to repeat what works or to try something different when necessary.

Not everyone can be a super salesperson. But every salesperson can achieve his own optimum performance by paying attention to the responses of other people.

Once a salesperson is *willing* to sell, he only needs to know what good performance *looks* like, *sounds* like, and *feels* like to sell better.

THE SIX STEPS OF SELLING

Very few salespeople come to our seminars knowing how to stay in touch with "the feel of the sale." They don't have a simple way to organize their selling so they know what they're doing *right*, and what's not working.

Your management of the sales process should focus on the steps the *customer* takes in making decisions, not the steps that you take. You'll seem more flexible and be more on track with the customer's thinking.

At the same time, you have to see that your own agenda for customer action is met. If you can shorten the average time between initiating contact, and making sales, you can substantially increase the payoff for you and the customer.

Most salespeople spend their sales time thinking of themselves and their techniques, not of their customer and his responses.

In contrast, peak performance sellers are able to temporarily forget their fears and their other customers, to concentrate entirely on the customer they're with. They immerse themselves in the interaction.

As a result, peak performance sellers are able to sense resistance to their products, or significant movement toward agreement. They can *feel* their success, and can recognize when they should change their strategy.

A sale has to *move*. There has to be a drive toward action. Without movement and a sense that something good is unfolding, there won't be a sale.

When the momentum of the sale shifts, you can sense it. If you're in touch with this momentum, you can exert control over it. Peak performance sellers use momentum to move the sale forward even faster.

To get this "feel of the sale" think of selling as a simple, six-step process as illustrated in the diagram on the next page. By having a six-step "memory hook" for the sales process, you'll find it easier in *any* sales situation to think of what to do to stay on track for the sale. As the diagram illustrates, the six steps of selling flow from how *customers* think.

Every selling situation is different. There are substantial differences in selling an idea versus selling a product, or selling an expensive product to a company versus selling an inexpensive product to an individual.

Large systems sales require patience, analysis, and creativity. Small "now or never" sales require fast response and high assertiveness. But every sale involves the six steps of selling.

The six steps of selling are based on Schneider's Law of Accumulative Momentum. Success builds on success. The customer and salesperson move toward the sale *together*, one step at a time.

Most beginning salespeople move to each succeeding step too soon, without building a solid foundation. They lock the customer out by overstructuring their presentation.

Selling is really as simple, and as difficult, as following these six steps.

First, relax and strengthen your confidence before each selling situation. If you're *feeling successful*, you're more likely to get "the feel of the sale" and to recognize and use what you do *right*. You're also likely to transfer that feeling of confidence to your customer.

Second, *develop* trust. Once the customer trusts you, he's more likely to talk openly about his problems and objectives, and to believe what you say.

Third, identify the customer's objectives with effective questioning

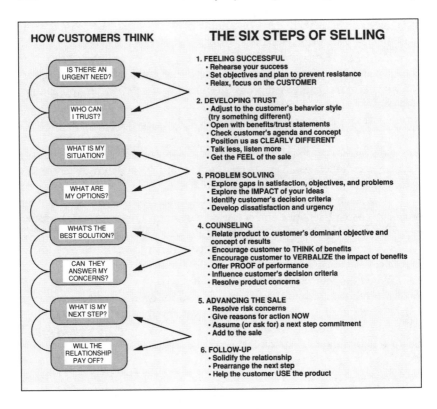

HOW CUSTOMERS THINK

- IS THERE AN URGENT NEED?
- WHO CAN I TRUST?
- WHAT IS MY SITUATION?
- WHAT ARE MY OPTIONS?
- WHAT'S THE BEST SOLUTION?
- CAN THEY ANSWER MY CONCERNS?
- WHAT IS MY NEXT STEP?
- WILL THE RELATIONSHIP PAY OFF?

THE SIX STEPS OF SELLING

1. FEELING SUCCESSFUL
   - Rehearse your success
   - Set objectives and plan to prevent resistance
   - Relax, focus on the CUSTOMER

2. DEVELOPING TRUST
   - Adjust to the customer's behavior style (try something different)
   - Open with benefits/trust statements
   - Check customer's agenda and concept
   - Position us as CLEARLY DIFFERENT
   - Talk less, listen more
   - Get the FEEL of the sale

3. PROBLEM SOLVING
   - Explore gaps in satisfaction, objectives, and problems
   - Explore the IMPACT of your ideas
   - Identify customer's decision criteria
   - Develop dissatisfaction and urgency

4. COUNSELING
   - Relate product to customer's dominant objective and concept of results
   - Encourage customer to THINK of benefits
   - Encourage customer to VERBALIZE the impact of benefits
   - Offer PROOF of performance
   - Influence customer's decision criteria
   - Resolve product concerns

5. ADVANCING THE SALE
   - Resolve risk concerns
   - Give reasons for action NOW
   - Assume (or ask for) a next step commitment
   - Add to the sale

6. FOLLOW-UP
   - Solidify the relationship
   - Prearrange the next step
   - Help the customer USE the product

problem-solving. Once you and the customer agree on his objectives, you can target your selling to his needs.

Fourth, link your product to the customer's objectives with sales *counseling* about what the customer should *do*, and how it will benefit him.

Fifth, *advance* the customer closer to a sale by moving the customer to a commitment to action. Closing the sale is the *natural* outcome of a sales conversation if you have followed the other steps of selling. Once a customer has agreed your product can solve his problem or help him reach his objectives, it can't possibly be pushy to ask him to buy your product or to take action that moves your relationship forward so he can have these benefits.

Sixth, whether you make the sale or the sale is still pending, *follow* up to strengthen your relationship with the customer.

At each step in this process, you're likely to encounter sales resistance that can move you *away* from the sale. Following the six steps of selling helps you sustain your momentum *forward*, toward the sale.

One saleswomen I taught compared this process to putting on make-up. She says that when you're all done, selling should have been so smooth and natural that the customer doesn't even know you've done it.

This simple checklist has helped thousands of salespeople avoid the most common mistakes of selling. It forces you to sell to the *customer's* viewpoint, and helps you organize your selling so you can recognize what you're doing *right* and repeat it.

The most frequent comment I hear from salespeople after they've watched themselves rehearse selling skills on videotape is, "I never realized I was doing so many things *right*. I just need to do them more consistently."

Following the six steps of selling can give you the *consistent* success of the peak performance seller.

WHY SELLERS DON'T SELL

Step one, *feeling successful*, is so important that I've devoted much of this book to increasing your confidence in selling. But negative thinking isn't the only common error in selling.

The error I see most frequently is the tendency of salespeople to jump from developing trust to recommendations and counseling, without problem solving to identify the customer's objectives. This mistake is the major reason so many salespeople are considered pushy. It causes salespeople to waste time talking about the wrong issues, or make recommendations before the customer's needs are fully developed.

Even worse, many salespeople skip both the developing-trust and problem-solving steps. As a result, they have no idea who their customer is as a *person* or what his objectives are. Without steps two and three, their selling meets maximum resistance.

Another frequent error in selling is to end sales conversations without asking for customer *action*.

The momentum of selling should lead somewhere. Without a closing, people can be committed to your idea or product in principle, and not take action to support it. You don't have commitment until you have customer *action*.

Salespeople lose control of the sales process by allowing the customer to move them *away* from the sale. This inability to lead sales conversations is one of the principal reasons salespeople have trouble closing sales.

I've watched thousands of salespeople, on video-tape or live in seminars and sales calls. Most of them follow a self-defeating pattern of "talk and stop" in their conversations. They find themselves backed into the role of "answer man" to the customer's questions.

In this chapter and in chapter eight, you'll learn how to stay on track toward closing the sale by organizing your selling around the six steps of selling.

Who do you think should be doing most of the talking in your selling, you or the customer? The answer is the *customer*. But most salespeople jump into their "sales pitch," and talk themselves out of the sale.

THE SECRETS OF SELLING:
The most frequent error in selling is that salespeople *talk* too much!

I've made hundreds of calls with salespeople, and 95 percent talk too much. They figure that if *they* do all the talking, the customer can't ask a question they can't answer!

The truth is, the more you talk, the *more* likely it is you'll be asked something you don't know, or you'll say the wrong thing.

To calm their nervousness or to overwhelm the customer with evidence, salespeople *sell* their products instead of helping customers *buy* them. They talk so much there's no time left to identify the customer's problems or to close the sale.

Remember, selling requires more *listening* than talking, more *getting* information than giving information. Relax. You're not on stage. You'll reduce your nervousness and seem more confident if you talk less and listen more.

Try to keep your talking to 30 percent or less of the conversation in a sales contact. Let the customer know you want his participation.

The six steps of selling are not a "one way" success formula. They're a guide, a way to organize your selling around the customer and his responses. Every salesperson will use them in his own way, with his own selling style.

The six steps of selling are designed to make your selling *more* flexible, not less. If your customer begins by telling you he wants to buy something, *close the sale.* You certainly don't want to say, "I can't sell you this yet. I haven't finished steps two, three, and four." As ridiculous as that response sounds, some salespeople are almost that rigid.

While you're closing one of these quick sales, you can move back to the problem-solving step to find ways to *add* to the sale.

The six steps of selling are simply a reminder to keep your momentum moving towards a "yes," and to avoid the common errors of selling.

In my company, we call our presentation on the six steps of selling "the ten-minute drill." In ten minutes we can explain 80 percent of the *technique* of selling by explaining the relationship among these six steps. It's getting the *feel* of the sale that takes time to learn.

The six steps of selling work whether you're face-to-face with one person, making a group presentation, or on the telephone. In fact, the more you learn about negotiation, public speaking, and coaching, the more you'll realize how well the six steps of selling apply to these skills, too.

In this chapter, we'll review the first three steps of selling, those that build your customer relationship into a problem-solving partnership. In the next chapter, we'll review the final three steps, those that close the sale.

STEP ONE: FEELING SUCCESSFUL

Peak performance sellers are as interested in selling with confidence as they are in selling more. They know they have to *feel* successful before they can *be* successful.

Salespeople who feel successful can concentrate on the *customer* and what they *want* to happen, instead of what *could* happen. They're not distracted from the customer by negative thinking.

Most of this book is devoted to developing your confidence and relaxation *before* you enter the sales arena, so you can relax and do what you know how to do during your interaction with customers.

The success cues and mental rehearsal techniques you learned in Chapter 2 will help you trigger the feelings and behaviors you've found effective. They're readily-accessible resources you can use to increase your confidence, and to recall successful selling actions you can use in new selling situations.

Feeling successful also leads to *enthusiasm*, one of the greatest sales motivators of all.

In his book *Leaders,* Richard Nixon writes, "People are persuaded by reason, but moved by emotion; he (the leader) must both persuade them and move them."

If you're feeling successful, you'll project energy and believability to your customers. But you won't stir the interest and emotions of other people until you first stir your own. Get excited about who you are and what you're doing!

Get enthused! It sounds "hokey" when you say it, but sparks set off sparks. People are persuaded as much by the strength of your enthusiasm as by your logic, since enthusiasm is interpreted as *conviction*.

David Mahoney, former CEO of Norton Simon, Inc., writes, "Sometimes a medium-good idea presented with lots of conviction can work. A great idea, presented tepidly, will fall on its ass."

To feel successful, *act* successful. To feel enthused, *act* enthused. Work like an actor, taking on the small gestures of your successful salesperson character and working backward to the feelings associated with those behaviors.

One story has it that during the filming of the movie *Marathon Man,* actor Dustin Hoffman told actor Laurence Olivier that he couldn't feel a scene. Olivier replied, "If you don't feel it, dear boy, try *acting* it."

Once you're feeling successful, you've entered your optimum performance state. *You're ready to sell.*

STEP TWO: DEVELOPING TRUST

Trust is one of the critical success factors in selling. Peak performance sellers make some of their sales on trust alone.

If a prospect believes in you, he'll find a way to buy from you. Without his trust, you *start* from a position of resistance.

In selling, trust is a sense of reliability and a feeling of working *with* someone. It's the reason customers believe what some salespeople say, and open themselves up to these salespeople to give them the information they need to make the sale.

Buyers can sense when your selling purpose is to *help* them.

Harvard University marketing professor Theodore Levitt writes, "The offered product will be judged in part by who personally offers it—not just 'who' the vendor corporation is but also 'who' the corporation representative is."

It's difficult to separate the salesperson from the product. If a customer sizes up your appearance and selling style and decides you're *not* reliable, he's likely to assume your product won't work either.

Studies by the Forum Corporation, the New York Sales and Marketing Club, neurolinguistics experts and other researchers have confirmed that the salesperson's ability to develop trust is one of the key traits that separates successful salespeople from the rest.

THE SECRETS OF SELLING:
There's no sliding scale of credibility in selling. Either you have it, or you don't, so do everything you can to maintain it.

Your success in developing trust and gaining people's interest in your first seconds with them determines whether you even get the *chance* to sell your ideas.

Here's what several salespeople in our seminars had to say about developing trust:

> Believe me, no one's going to sign a two-million-dollar contract with me unless he's sure our system will do what I say it will. My credibility is always on the line.

> I see the difference trust makes in my commission checks. I live off repeat sales and my customers remember me and ask for me by name. Some of my customers even trust me enough to let me order for them when I find something I think they'll like.

> I save a lot of time with customers by telling them we'll only look at houses they can afford. Sometimes they're so worried they're going to get sold something they can't afford that they miss some of the homes that might be right for them with creative financing. They won't even look at those houses with me unless I gain their trust.

Customers want to do business with salespeople they can believe in. They buy *you* before they buy your product.

One of the most famous ads in the history of industrial advertising was created by McGraw-Hill to point out the value of advertising in developing trust before the salesperson's call. The ad featured a stern-looking buyer saying the following words to the salesperson:

"I don't know who you are.
I don't know your company.
I don't know your company's product.
I don't know what your company stands for.
I don't know your company's customers.
I don't know your company's record.
I don't know your company's reputation.
Now, what is it you wanted to sell me?"

This ad makes a good case for creating specific sales strategies to develop trust.

STRATEGIES FOR DEVELOPING TRUST

Salespeople frequently say to me, "Customers don't want to deal with me. They want to deal with the more 'experienced' people in the office."

Why do they want to deal with the "experienced" people? They have a *reason* for trusting those salespeople more.

Customers take their cues for their behavior from you.

If you find that customers resist you or withdraw from you, it may be because you're giving off the wrong cues, *creating* resistance to yourself.

Developing trust begins with the human relations skills covered in Chapter 4: First Impressions. Research has proven that peak performance sellers are highly effective in establishing trust because they use these simple fundamentals of human relations.

In the early stages of a relationship, you're really trying to say, "I'm like you. You can trust me."

The peak performance seller adjusts to the customer's responses at each step of the sale. Average salespeople don't. Psychologist Donald J. Moine writes,

Sales agents with only average success tend to jump immediately into their memorized sales pitches or to hit the customer with a barrage of questions. Neglecting to pace the customer, the mediocre sales agent creates no common ground on which to build trust.

Many salespeople think of trust building as time-wasting. They're so busy thinking about what they're going to say, they miss the *feel* of the sale.

When I speak to groups of salespeople, I ask people in the audience what they think they're selling every day. Usually the answers are *products* such as cars, insurance, houses, or machinery.

What you're really selling is *you* and the *results* of your products. And the less difference there is between your product and the products of your competitors, the more you're selling yourself.

Supersalesman Joe Girard, the world's leading car salesman every year from 1967 to 1977, suggests that before you meet with a prospect you should ask yourself, "Would I buy me?" If the answer is "yes," you're on your way to the feel of success in selling.

To sell yourself, you have to make the customer feel important. The salesperson who talks about his product nonstop, who won't let the customer participate, *destroys* trust. How can you trust someone who tries to keep you out of your own decision?

The more the customer contributes to the sale, the better the outcome will be. Customers want to know they're a full partner in working out solutions to their problems and in evaluating your product.

Talking only gives you the *illusion* you're in control of a conversation. In reality, the other person may be tuning out.

Of course, trust requires more than rapport and involvement. Getting a customer's attention requires gaining his trust that your conversation will be important from *his* viewpoint. You've got to sell your conversation just as you have to sell yourself and your product.

Why *should* the customer talk to you? What are the benefits to him?

Closing the sale actually begins in the developing trust step when you identify the objective you're going to talk about and create a frame for your conversation. Start your selling at the *end*, with your bottom-line reason for being there.

IBM salespeople are taught to tell prospects why they're there and what they hope to accomplish.

Tell the customer what you want, what he'll gain and why you think he'll get it. You might say, "Mr. Johnson, Tom Wycoff wanted me to tell you about a way you can cut your employee-benefit costs with a new health care program that has saved thousands of dollars for two companies very similar to yours."

No matter how long you have to make your point, try to get to the heart of the customer's objectives in the first seconds.

By stating your objective early in the conversation you'll sound organized, and prevent unnecessary tension about your motives. Let people know your game plan up front so they can be part of it. Customers are uncomfortable if they don't know where you're going with your presentation.

Mentioning a third-party referral strengthens the customer's trust in the credibility of what you have to say. Frequently, I've noticed a prospect's entire body relax after I've mentioned the name of a referral.

A third-party referral almost always buys you enough credibility to earn you a fair hearing for your product story, and that's all any salesperson can ask for.

Stating your credentials or your track record of success with other customers in similar situations also builds trust. Customers won't know your credentials unless you tell them.

In this developing-trust stage, customers want to know you're *similar to them* and *different from other salespeople.*

THE SECRETS OF SELLING:
Position your product as *clearly different* and *better* than the competition.

It's not enough to demonstrate that you can get the results the customer wants. To justify differences in price or the effort to switch suppliers, you also need to establish that your product is *clearly different* and better than your competitors products on the decision criteria that are important to the customer.

Think of yourself and your competition as each having a place, or a *position*, in the customer's mind and position yourself and your product as *clearly different* and *better* than other options. If possible, that positioning should link you and your product to the customer's key objectives.

This sales positioning is what makes you memorable and credible. When you and the customer part company, the customer should be able to describe you, what you do, and what's different about you in a few sentences. If you can't establish how your product is clearly different, why would the customer pay more for it or go through the hassle of changing suppliers? Price will become the only issue.

Make a "clearly different statement" in the first moments of contact to establish value, and then tailor statements more specifically to the customer as you learn more about him. Use words such as clearly, definitely, fastest or most to replace any "same as everyone" descriptions and really set you apart.

In any sales situation, there's a certain amount of tension in the relationship.

Life insurance salespeople, in particular, encounter high prospect tension in the first moments of a sale. Their prospects often resist the idea of being sold, and feel uncomfortable with facing the idea of their own mortality.

Some tension is healthy in selling because it keeps the customer involved and thinking of a potential commitment. But often it's necessary to make special tension-relieving statements to relax the customer's defenses. These statements are particularly important when you're selling by telephone, when a customer's budget or time is limited, or when a customer is satisfied with his current supplier.

In these high-tension situations, a simple statement such as, "I know you're working with a tight budget, Ted," is usually enough to relieve the tension and to open the prospect's mind to your conversation.

I've found that when I relieve the tension this way, I can actually see the person relax. And once he's giving a fair hearing to my presentation, he'll put aside any early reservations if I'm on target with his dominant objectives.

People tend to trust the salespeople who can show them they understand their situation. The more you know about a customer, the higher the chance of building trust and selling to his objectives.

STEP THREE: PROBLEM SOLVING

Most sales are made in the problem-solving step of selling. That's when the objectives of the sale are negotiated.

Success in problem solving requires an ability to screen quickly for the best prospects and for the buyer's objectives and problems. In selling, *getting* information is more important than giving it.

When a customer says, "Just looking," he *means* it. He's looking for someone who will take the time to find out what he needs and to sell it to him.

As a customer, it isn't easy to find a salesperson who will do any problem solving. Mail order millionaire Richard Thalheimer writes, "It's amazing how many people either don't know what people want, or don't know how to find out."

The problem-solving step saves you time by isolating what the customer wants and how he thinks about his problems. It keeps the customer involved in the sale, thinking fully about your ideas.

THE SECRETS OF SELLING:
Coach your customers with questions to help them think about and verbalize the impact of your ideas. Customers have to *share* to care.

The peak performance seller thinks about more than making the sale. He thinks about solving the customer's problems. He sells with the purpose to *help the customer.*

Almost every customer you see has a problem you might be able to solve. In our business, I've found customers seldom come to us with well-defined problems, only symptoms they want resolved. By problem solving, I've found I can *create* sales opportunities.

In problem solving, you're sifting through the customer's objectives, and the symptoms of these problems, until you agree on a problem you can solve together. In the process, you're negotiating the sale.

Your questions also help coach the customer to think through his objectives and problems. Often a customer isn't sure what he wants because he doesn't know all the benefits of your products. Nobody wanted television until they saw it.

Salespeople tend to believe the customer always knows what he wants. He often doesn't. He may know his problems or his objectives, but there's a good chance he doesn't know his options, or the impact of those options.

Think of problem solving as you might think of a detergent ad on television. Picture eight detergent boxes labelled brand A though brand H.

You ask your first question and, based on the customer's answer, a pair of hands slides four boxes off the screen. You ask a second question and, with that answer, two more boxes are pushed aside. Finally, you ask a third question and, based on that answer, there's only *one* box left, the box the customer wants.

Who chose the box, a pushy salesperson? No. The *customer* chose the box with his answers to your questions about his objectives and problems.

This approach to selling puts you in the role of a *coach and counselor*. Counselors help people make their own decisions.

When salespeople tell me they run out of time before they can close the sale, I know they don't do enough problem solving.

Philosopher and poet George Santayana described a fanatic as "someone who redoubles his efforts after he has forgotten his aim." In reviewing hundreds of sales presentations on videotape, I've found salespeople often temporarily lose sight of their aim of moving conversations toward the customer's objectives and redouble their efforts by talking too much.

Salespeople are often reluctant to ask questions because they're concerned they might seem pushy, or they might lose control once the customer starts talking. Actually, the problem-solving step is what takes the pushiness *out* of selling and gives you *more* control over the outcome of your conversation.

The easiest path to what customers want is *their* path. Once you find the customer's path to the sale, you can cut your sales time by 50 percent and increase your success rate.

Here's what a real estate saleswomen said at one of our corporate seminars about the value of problem solving:

> Sometimes I have to spend two or three days showing homes to one couple. I used to show home buyers whatever properties they would see from the multiple listing book. I finally figured out that if I show them the wrong types of homes, I've lost money, not just time. It used to seem pushy to ask questions, but not any more.

The problem-solving step saves time by identifying the prospects and the decision makers who are able to *act* on your ideas. It separates the "lookers" from the serious buyers.

Qualified buyers have answers to questions such as "Why do you want this?" or "When do you need it?" Lookers don't.

Doing some problem solving before you "sell" your ideas is just good common sense. Yet a visit to almost any business will convince you that the vast majority of salespeople waste their time by not screening which "lookers" have the money or the clout to buy.

When I was in the market for my previous home, only one of ten real estate agents took the minutes necessary to qualify my interest before investing hours to see specific homes. She was the only one to discover how much I wanted a swimming pool. And she got the sale.

Are you asking enough questions? My first sales manager helped me build the right habits in problem solving by asking me questions about my prospects after each call. Once I saw how little I knew about the customer I had just called on, I learned to ask more questions.

THE RIGHT QUESTIONS FOR THE RIGHT ANSWERS

Sometimes customers may resist giving you the information you need, or give you only superficial answers.

To minimize resistance as you begin a series of questions, mention something you *do* know about the customer's situation and state the benefits to him for answering your questions. You might say, "Dave, I know you're primarily interested in word processing capability. To save you time and help you select the product that's right for you, I'll need some information." Or you might say, "You'd like something to match the living room paper. So we both have the same thing in mind, could you tell me a little more about what you're looking for?"

If you preface your questions with benefit statements, your customer will tell you almost anything you need to know to make the sale.

Even the *way* you ask questions can cut resistance. Try to get across a problem-solving, "we're in this together" manner so you don't seem pushy.

To stay on track toward the sale, peak performance sellers also think through a well-planned *series* of questions.

You won't need many prepared questions. As ABC anchorman and expert interviewer Ted Koppel says, "Most of the time, if you give people a halfway decent opening question they end up telling you fairly interesting things."

A well-planned series of questions will result first in some fast, time-saving screening, then in getting the customer to talk and display his style.

As you move on, your questions should focus on identifying the customer's objectives, his experience, his current problems or losses, and what he might gain by buying your product. During this phase of the sale, it's important to take the prospect as deep into his thinking as you can.

As you move into the counseling step, your questions should be used more to make the customer *think* about and *verbalize* the consequences of his current actions and the benefits of your ideas.

No one understands the customer's viewpoint and concept of desired results better than the customer. The key selling strategy is to get the customer to explain his thinking to you *in his own words*.

When you're in doubt, or just plain curious about something, check it out. Your intuition is telling you that you're at the leading edge of something important.

Of course, asking the wrong questions can cause a customer to *stop* talking. That raises the question, "*What* questions should you ask?"

SCREENING QUESTIONS

Screening questions are used to save time by qualifying the customer's potential, identifying his style, and sorting out his objectives. An example from financial industry selling is, "Are you more interested in an investment that gives you the highest return possible, or in something that gives you monthly income?"

There's no need to talk about six different products if a customer is interested in only one, or if he can't afford any.

One of my banking clients offered four similar products which had the same descriptive phrase in their names. Their employees became frustrated because customers frequently asked for their products by the descriptive phrase alone. They were losing sales time by having to describe all four products to every customer, to determine which one he was really interested in. This approach frequently confused the customer, and they lost even more sales time.

We saved these salespeople time by teaching them how to ask two or three screening questions before they talked about *any* of the products. Based on the answers to those questions, they normally had to talk about only one.

PROBLEM SOLVING QUESTIONS

Problem-solving questions, such as "What do you want to happen that's not happening now?" are used to get the customer talking, and to identify his thinking, his experience, his objectives, his preferences, his feelings, and his problems. You're looking for at least one customer objective or problem you can build the sale on.

Try to focus your questions on the *gap* between the customer's objectives and his current results. Be sure that what he wants is what he *needs*.

Most problem-solving questions start with *who, where, when,* or *how.* Obviously, it's more helpful to know *what* plans are being made for a company's growth than whether plans are being made.

If you really get into their problems, customers will become more interested in solving them too.

Your questions should focus on the customer's current way of operating, and the strengths and weaknesses he finds in operating without your product.

You might ask, "What are some of the problems you're having with the current system?" "Which way do you prefer doing it?" or "What is it you want the product to do for you?"

Don't be disappointed if your customer is already using a competitor's product. In many cases, that customer is an *even better* prospect because you only have to sell him *your* product, not on using the product itself.

HIGHLIGHT QUESTIONS

During the problem-solving step, and later in the counseling step, you should always use questions to highlight sales points you want the customer to *think about* and *verbalize* so the customer thinks fully about the consequences of your idea and states those consequences *in his own language.*

Highlight questions are used to *give* insight, not to gain it. For example, an insurance salesperson might ask a customer, "If something happened to one of you, what would the effect be on your finances?" or "What would it mean to you if you had this much extra income each month?"

Highlight questions are effective in dramatizing what the customer is losing by not using your product, or what the customer will gain as a result of the benefits provided.

You may know the answer to a highlight question before you ask it, but ask it anyway to register the thought in the customer's mind. For example, you might ask, "Are you paying more, now? or, "How much could that save you?"

FOLLOW-UP QUESTIONS

You'll also need to follow up most of your questions with other questions that take the customer *deeper* into his thinking. For example, you might ask, "What causes that?" or "Is there anything else that concerns you?"

Follow-up questions enable you to get to the causes behind the customer's problems, and to his underlying reasons for liking or resisting your product while there's still time to respond to those reasons.

If you don't know why a customer is resisting or what's *really* causing his problems, you'll find it difficult to help.

When a customer seems to have trouble expressing his real feelings, ask him how he would *like* things to be. If that doesn't work, ask him to *guess* what he thinks the impact of your product would be.

To help a customer get his thinking unstuck, it sometimes helps to change senses and ask the customer what he's *feeling,* how he *pictures* the solutions, or what he's *hearing.*

CHECK QUESTIONS

Check questions are used to check the customer's response to your ideas, to make him think about your sales points, and to test his readiness to buy. A simple example is, "How does that sound?"

Peak performance sellers use check questions *throughout* their conversations to keep the customer involved and to stay in touch with "the feel of the sale."

Throughout the sale, think to yourself, "Talk and check. Talk and check." This will fight your natural tendency to talk about your product too long. You'll stay in touch with the customer's thinking.

Some salespeople are reluctant to ask customers what they think of their product because they're afraid of a negative response. You can't stick your head in the sand if you're going to make sales. You've got to stay on track with the customer's thinking.

This checking process keeps your conversation free of false assumptions, gives the customer opportunities to express his feelings, and clears his mind for the next idea. It also helps you determine if the customer understands and accepts what you've just said. For example, you might ask, "Can you see how this will save you time?"

THE SECRETS OF SELLING:
Checking customer reaction keeps you in touch with "the feel of the sale."

The answers to your check questions provide the information you need to make adjustments in your selling style. Can you see how asking more check questions could save you time? (Check!)

As much as possible, try to sell with *questions.*

After you've made a sales contact, ask yourself if you were able to sell without doing much of the talking. How did it feel, sound, and look to be talking less? Was there a difference in the way the customer responded to you, compared to the way customers respond to you on most of your sales contacts? Did your selling seem less pushy? Which questions *worked best*?

If you ask more questions, your selling will *feel* different. Your customers will be talking more, you'll be more on target with the customer's objectives, and selling will seem less pushy. The effective use of problem-solving saves time and helps you create sales opportunities.

Sales motivation speaker Zig Ziglar writes, "... the question approach to selling is a way of life for me." It is for all peak performance sellers. Make it a way of life for you, too.

The first three steps of selling build your relationship with the customer. You become partners moving through the sales process together, one step at a time. It's during these steps that you lay the foundation of trust and negotiate the objectives for the sale.

In the next chapter, you'll learn how to help the customer achieve those objectives, and close the sale.

CHAPTER 8

The Six Steps of Selling: Closing the Sale

Sales almost never go the way you plan. They unfold before you in the first steps of selling.

Once you've developed a good relationship with the customer and negotiated the problem to be solved or the objective to be achieved, the sale begins to *move*.

No word is more frequently associated with selling than the word *motivation*, the drive toward a dominant desire. Since all motivation is *self*-motivation, the customer's drive comes from the inside, not from the seller.

The last three steps of selling focus on *solving* the customer's problems and giving him a *direction* to move, a way to drive himself to take action for what he wants.

This chapter is about *closing* sales.

Most salespeople either do no planning at all for closing sales or they overplan, losing touch entirely with "the feel of the sale." Remember, the *customer* is your guide.

Get to know as much as you can about the customer's problems and objectives. Anticipate his objectives. Plan your questions, your sales *positioning*, your presentation of the benefits, and your strategy for closing. But don't allow your planning to distract you from the customer's *responses*.

The most important rule of thumb for the counseling, closing, and follow-up steps of selling is: when what you're doing isn't working, *try something else*. The customer is constantly rewriting your presentation.

Once you've disciplined yourself to think from the customer's viewpoint, you can prepare for a sale in minutes.

STEP FOUR: COUNSELING

The counseling step of selling should be the briefest of the six steps of selling. For most salespeople, it's the longest. They're determined to sell products instead of *solutions*.

As the term counseling implies, selling is a two-way process. If you've done a good job of negotiating what the customer wants, you can sell to his objectives. You can sell with customer purpose.

Your counselor role is to help the customer recognize his problem, to understand *how* it can be solved, and to know *why* it's in his best interest to solve it.

Holding your sales counseling suggestions until you know what the customer wants is like archery. You wouldn't think of releasing your arrow until you had sighted the target and stretched the bow to its point of maximum leverage.

One of the salespeople in seminars put it this way:

> I used to try to tell everything I could about our products and that led to
> a lot of questions I didn't want. Now I ask a few questions to identify
> what the customer really wants and then *I get right to it.*

In virtually every sales contact, the customer will provide you with at least one problem or one objective you can build a sale on. These openings are doors of opportunity.

When an opening occurs, it may be your only opportunity with that customer. You can't afford to let it pass by. The door may never open again.

THE SECRETS OF SELLING:
Sales counseling is recommending
the *right* solution to the *right* customer
at the *right* time.

In earlier chapters, we explored how to focus your selling on the customer's viewpoint. Benefit selling is the greatest secret in selling and the heart of sales counseling.

In Kaplan's *The Big Time*, he quotes Stephen Schwarzman, a partner at Shearson/Lehman Brothers:

> Ultimately, I am distinguished by my verbal ability, to synthesize, and
> to figure out what other people are thinking without telling me. And if
> you know what they are thinking that means in a real sense you know
> what a politician or any leader does, which is to make explicit what's
> on people's minds... that, of course, is the essential gift all good sales-
> men share.

Peak performance sellers talk only about those few benefits that relate directly to the customer's objectives. They don't waste time talking about anything that isn't important to the customer, even if it's important to other customers. They don't get trapped into a technical, detail-by-detail presentation of their product.

Laser-like, they cut through to what their customer really cares about. The key stretch benefits seem stronger if they're not watered down by a lot of details or by too many benefits.

Sales counseling requires fast response, not fast talking about the product. If you don't make your point fast, you won't make it at all.

The fastest and smoothest transition from the problem-solving step to the counseling step is to link your recommendations to the customer's objectives.

Think, "Repeat the customer's words." This simple action will remind you to think from the *customer's* viewpoint.

If the customer mentions a problem you can solve, use that problem as a transition to your recommendation.

In counseling the customer, you're really saying, "Based on what you've told me, we have a way to resolve your problem and to help you get what you want." You might simply say, "Since you want maximum durability, I'd recommend product X."

Another way to make a smooth transition from an identified problem to the counseling step is a selling sequence best described as *support it, explore it, make it hurt*, and *solve it*. The objective of this sequence is to help the customer talk more about his problem until he can see for himself how he's being hurt by his current course of action.

If a customer says, "I'm concerned about the time it's taking me to do this," you might respond,

> You're right. It does seem to be taking a lot of time (*support it*). Why is that (*explore it*)? What could that cost your department several thousand dollars in overtime over the course of a year (*make it hurt*). We could save you that $3,500 in overtime costs and free some money for the word processing system you want with our beta product (*solve it*).

In this example, you've developed the customer's problem fully before making your sales point.

How you say things is important.

For starters, always mention a stretch benefit *before* you introduce your recommendation or discuss the features of your product. Why risk turning the customer off with the costs and details of your product before he knows what your product can do for him?

Picture yourself walking into your boss's office to suggest an idea. The first time you walk in, you say, "I've got an idea I'd like to talk to you about. Do you have a few minutes?" If your boss is as busy as most of mine were, he's likely to check the time and say, "I'm busy today. Can we do it tomorrow?"

Now picture going in to your boss with the same idea and saying, "I've been thinking about a way you can save a thousand dollars a month in mailing costs. Do you have a few minutes?"

Same idea. Same boss. But where do you go on your boss's priority list? Chances are, you go *up*. Why? Because there's a benefit for your boss to talk to you.

Over time, you can develop your own list of tested opening sentences that work best in the selling situations you encounter most frequently. For example, some peak performance sellers who sell to investors have found that the benefit statement, "You'll get all your money back *first*," is a powerful opening with investors.

Think back to the benefit sequence you completed in Chapter3.

Here's how it would sound to use this format in counseling a customer:

> Mr. Davis, we've found a way to *save you as much as $8,000 a year* on your office supplies (stretch benefit). If you would consolidate more of your buying with us (*your objective*), we could increase your discounts to *save you money* and *you would have more time for management of your business* (stretch benefits).

> When people with your volume buy from many suppliers (customer's current action), *they lose the extra service and big cost savings* they deserve (losses). We'll *save you time* by coming to your office for your orders and we'll work on a 25 percent discount which will *save you an extra $15 on each $100 order* (stretch benefits). How much extra money would this give you for your operation (question)?

Throughout the counseling step, use the word "we" as you talk about solving the customer's problem so the customer feels you're working as *partners*.

NAIL DOWN THE BENEFITS

THE SECRETS OF SELLING:
If your sales points don't stick in the customer's mind, you're not selling.
A seller has to *nail down* the benefits.

If your customer isn't *thinking* about his losses or about the stretch benefits of your product, your sales point can't possibly influence his decisions.

Peak performance sellers "nail down" their sales points by forcing customers to *think* about them, and by *proving* the benefits.

To be sure the customer thinks about key sales points, and to check his response, wrap each key loss or benefit in a check question: "This could save you several hours a day. Can you see how this would save you time?" or "This is a timesaver, *isn't it*?"

This checking strategy is particularly useful in pointing out potential trouble to customers who are satisfied with their current way of doing things.

To nail down product benefits in the customer's mind, it may help to number them: "First, you'll save time. Second, you'll have fewer hassles." or "*This* is an important point."

No one knows the potential of your products as well as you do. Most customers need a little help in recognizing exactly what your product means to them or how they'll feel if your product works well for them.

Store the customer's words in your selling memory so you can repeat them, particularly the words the customer uses frequently. Let him know how he'll feel using your product, and what he'll *tell* himself after he's used it. Help him *picture* himself enjoying the results.

If you're selling a tangible product, stress the intangible aspects, such as service. If you're selling a service, stress the tangible evidence of results.

For every major selling point, *prove* your product gets the results you claim it does.

The customer is buying your promise of satisfaction. He wants to know that someone like him tried the product and it *worked*. Your proof minimizes his risk, and helps him justify the purchase to other people. It demonstrates you've done your homework.

Proof of performance can include demonstrations, sampling the product, hand or computer calculations, statistics, stories, articles, brochures and other sales aids, client lists, letters or referrals from satisfied customers, estimates, and even your personal experience with your product.

Choose the type of proof that best fits the customer. An analytical customer might prefer statistics, but a people-oriented customer might prefer a personal reference.

Proof of good service could be worth up to a 25 percent mark-up in price.

Most customers appreciate a good story about the results of your product. The plot is almost always the same. One of your customers had a problem. Things got worse, and you saved him.

Veteran salespeople from the early medicine shows in the West found the more specific and colorful their stories were, the more successful they were. That's still true today.

The Rev. Jesse Jackson provides a good example of the powerful impact of proof in this excerpt from one of his speeches from the 1984 Presidential primary campaign:

> In 1964, Hart and Mondale *believed* in integrated public accommodations, but I marched for it. In 1965, Hart and Mondale *favored* the

Voting Rights Act, but I risked my life for it. In 1966, they *supported* open housing, but I dodged bricks with Dr. King for it.

If you don't have any proof, or if the dollar impact of your product is difficult to calculate, ask the customer to estimate or guess how great the benefits would have to be to justify your product. Make some assumptions with the customer and "prove" you could achieve that result. You could also base your proof on a similar experience your customer has had.

Through comparisons and proof, you can establish the comparative framework your customer uses in evaluating your product and *position* your product favorably against other products.

You can compare the results of your product to the results of competing options, compare the benefits of having your product to the losses without it, or compare the benefits of starting now to the dangers of waiting.

Prove the results of your products in *financial* terms. Add up the financial impact of cost savings, productivity gains, reduced losses, and other factors. Make the customer think about the dollar amount of risk he's reducing, and the financial impact of your *continuing* to solve his problem.

Position your product by comparing it to one with which your customer is familiar. For a customer most concerned with quality, you could position your product as similar but better than premium brands he's familiar with. Sometimes the association with a more expensive product will increase your product's perceived value.

To strengthen a comparison, maximize the benefits and minimize the losses. A savings of $10 a week for the customer will register more strongly if you remind him that he will save $520 a year—and that your $100 annual fee is only 27 cents a day.

Get the customer to *use* your product so he can experience the benefits and prove your sales points to himself. By asking a customer to "Try it," "Take a test drive," or "Put it on," you nail down the benefits.

SELLING WITH SALES AIDS

Research has proven that visual aids can double the impact and retention of what you say. Brochures and other visual aids can also help you keep sales alive after the customer leaves you.

Visual aids work, but be careful. If you're too quick to hand a customer materials describing your product, two negative things are likely to happen.

First, the customer may *read* them. He's likely to be turned off by one of the product features he sees before you have a chance to sell him on the stretch benefits.

Second, the customer may use the visual aid as an excuse to leave, saying he'll read it at home or he wants to show it to someone else.

In either case, you've lost control of the sale.

Try not to release your visual aids to the customer until he's made a decision, or until your conversation has ended.

Use your sales aids to focus interest and to emphasize key points by underlining and circling them as you speak. This highlighting will also encourage the customer not to toss your materials away later. But don't get too attached to visual aids. The goal is to keep the customer *participating* in the sale, and to build your counseling around the customer's responses.

A growing number of salespeople work with their customers at a computer screen. By turning the screen toward the customer at *selected* times, you can use the terminal to *prove* key points, and to get the customer involved without confusing him with too many choices or details.

When you use your product itself as a visual aid, handle it as though it's *gold* and the customer will respect its value. And *practice* your presentation so your selling is confident and natural.

Probably the best visual aid of all is your own body. Pick up your energy and your pace as you move into counseling. If you're animated and enthused as you speak, you can build excitement and credibility for your product.

Since people remember most what they hear *last*, close the counseling step by repeating the stretch benefits that the customer seemed to accept best, those that fit best with his dominant objectives. Stick with what *works*.

STEP FIVE: ADVANCING THE SALE

If you follow the six steps of selling, the natural conclusion to your conversation is to help the customer take action to get the benefits he wants from your product. In selling, this is called *closing the sale*.

If you can't close, you can't sell. Sales effectiveness is measured by *customer action*.

This is the moment of truth, the time when you put your idea on the line. It's the step in selling that counts most in a salesperson's compensation. Salespeople are paid to sell, not to "try" to sell.

Increasing your closing ratio from 20 percent to 40 percent, or from 50 percent to 60 percent, will substantially increase your income, dramatically cut the pressure on your time, or both.

A closed sale is really the result of a series of customer actions that advance the customer toward a decision and toward effective use of your product.

There are three possible outcomes for a sales contact:
a) Refusal—The sale is dead
b) Delay—discussion will continue, but the customer has not agreed to take any actions to advance the sale
c) Customer Action—the customer has agreed to buy or to take actions to advance the sale

Most sales contacts end in delays, but effective closers get more *cus-*

tomer action. The difference between top performers and average performers in the outcome of their sales contacts isn't just their higher ratio of sales to refusals. They also achieve a much higher ratio of next step customer actions to advance the sale.

For many salespeople, this final step is a difficult one. Here is what several participants in my seminars have said about closing sales:

> Closing the sale is the only thing that shows up in the district sales figures. The other salespeople can talk all they want about the big deals they're working on, but if they don't close sales, they don't have anything. I have the best closing rate in the office, and I think it's simply because I don't have any hang-ups about asking for the business.

> I guess I had the same negative feelings about closing sales that most salespeople do. But what can a customer say but 'yes' or 'no'? Actually, I don't feel I've closed a sale until I've sold several items.

C. Peter McColough, former Chief Executive Officer of the Xerox Corporation, said in an interview for *Working Woman* that the prime cause for failure among salespeople is not asking for the order.

Even schoolgirl Markita Andrews, who became known as "The Cookie Kid" after setting records for the sale of Girl Scout Cookies, says, "You can't just chat. You have to ask for the order."

Salespeople may think they've closed a sale because they've suggested a product. They've pointed the gun, but they haven't pulled the trigger.

Many salespeople are afraid of the customer's reaction to their closing attempts. They're afraid of seeming pushy or of being rejected.

Other salespeople have difficulty focusing on precisely what they want the customer to do, or hesitate to close a sale because they're afraid the customer will hold them personally accountable if their recommendation doesn't work out.

To increase your motivation to close a sale, remind yourself how much the *customer* will benefit by meeting his objective. Usually, he'll benefit much more than you will by the sale.

If you're selling with purpose, with real interest in solving the customer's problems, you won't feel any hesitation in closing.

Customers come to you hoping you can help them. By closing the sale, you save them time in getting what they want, and help them enjoy the benefits of your product sooner.

If you've followed the six steps of selling, and checked out the customer's interest, closing the sale can't possibly be pushy.

A customer is no different from anyone else. He wants to feel important as a person. And asking him for his business makes him feel important.

Every time you have an interested customer in front of you and you don't ask for the sale, *two* people lose—you and the customer. You both could have saved time, and the customer could have enjoyed the benefits of your product sooner.

Often you're able to see the customer's situation more clearly than the customer. He may see it short-range, or from only one perspective.

Salespeople have to *close* sales to help people.

THE RIGHT TIME TO CLOSE

To increase your comfort with advancing the sale, you may need to frame it in a wider perspective.

A sale actually begins in the developing-trust step, when you discuss with the customer why you're getting together. From the beginning, you need to frame your conversation as one that is going to lead somewhere.

Research on peak performance "relationship" sellers has shown that in about half of their successful closing attempts, they do little more than "nudge" the customer to buy. They're so effective in establishing the need and the urgency for action that the customer asks for the product himself.

You've taken a giant step toward a sale it you can get the customer to agree to a timetable of things that have to happen to complete the sale. If the customer has agreed to a deadline for action or a timetable of events, you can remind him of that timetable later to create a sense of urgency for the sale.

There's no one right time to close a sale. If a customer walks in ready to buy, you can move straight to asking for customer action.

In my experience with thousands of salespeople, I've found most of them need more assertiveness, more patience, and better timing in closing, not more ways to close. They need to *do* what they already know how to do.

Most salespeople ask for the sale too soon, before the customer's need is fully developed, or not at all.

THE SECRETS OF SELLING:
There's only one way to know for sure that the timing is right to close a sale. Ask the customer.

Test the customer's interest throughout the sale with check questions such as, "How does that sound?" or "What's the next step?"

The customer's answers will provide you with "check points" for your transition from the counseling step to advancing the sale.

You'll be able to sense the chemistry when another person is close to making a commitment. You can also sense when a person turns resistant or evasive—for example, you may feel a little uneasy when a customer says, "*Generally*, it looks good."

It's probably a good time to ask for customer action when you notice the customer react in one or more of the following ways:

CLOSING CLUES

- The customer repeatedly gives you positive responses to your check questions.
- The customer's questions switch to details such as rate, price, delivery, or how long it will take to get started.
- The customer reaches for his money, a pen, an application or an order form.
- The customer makes strong positive comments such as "Sounds good."
- The customer expresses a strong preference for one selection over another.
- The customer asks a third party for his opinion, or a third party makes encouraging comments such as, "That seems like a good deal."
- The customer leans forward and his body and tone of voice seem to relax.
- The customer appears satisfied with your answer to his objection about price.
- The customer makes a negative/positive statement such as, "Of course, I couldn't transfer the funds before Tuesday."
- The customer reaches for your product, looks at it fondly, or is using it.
- The customer asks for assurance with comments such as, "I've never used one like this before," or "What do *you* think?"
- The customer becomes silent, as if he's considering his decision.
- The customer talks about how he'll *feel* using the product, or tries to picture himself using it.
- The participants in a group presentation look to one person for his or her reaction.

When all signs are "go," you can leave the next step action to the customer and risk losing the sale, or you can take responsibility for advancing the sale.

If you think about how much the customer will benefit by acting now, your confidence will tell the customer you expect a yes.

In *How to Sell Anything to Anybody*, master car salesman Joe Girard says that sustaining his confidence at the moment of closing was critical to his success. So critical, in fact, that he didn't even look at the buyer when he asked for a deposit because he feared the customer's reaction might weaken his resolve. He says he had seen too many car salesmen sell a car, then buy it back.

MAKING IT EASY TO BUY

During the problem-solving and counseling steps, you may adjust your objective several times. But once you've negotiated the customer's objectives, set a sales goal for yourself and don't lose sight of it.

A lot of sales are lost because the salesperson tried to make the wrong sale.

Many salespeople do so little problem solving, and talk about so many products, they confuse their customers and themselves. They end the sale with no focus on what they want the customer to do.

Make the sale *simple*, even if you have to cut the buyer's risk by closing on a smaller, first-step sale.

You'll find it difficult to close a sale unless you can state your sales goal in one sentence. If you can't describe it in one sentence, how can you expect the customer to know exactly what you want him to do?

Try to set a maximum and minimum customer action goal for yourself based on the customer's objectives, and use these goals to focus your selling. Make sure that the action you ask for is observable and measurable, specific as to actions and quantities, and tied to a timetable.

If your goal is to close the sale, ask for the sale. If it's to gain the opportunity for a follow-up presentation to someone else at a higher level, ask for that.

Many sales are really mini-sales on the way to something bigger. If you've set a dollar goal for the sale, you're more likely to ask for as much business as you really want. But remember, your goal is determined by the *customer's* agenda.

I've found I can make closing a sale seem less formidable by thinking of my objectives as the difference between what the customer has already sold himself (let's say he has the figure $30,000 in mind) and what he actually needs (we'll say $36,000.) In this example, I only have to make a $6,000 sale, not a $36,000 sale.

To make sure the customer is thinking about how your product fits his dominant objective, remind him again. As you remind him, use *his* words.

As people make their decisions, their last step is often to think what *using* the product would be like. They search for a gut feeling that says, "This is what I want," and tells them they would like living with the product's results.

The peak performance seller might ask, "Won't it *feel* good not having to worry about this any more?" or "Can you *picture* how much easier this will be for you?"

Some real estate agents ask their customers to imagine one last time how they'll feel living in the house they're being shown.

Your chances for a sale are best if your customer makes his yes/no decision while he's with you, so you're available to answer any concerns or objections, and lock out your competition.

In selling, *anything* can happen, and usually does. Any delay reduces the chances you'll make the sale. If you part company without a decision, the probability for a sale drops substantially.

THE SECRETS OF SELLING:
In closing sales, *always* give your customers reasons for acting *now*.

The iron rule of closing is: always give people reasons to buy *now*. Point out what they'll lose by delaying, or what they'll gain by acting immediately.

Since the most frequent objection in selling is, "I'll think it over," the obvious counter is to give people reasons why they shouldn't think it over any longer. Even though a customer has agreed that your product meets his need, you won't make the sale unless you can establish *priority* for that need in relation to his other needs.

You have to convince the customer that delaying will cost more than going ahead, or that he may pay the cost of your product in losses if he doesn't buy, without ever having its benefits.

The peak performance seller can always find *some* reason for the customer not to delay his decision.

The reasons for the customer to act quickly include gaining stretch benefits, such as saving money while a product is on sale, or to prevent losses he's incurring now, such as losing money on maintenance costs. The reason may simply be relief from the agony of making the decision.

With new prospects, you may need to make it easier to become a customer by suggesting a low-risk first step, or by making the sale conditional on the approval of someone else. The key is to get things going so you can earn the additional business.

Don't let paperwork or inconveniences delay or block a sale. Complete paperwork after the customer leaves, and make the extra effort necessary to prevent any inconvenient delays. They could easily cost you the sale.

Most professional salespeople write on the order form or application as they're counseling the customer so he gets comfortable with the idea of closing the sale, and so the salesperson won't have to stop his momentum at a crucial moment to look for the closing documents.

ASKING FOR ACTION

There are hundreds of closing techniques described in the many books on selling. You can forget about most of them. Many of them are simply ways to overcome objections (see Chapter 9), and most of the others are openly manipulative, something your customers will sense immediately.

Salespeople often try to close a sale by asking a direct question such as "Would you like it?, Will you want to start today? Shall I write this up?" or "Do we have a deal, then?"

If you're sure the customer will say yes, this close is direct and effective. In other cases, it leaves the customer with too big a decision. It's too easy to say no.

However, the direct question can be used effectively in response to another question. If a customer asks, "Does this come in blue?" you can make a quick transition to closing by asking, "Do you want it in blue?"This direct approach certainly works much better than statements such as, "We would sure like your business." So would a lot of people. What kind of commitment can you get from a statement like that?

Still, asking a direct question makes it too easy for the customer to say no.

THE SECRETS OF SELLING:
When you close the sale, *limit the customer's options.*

Think of what happens when you shop in a fine jewelry store. If you ask to look at necklaces, the jeweler will probably show you several items at several tiers of pricing, laying them on the counter for your selection. As you lose interest in an item, he immediately puts it back in the display case until only one or two are left to consider. He doesn't do that solely because he's worried you're a shoplifter! He wants to simplify your decision by limiting your options.

All the strong closers in selling *limit* the customer's choices.

The first way is to offer the customer a choice, with either option meaning acceptance of your product. For example, you might say, "Would you prefer the red one or the blue one?" (Notice that "neither" is not one of the choices.) This is the closing method used most often in retail stores, where customers are faced with a dizzying array of choices that could confuse them or delay the sale.

By narrowing the customer's selection, his attention becomes focused on the small decision of *which* product to buy rather than the larger question of *whether* to buy.

You can strengthen this close even more by adding your recommendation. You might say, "From what you've said, I think the blue one will work better for you."

The second way to limit choice is to *assume* the sale is made. This is the way most sales are closed.

By assuming the sale, you skip right past the yes/no decision to details such as, "What type of wrapping will you want on this?" or "Where will you want this shipped?" Sometimes this close is made by physical gestures such as sliding the order form toward the customer and saying "I'll just need your approval on this," or by starting to package the product.

Assuming the sale is the most forceful way to close so *always* check the customer's interest first with check questions.

Assuming a sale can also be used to turn an objection into a request to buy. You might say, "I understand your concern about the timing, so we'll guarantee overnight delivery starting tonight on your first shipment," or "I can understand your concern on the price, so I'll write it up at the old price."

A third way to limit the options in closing a sale is the "If, then?" technique: "If you can convince yourself this will save you money in the long run, *then* will you buy it?" By saying yes, the customer *limits himself* to one option if you can answer his concerns.

No matter how you ask for the sale, once you've asked, *stop talking*. Experienced salespeople have a saying, "The first one to talk loses."

Your silence reinforces the need for a decision; and by not talking, you're less likely to offer the customer excuses for not taking action now.

You're also more likely to hear the customer's first words *exactly*, so you can accurately evaluate his response. If the customer's answer is "no" or "maybe," it's important to hear the *intensity* of his resistance and his reasons for objecting.

If the customer hesitates, but can't explain why, you may need to explore whether he has the *authority* to make the decision. If he isn't sure he does, show him he's exercised similar authority in other cases, or ask to meet with both him and the person who can release the dollars.

If the customer's answer is yes, assure him his decision is a good one. Tell him about other people who made the same decision and felt good about it later.

Every time you close a sale, thank the customer for his business, restate the benefits, and assure him he'll have your personal attention after the sale.

Next, *get out of there*! You don't want to say something that *unsells* the customer. You may think you're telling the customer one extra benefit only to find you've raised a concern he had overlooked.

THE SECRETS OF SELLING:
Make sure the sale *stays* a sale.

A sale isn't a sale unless it stays a sale. It can be a long way from the close to the order, and the customer can always change his mind. I lost one $100,000 sale by one day because the buyer resigned the day before we were supposed to sign the contract.

Customers want reassurance.

Did you ever notice that when you buy a car, let's say a blue Oldsmobile, it seems as though all you see on the street for the next few weeks are blue Oldsmobiles? And the salespeople you remember most are the ones who call you *after* the sale to see if everything was right with your purchase?

Our sales force is trained to give our clients more than they expect when they close a sale. By doing something extra, and taking responsibility for seeing that supporting service work is done and done right, their sales *stay* sales.

On a closing call to a *major* customer, ask a senior manager to make the call with you. Too many salespeople are afraid to ask for their boss's help when it can make a difference. They're worried about looking bad, instead of focusing on *results*.

Customers find it reassuring that you're involving someone important in the final negotiations. It says you really want their business.

ADDING TO THE SALE

Every sale can be a springboard for even more success.

When a customer trusts you enough to make one commitment to you, he's immediately your best prospect for your next sale. Like the billiards player who analyzes how he will use one shot to set up his next one, the peak performance seller plans for multi-product sales.

To increase the average size of each sale, think in terms of *customers*, not products. Think of *adding* to the sale to strengthen the customer relationship and to improve product usage.

Adding to the sale helps lock in the first sale. The more you do for a customer, the more loyalty you build and the longer your customer will do business with you.

Each sale, each proposal, should lead to information that provides the first step to your next sale.

Most salespeople are so happy when they make a sale, they hesitate to ask the customer for more. They may think it seems ungrateful or pushy.

By thinking this way, salespeople limit the size of their average sale and set *imaginary* limits on their results. They also lose opportunities to really help people.

I've found that customers never resent the implication that they're more important than they really are.

THE SECRETS OF SELLING:
Why not ask for *more*?

If providing more service will help the customer and increase your sales, why not ask for more? Suggesting additional ways to help is one of the things that makes you stand out as someone really interested in the customer.

How can you add to the sale without seeming pushy and taking too much of the customer's time? You probably can't if you try to sell features. But if you ask questions and sell with stretch benefits, you can add to a sale in one or two sentences.

Of course, you want to be sure you have a commitment on the *first* sale before explaining the benefits of ordering everything the customer needs while he's with you. It only takes a few seconds to ask, "You'll want a second one, won't you, while you're getting the 30 percent discount?"

Sales pioneer Elmer Wheeler revolutionized retail selling when he convinced food counters to switch from "Large or small?" to "Large?" and gas stations to switch from "How much?" to "Fill'er up?"

The day after attending one of our seminars, a banker asked one of his new checking account customers it there were any other funds that he would like to add to the account while he was there, and the man transferred $200,000 in certificates of deposit from another bank.

When a customer seems confused by how much to buy, tell him how much customers in his situation *usually* buy. This will get you past his fears of seeming either too cheap or too extravagant. You'll almost always increase your average sale if *you* suggest the order size.

Second, suggest a product that enhances the first product.

Third, sell the customer up to a higher-priced product or to a more profitable product on the basis of quality or value. Most customers are willing to pay a small difference in cost for extra value.

If you sell an expensive item *first*, by contrast, the next item will seem less expensive than it really is.

In *The New Psychology of Persuasion and Motivation*, Robert Whitney writes, "Even when a man enters a clothing store with the express purpose of purchasing a suit, he will almost always pay more for whatever accessories he buys for them after the suit purchase than before."

Fourth, ask the customer for a longer commitment, or sell products which lock the customer in to continued use or repeat purchases. Persuading a customer to open a charge account is a good example of how a salesperson can use a second sale to encourage regular use of his product.

Fifth, present the first product with others as one *package* of products that meet the customer's objectives and together enhance their respective values. This approach can sometimes make your product appear more comprehensive than the competition, and give you an edge. A cosmetic salesperson might say, "We sell these cosmetics together because they work together to keep your skin in perfect balance."

Sixth, put your satisfied customers to work for you by asking them for referrals to other people who might want your product. But ask for *specific names* or you haven't asked for the sale.

Seventh, give the customer information that builds *future* product use, such as information about upcoming price changes, special promotions, reminders of special seasonal needs, information about credit arrangements, or information about when a product will be available or on sale.

If necessary, keep a sales notebook of customer interests, and follow up at the appropriate time.

Eighth, add *protection* to the first product with products that make it last longer, insure it against loss, or guarantee results, such as insurance contracts or warranty protection.

In our business, we've found that the limits to our assignments have been set by *us*, not by our customers. After more than one large gulp, we were able to double the average dollar size of our assignments in one year simply by asking for more comprehensive assignments.

Are our clients offended by the larger size of these contracts? Absolutely not. As a result of our success, we've been able to *help* our clients more, too. We now have close to a 100 percent rate of repeat assignments, much higher than before, because now we're doing enough work for our clients to have substantial impact on their results.

Most add-on selling boils down to two basic strategies. Show how the add-on makes the first product better, or link it to one of the problems or objectives mentioned by the customer in the problem-solving step.

After I've bought a suit, an experienced sales clerk might ask me if I'd like a second suit in the same style since it fits me so well. If that doesn't work, he'll suggest a shirt that will bring out the color of the suit I bought—a one sentence sale. He may say that the suit will look more expensive, because the color in the shirt brings out the stripe in the suit.

Next, he's likely to suggest a tie that coordinates with the suit and the shirt so all three look better—another one sentence sale. Finally, he'll probably suggest a pair of shoes that will give me that *total*, finished look that will give me the feel of success—again, a one sentence sale.

The goal in each of these sales is to make me look better in my suit. The add-on sales are a logical extension of what I've bought.

What would have happened if the sales clerk suddenly asked me, "How about a blender today?" That's a 300-sentence, 20 minute sale, if he can make it at all. (Unless, of course the salesperson can convince me I'd better go home with something for my wife!)

The blender would be a tough sale, because it doesn't relate to the first sale, or to *any* interests I expressed to the salesperson.

When you're selling on limited time, make sure your attempts to add to the sale enhance the first product sold.

Learn to include in your problem solving some early screening for the most likely add-on sales. Mix in questions about the customer's possible additional needs while you're getting information for the first sale. With a little experience, you'll be able to anticipate these add-on possibilities and ask the right questions.

In my experience, adding to a sale feels almost rhythmic. Benefit ... Close ... Benefit ... Close ... Benefit ... Close.

STEP SIX: FOLLOW-UP

There's a forgotten sixth step in closing sales—persistent, strategic *follow-up*. This is the point at which the average salesperson stops. He may have invested considerable time with a qualified prospect, and be inches from the sale, but he quits.

Persistence pays off in selling. Persistent follow-up to inquiries, to pending sales, to new customers, to key accounts, even to prospects who say "no," will substantially improve your results.

THE SECRETS OF SELLING:
In selling, failing to follow through is like boating to where the fish are and not dropping your line in the water. The fish know you've been there, but they don't remember why.

For most businesses, the return on your investment in follow-up to qualified leads is almost always better than the return on more calls to new prospects.

INQUIRIES

There's a saying among salespeople that a cold lead is a *dead* lead. Referrals and inquiries are top sales priorities. These prospects are ready to make a decision, and they apparently have some reason for being interested in your product. *They're prospects with their hands up.*

Yet what happens at most businesses when a prospect stops in or calls to ask for information regarding a possible large order? Research has proven that the average salesperson is very helpful on inquiries, spending ten to fifteen minutes with the prospect, if necessary. But after the prospect has left or hung up, it's very seldom the salesperson has *any* information to make successful follow-up possible.

On most inquiries you have only two objectives: get the prospect involved with you so you can identify his objectives and obtain an appointment. That's all.

Of all times in selling, responding to inquiries is the time to be assertive, and organized for follow-up.

PENDING COMMITMENTS

Moving pending commitments to action is one of the critical skills of peak performance selling. Most commercial sales are closed on the fourth or fifth sales call, not on the first. Peak performance salespeople are known for their relentless follow-up on key prospects.

Salespeople often get hung up on the issue of how much follow-up is too much. It varies with every prospect. The rule of thumb is to make as many calls as are economically justified, and to track your results so you know how many calls that is.

It's almost always better to err on the side of *too much* follow-up. At least you'll stay in touch with the prospect's changing thinking, and the prospect will know you want his business.

Once the decision to buy is made, buyers move fast. If you're in close contact, you may get the sale by default.

In follow-up, you have to constantly reassess your position. You may have to change strategy several times before you close the sale. You may even have to decide that the prospect is no longer the best use of your time.

You *will* become a nuisance to your prospects if you call only to see if they have made a decision on your product. Make your follow-up valuable from the customer's viewpoint by calling to give your prospect *new information.*

When a decision is pending, find a reason (usually new information) to be the last competitor to meet with your prospect. Follow the guideline, "Last in, first out with the sale." Your competition almost always raises some new concern or comparison to your product that you'll want to counter.

No one sells your product better than you do. If the person you're dealing with will have to persuade someone else, ask if he would like you to be present for that discussion, or if you can submit a letter proposal that will help him sell it.

The key to closing pending commitments is to create a sense of **movement** for the sale. There may be movement in the fact that information is being pulled together, obstacles are being overcome, people are being won over, or progress is being make on an agreed-upon schedule.

After a sales call or submission of a proposal, send the prospect a thank-you letter summarizing your key sales points and any agreements that were made between you and the prospect regarding the next step.

Always *pre*arrange your follow-up with your prospect, so when you call you're doing something the prospect agreed he wanted.

When you lose a sale, ask the prospect who did get the sale and why. There may still be some way to get *part* of the sale.

If a "no" is final, thank the prospect cheerfully for the opportunity to be considered, and ask for a meeting in the future to determine if there is any way for you to be of help as his needs change. A surprising amount of my own business has come from referrals by people who weren't able to buy our services, but who recognized the value of our product and our genuine interest in their problems and objectives.

RELATIONSHIP SELLING

The true test of your commitment to excellence in selling is whether you care *after* the sale is made.

Your selling doesn't stop with a sale. To develop *repeat* sales, you need to develop a strong problem-solving relationship with your customer after the sale.

For the customer, the sale is the *beginning*, not the end. He has to live with your promises, and his relationship with you intensifies.

Top salespeople commit themselves to keeping these new customer relationships strong, and to keeping their products in use. For example, the real competitors for people selling to distributors or retailers are their customer's other product lines. These salespeople have to fight to keep their product visible and coach their customers in how to sell their product.

Your key accounts today are your most profitable sales tomorrow, particularly if you count your low sales expense on repeat sales.

Building customer loyalty for *future* sales has proven to be a significant aspect of salesmanship. If you've built a strong relationship and become a customer's trusted advisor, you'll be his obvious choice the next time he needs your product. No one else knows his needs as well as you do.

Be sure to use your relationship with the buyer to sell deeper into the family or organization to form relationships with other possible buyers. You never know when the person you're working with will leave, or when another person will have the primary influence on a different sale.

The best transition to an advisor relationship after the sale is follow-up with the customer to help him *use* your product. A call to see that things got done, and that your product is working for the customer, will enable you to identify opportunities for reorders and add-on sales, head off problems before they get started, and demonstrate your interest in the *person*, not just the sale.

In all your selling, try to build a selling memory (or notebook) for prospect names, likes, dislikes, problems, objectives, etc. to guide your follow-up selling.

Relationship selling locks out your competition, cuts attrition in your accounts and increases your opportunities for referrals and repeat sales.

Peak performance sellers gain their selling edge by persistent attention to hundreds of small details done a little better in caring for their customers.

In the next chapter, you'll learn how to plan so you can use objections and other forms of sales resistance to your advantage throughout the six steps of selling.

PLAN AHEAD

Sales conversations seldom go the way you plan them. They unfold before you based on the objectives, problems, and reactions of the customer. The customer is a moving target with changing objectives and priorities. From the start, *expect* the unexpected, and stay flexible.

Despite the flexibility displayed by effective sellers, they also stay on track toward their *customer action* objectives. They have quality relationships because they do quality planning. One minute of planning can save ten minutes of floundering.

Your plan may simply be to set maximum and minimum objectives and make a few scribbled notes, or it may be to prepare a detailed analysis of the situation similar to the Feel of Success® Sales Planner in this unit. The more important the contact, the more planning you should do.

The Sales Planner form used in this unit will help you organize your strategy from the *customer's* point of view and focus your attention on the exact customer action results you want for your efforts. Your plan should focus on **what the customer must do** to invest in your relationship as well as **what you must do.** With a little practice, you'll be able to complete this analysis mentally for each contact in a few minutes of preparation.

SALES PLANNER GUIDELINES

1. **Always** begin your analysis in the far left column with the **customer's** objectives and problems in mind **before** you consider what solution to propose or what customer action to ask for.

2. Identify the objectives and problems you rate most important from the customer's viewpoint and look for benefits and losses that match.

3. Plan your approach based on our product's best match with the customer's dominant objective or problem.

4. Ask yourself why the problems and objectives you've written down for the customer may have **urgent impact** and convert those issues into highlight questions to ask the customer.

5. Plan to ask the customer about problems and dissatisfactions at least five times.

THE FEEL OF SUCCESS® SALES PLANNER

(1) THE CUSTOMER'S VIEWPOINT	(2) THE SATISFACTION GAP	(3) YOUR IDEA	(4) YOUR STRATEGY
DESIRED PERSONAL OR BUSINESS RESULTS	**EXISTING SITUATION**	**PROPOSED CUSTOMER ACTION AND RESULTS**	**YOUR ACTION PLAN**
Objectives / Problems	Poor Action Resulting in Losses	What You Want Your Customer To Do — Max. Customer Action — Min. Customer Action	Key Questions
	LOSSES	GOOD FEATURES ⬆ STRETCH BENEFITS	Expected Resistance
TOP THREE DOMINANT ISSUES (Rank)	Possible Consequences that Make the Problem Serious	⬇ DOMINANT OBJECTIVE	Resistance Prevention Statements
Behavior Style Strategies	Customer's Top Three Decision Criteria (Rank)	Possible Impact of Benefits that Create Urgency / PROOF	Reason for Acting NOW / ADD-ONS
SUPPORTER · Focus on Relationships · Slow Your Pace · Give Assurance · Secure Action Steps **PROMOTER** · Focus on Concepts · Show Enthusiasm · Stress Relationships · Avoid Details **THINKER** · Focus on Facts · Give Proof · Sell Step-by-Step · Be Organized **DRIVER** · Focus on Goals · Get to the Point · Pick up Your Pace · Avoid Small Talk		HOW IS IT CLEARLY DIFFERENT?	

CHAPTER 9

Sales Resistance: The Force is with You

In selling, there's almost always resistance to you or your product. As you move through the six steps of selling, you're likely to encounter resistance each step of the way.

You may encounter resistance as you seek information, as you make recommendations, as you attempt to close the sale, and as you follow up your sales contacts. And every salesperson faces it when resolving complaints with angry customers.

You can actually *feel* sales resistance. It's like hitting an invisible wall that's pushing you away from another person. And you can *see* it and *hear* it in the responses of your customers.

I'd like you to change the way you think about sales resistance. I'd like you to think of resistance as a *success* force.

In this chapter, you're going to learn judo salesmanship. As in judo, you can turn the force of resistance into *advantage*.

In the movie *Star Wars*, sage Obi Wan Kenobi gives hero Luke Skywalker a charge that will defeat all resistance: "May the force be with you." As a salesperson, you can turn the force of resistance back on itself so it becomes a force of success.

It's frustrating when people block you from the things you want. But people resist change because what they're doing meets certain needs for them. People aren't against you; they're *for* themselves.

Sometimes your ideas simply aren't right for someone at that point in time. As Supreme Court Justice Oliver Wendell Holmes wrote, "You cannot argue a man into liking a glass of beer."

If you understand *why* other people resist, you'll understand better how *you* contribute to that resistance. It may be your resistance to changing your style of communicating that's creating much of the sales resistance you encounter.

143

When a customer resists, his resistance is usually also a statement about what *you're* doing. Out of all the ways you've attempted to make contact and establish rapport, you haven't yet found a way that *works*.

If you relax in the face of resistance, you can get a handle on what stands between you and the sale.

THE POSITIVE SIDE OF RESISTANCE

Is there anything *positive* about sales resistance?

The answer is *yes*. With his resistance, the customer is telling you exactly what stands between you and the sale, what it takes to make the sale. That's *good* news.

Sales resistance is almost always a sign of involvement, and a source of information about what's really important to your customer. And once a customer's resistance is out in the open it doesn't seem so serious to him.

Many salespeople are threatened by *any* show of resistance. But resistance doesn't mean the prospect isn't eventually going to go along with you. It's not the same as "no." Even "no" is nothing more than resistance to your idea at one point in time.

Resistance cannot only be overcome, it can be *used* to your advantage. The more you know about what's causing it, the easier it is to use it as a success force.

I've found many salespeople hold back from doing what needs to be done because of the fear they might not be able to answer *unexpected* sales resistance. Ironically, their fear of the unexpected is more paralyzing and destructive to their selling than the resistance itself.

At the time it occurs, sales resistance seems like a pain to most salespeople. But most of the damage to their selling is done by their *response* to that resistance.

In *Psychology Today,* social worker Stephen Levine provided insight into psychological resistance from his work with the terminally ill:

> What is pain? They'll say it's awful, or it's unbearable. But that's their response—not the pain itself. Most of what people call pain is actually resistance. The reflex is to see pain as the enemy, as something to be eradicated under any circumstances. But we get people to look at it in detail. Is it steady? Does it move? Does it vibrate? Is it hot? Burning? Cold? Does it have tendrils? The idea is not to get rid of the pain, but just to see what it is. When people look directly at their pain, they can see how their resistance is like an amplifier, magnifying the pain.

Have you really thought about the resistance you get from other people? How much of it is caused by your own actions and selling style? How could you use it or go around it?

Think of yourself as driving a wind-up car that simply changes directions as you bump into one wall of resistance after another until you find the right path. It's the resistance that guides you down the right path.

In *Sports Illustrated*, speed cyclist John Howard explains how he minimizes wind resistance in cycling by cycling behind a car: "The car bores a hole through the wind, in essence moving the air molecules away. You just sit there with no resistance."

By the objections they raise, your prospects are also moving obstacles out of your way and clearing a path of less resistance.

THE MANY FACES OF RESISTANCE

Occasionally I make a sales call to a prospect who welcomes me warmly and immediately says, "Jim, I should tell you first I have absolutely no budget for training this year. But please sit down and tell me what you're doing with your company."

Now what? My reaction *could* damage my selling. But I've learned not to be discouraged in these situations.

In my experience, the quick, open resistance of prospects like these has been the *easiest* sales resistance of all to overcome. You know what you're dealing with. Knowing that, you can keep your confidence and your enthusiasm in these situations.

The most difficult person to sell is the person who agrees with everything you say ... until you ask for the sale. Then he gives you a rock-hard, resounding "no" with no explanation. Others tell you "yes" and then simply don't act on that "yes."

Never assume that because someone acts agreeable there isn't any resistance. There almost always is.

Even emotions such as anger, fear, or overexcitment are resistance in that they can prevent a fair hearing of your product. Peak performance sellers learn to give people time to discharge their feelings before they try to influence them.

Some of your customers will be preoccupied with other thoughts or activities as you begin your selling. Some will be low reactors to almost any idea. Hold your selling until you have their full attention.

More often, you'll encounter customers who are indifferent or who doubt the benefits of your products. These forms of resistance can usually be resolved with more information, and with proof of the losses they're incurring or the benefit they'll gain from your product.

Some prospects will even try to "escape." They may cut you short, stall, withdraw, become overly aggressive, or hide behind nonnegotiable statements like "My mind is made up. This is the way it's going to be."

Most salespeople either back down or push too hard when they see their prospect escaping. Instead, back off to relax the person. Then continue on course in a gently persistent selling style.

Some prospects become *defensive* trying to protect their position with their familiar ways of doing things. They may feel as if they're giving up something if they accept your ideas. Or, their defensiveness may be an attempt to put *you* on the defensive to test the strength of your conviction.

Read the message behind this defensiveness. It may reveal a lot about the customer and about you. Ask yourself what might be causing anxiety for this person, how he may need this defense, and what you can do to adapt your selling style in response.

Most sales resistance results from concerns about the *value* of your product. Because the customer doesn't think the benefits outweigh the "costs" of making a change, he raises objections. Most objections, even "no," are really nothing more than *questions* about how well your product meets the customer's objectives or solves his problems.

Some objections are the result of misunderstanding your product. These are easy to resolve. You can answer them quickly and directly, and they're out of your way. Others, like those below, are valid drawbacks and are more difficult to answer.

As you read these objections, think of how your customers would state them, and how you would answer them:

> I just don't have time right now.
> I don't like the way it looks.
> I like it, but Harry would never go for it.
> I've got a friend in the business.
> It costs too much. I just can't afford it.
> My current supplier has always been good to me.
> Well, we'll think it over.
> I tried it before and your service was lousy.
> We're just shopping around.
> I don't need it right now.
> No.
> See us after the first of the year.

A prospect can find a hundred ways to sell you on the idea that he can't buy. If you're encountering the same objections over and over again, it's time to ask yourself why.

You may be causing the resistance you're encountering by your manner or actions, or you may be using ineffective strategies to reduce it or overcome it. Salespeople typically try to break resistance down by talking more, avoiding or "not hearing" it, or discounting it. While these low-yield strategies often get a momentary positive response, they usually *increase* resistance in the long run.

Some sales resistance isn't worth trying to overcome. Sometimes your product just isn't right for the customer at this point in time.

Fortunately, most sales resistance *can* be overcome. With a little planning, you can avoid much of the resistance you encounter. You can reduce the number of objections you have to deal with, and you can soften the *intensity* of the resistance.

As the Japanese say, "To fight and conquer in one hundred battles is not the highest skill. To subdue the enemy with no fight at all, is."

AN OUNCE OF PREVENTION

Every sales training course teaches salespeople how to *answer o*bjections. But most of them miss one of the greatest secrets of selling: you can *prevent* most sales resistance from becoming serious by answering expected objections *before* they're raised by the customer.

The legendary Chinese leader Mao Zedong writes, "The only successful generals in the world are those who can accurately anticipate the strategic actions of their opponents and therefore tactically outmaneuver them." The tactics of anticipation work for salespeople, too.

THE SECRETS OF SELLING:
The real skill in handling sales resistance is *preventing* it in the first place.

Sales research confirms that by encouraging more customer participation, peak performance sellers permit their customers more opportunities to vent their concerns about the product.

One major study of several thousand salespeople compared the methods and results of high-performing salespeople (high sales results) to those of low-performing salespeople (low sales results). The researchers found that peak performance sellers encountered about one-tenth as many serious objections as low performance salespeople.

What conclusion can we draw? Peak performance sellers *anticipate* resistance and *prevent* it by developing trust, by selling stretch benefits, and by answering the anticipated objections in their presentation *before* they're raised by the customer.

You'll have more confidence in answering sales resistance if you've *planned* for it. Look for the gap in your defenses. When you expect to be confronted with an objection, wouldn't you rather talk about it *when* you want to and in the way you want to so you can counter it with stretch benefits?

Here's what a sales manager at one of our seminars had to say about anticipating sales resistance:

> There's no way I'd walk into a sale presentation without thinking
> through the advantages we have over the competition and my answers

to the objections I know I'm going to get. At my age, I don't need that kind of stress.

By admitting the shortcomings of your product *before* they're mentioned by the customer, the customer's sales resistance will seem less important. After all, how serious can an issue be if you're so willing to talk about it?

Customers *need* to vent their resistance in order to dissipate it. By raising the issue on your terms, you simply make it possible for them to do this in the most favorable way for you. (Naturally, you don't want to talk about the weak points of your product unless you're sure the customer will think of them.)

You're giving the customer an easy way to save face and change his current way of doing things, based on "new" information or conditions outside his control.

Nothing replaces good solid *planning* to prevent objections from becoming serious.

When we first began marketing sales training programs, one objection I knew we would get on every sales call was, "You haven't *proven* the effectiveness of these courses with any clients."

Following the precept that a good offense is the best defense in selling, we turned that objection into a major *plus* by beginning every sale with the statement, "We're a new company. And that's what exciting. We've put together the very latest, state-of-the-art training programs based on the proven experience of our top consultants."

As a result of a little planning, we almost never heard the objection we feared the most.

If you're certain you're going to encounter a price objection, you can use that fact to your advantage in developing trust with your customer. For example, you might begin,

> Today I'm going to tell you about a new product that will save you money for years to come. It's the most expensive product of it's kind, and that's what gives us the edge over our competition. For the small difference in price, you get a new level of *quality* that saves you up to 20 percent per year in maintenance costs.

If you know that a customer is likely to be upset by a price increase, you might prevent his objection from becoming serious by suggesting in advance that he increase his order size to keep his cost the same.

By preparing themselves to handle anticipated objections, salespeople are able to think of exactly what to say to prevent resistance. This saves them sales time, since they're less likely to get sidetracked from the positive aspects of their presentation.

Think of the people you need to sell in the next several days. What sales resistance do you expect? How are you going to *prevent* that resistance from becoming a serious obstacle?

JUDO SELLING

Even at your best you won't prevent *all* sales resistance. When objections surface, welcome them as an opportunity to use the customer's involvement and thinking to your advantage.

Your first reaction may be to meet force with force, to defend your point of view. Don't do it. Instead, use *judo salesmanship*. Use the force of the customer's resistance against itself by encouraging the customer to move in the direction he's already moving.

In *Mental Judo*, Lance Laeger and Amy Kraft write,

> If we are going to use the force of another person to our advantage, physically or mentally, we must give way to our opponent's force (this is the principal of nonresistance) and throw him in the direction in which he is moving.

The yielding art of jujitsu used the momentum of opponents to transfer their force back onto themselves.

To know what direction the customer is moving, you have to stay in touch with his resistance so you can move as his thinking moves. The peak performance seller stays focused on "the feel of the sale."

THE SECRETS OF SELLING:
The judo seller *uses* sales resistance to his advantage by learning more about the customer's viewpoint.

To use resistance to your advantage, you first have to know what it is. Then you can show concern for it, explore it, and *use* it to move the customer toward the *strengths* of your product.

As in jujitsu or fencing, once a person has committed himself to an attack, such as stating an objection, he can actually be more vulnerable than you. Pushing against a wall, he finds it has disappeared. And now you have the advantage of knowing what it takes to make the sale.

The force is with you.

ENTERING AND BLENDING:
THE CUSTOMER'S VIEWPOINT

In the self-defense art of aikido, one of the key tactics is called "entering and blending:" moving toward the attacker and turning momentarily to face the world from his viewpoint. Entering the customer's viewpoint and blending with his thinking is also the seller's primary tactic in defusing sales resistance.

The first step in answering an objection is to see it from the customer's viewpoint.

The seller has to free himself from resistance to the customer's thinking before he can free the customer from his resistance to the seller's ideas.

The concern you show for the customer's objection is more important than your answer. If a customer believes you've listened to him, he's more likely to listen fully to you.

If you let the customer know it's OK with you that he doesn't like everything about your product, you'll get to his real feelings and take some of the edge off his criticism. You'll also appear more confident by allowing your product to be seen as imperfect.

It's important to gain the customer's trust by stating that you *want* to hear his resistance. Avoid the words, "yes, but" entirely. They sound as if you've been thinking about *your* ideas, not the customer's.

The resistance you *sense*, or the objection a customer first gives you, may not really be the objection blocking the sale. It might even be a buying signal in disguise. As industrialist J.P. Morgan wrote, " A man generally has two reasons for doing a thing—one that sounds good and a real one."

A buyer may object to your price because that's what he's supposed to do in negotiating for his company.

Ask questions to get to the *underlying* reasons for a customer's resistance. The question I've found most effective in my selling is, "Is there something else that concerns you?"

Probe for *all* the resistance. How can you answer an objection if you don't know what a person needs, or how he arrived at his objection?

If someone says vaguely, "It doesn't seem like it'll work" or "My gut feeling is that it isn't right for me," answer, "With your experience we should look into that."

Ask him, "What tells you that it won't work? or "Could you tell me more about that?" The idea is to get the customer focusing on an obstacle that can be overcome.

Entering the customer's viewpoint deeply enough to identify the *real* objection will help you close sales faster. For example, if you ask, "Is that the only reason you're concerned?," and the customer's response is "yes," you have a commitment to buy if you can answer that one concern.

Let's say you're selling a product for $10,000 and the customer objects that it costs too much. By asking the customer *how much* is too much, you can instantly transform a $10,000 sale into a $1,500 sale, the difference between what the customer *expects* to pay—$8,500—and what you're asking. At that point you can redefine the sale as whether your product is *worth* an extra $1,500, or not.

Work hard to get resistance to surface *during* your discussion while you have a chance to answer it. By asking check questions like, "How does that sound?," you'll uncover resistance that may be boiling just under the surface.

If you sense the customer isn't telling you his real concerns, play your hunches. Whenever you sense resistance, check it out. Is there another supplier in the picture? Has he overcommitted his budget? Ask, "Some people have had a problem with this. Will it be a problem for you?"

If you sense the customer is trying to "escape" from telling you his concerns behind statements such as "Harry wouldn't go for it," ask, "What would it take for Harry to go for it?" And ask for an opportunity to talk to Harry.

Whatever you do, don't let your irritation with resistance show to the customer. Remind yourself that you can *use* this resistance to your advantage.

Once you've entered the customer's viewpoint and blended your concern with his, you can use your knowledge of the customer's resistance to sell him.

EXECUTING THE JUDO SELLING MOVE

The secret to answering objections is the judo selling move, moving the conversation so you're in position to discuss the *strengths* of your product instead of defending its weaknesses.

When confronted with objections, never push against them head on. Don't waste time trying to explain why your product isn't as *bad* as it sounds.

Think for a moment about the Japanese proverb, "Gain advantage over your opponent without sacrificing your strength." It's a key concept in judo selling.

THE SECRETS OF SELLING:
When you answer an objection, refocus the customer on your *strengths*.

When a customer says a price is too high, the seller's usual response is to explain *why* the charge is higher at his company than it is at other companies. When he's done, the customer still doesn't have a reason why the product is *worth* the small difference in price. And the salesperson has spent his sales time *reinforcing* his product's weakness. He may even have answered the *wrong* objection.

You can talk for an hour about why your price is higher than someone else's price, but when you're all done, *nothing has changed.* Your price is still higher, and you haven't shown why your product is *worth* the difference.

The judo selling process illustrated in the diagram below will move your customer to a discussion of the *strengths* of your product.

When a customer raises an objection, relax, pause, and show concern for the objection with a comment such as, "I can understand why that would concern you." Repeat the objection in your best "pass the butter" voice.

This *relax, pause*, and *understand* sequence (The RPU Response) should always be your base of leverage in building an effective reply. It's the first step of entering the customer's viewpoint and blending with his thinking.

To keep your voice calm and confident and your thinking clear, tell yourself, "Relax, I can handle this."

Pause for about three seconds, looking directly at the customer. This gives him the sense you're listening to his concerns and considering them.

Don't tell the customer you agree with his objection, only that you *understand* his concern or viewpoint. You might say, " I can understand why that would be important to you. I had the same concern when I first evaluated this investment for myself."

Since customers tend to overstate their objections, rephrase them and soften them as you repeat them.

Next, *clarify* the real objection. Check to be sure you really know what you're dealing with. This checking process also gives the customer a chance to vent his feelings. You might ask, "What is it that's really concerning you?" "What is it about our price that seems high?" or "What are you *comparing* us to?"

This clarifying step is particularly important when a customer says he wants to think over his decision. When that happens, *always* ask, "Is there anything that still concerns you?"

This clarifying step will assure you of an "apple to apple" comparison, and gets rid of most objections based on misinformation about the features, function, quality, usefulness, cost, or value of your product, or about what your

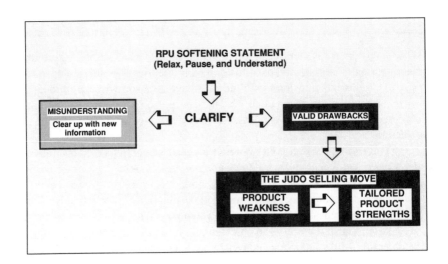

competition offers. Most important, you'll be sure you're answering the *right* objection.

Probably one third of the objections you encounter can be answered simply by clarifying an exact comparison or concern.

Once you know you're dealing with the right objection, you're ready to use one of the judo selling moves below to move the conversation to your product's strengths.

The judo selling move takes you off the defensive, and creates the opportunity for you to answer the objection *positively*. It's particularly effective in answering *price* objections, because the key to holding your price is establishing *value* for your product.

If the customer is still skeptical of your product after you've restated the benefits, offer *proof* the benefits are valid. Evidence moves the customer's thinking from "Will it work?" to "It does work." He knows you've planned and done your research, and he's just now thinking about it. Your evidence brings his risk down to where it's worth taking.

Participants in our seminars tell me that the easiest judo selling move for them to remember under stress is *"feel, felt, found."* How can you forget something that's this much fun to say!

It sounds like this:

> I understand how you *feel*. Others *felt* the same way when they first heard about it. But here's what most people have *found*. They've been able to cut their maintenance costs by 20 percent and save three to four hours of their time each week.

In one quick move, you're back to discussing the *strengths* of your product.

Some objections, such as price or loyalty to another a company, can easily be rephrased or reframed as a question you want to answer, one that brings out the strengths of your product. You might say:

> I can understand your concern. *I think what you're really asking is,* "what *more* do you get with us that makes our product *worth* that small difference in price?" For only a dollar more per week, you'll save at least $1,000 in repairs.

Again, you're back to a discussion of the strengths of your product.

When the spoken objection is loyalty to another supplier, the real issue is usually loyalty to a *person*. Your objective is to demonstrate that you add something new without disturbing that personal relationship. You might say, "*I think what you're really asking is,* What can we do for you that even your friend would want you to do for yourself? No one has a monopoly on *all* the good ideas."

Another version of the judo selling move is, "They've done a good job for you in the past. *I think what you're really asking is,* "How much *more* will you get from us in the future?"

Vice President Walter Mondale used this rephrasing strategy in the first presidential debate of the 1984 campaign. When Ronald Reagan asked, "Is America better off than it was four years ago?," Mondale reframed the question, saying "The real question is, *will* we be better off?"

The judo selling move that salespeople tell me feels most like an actual judo self-defense move is reversing an objection into a *plus*. A reason for not buying can almost always be used as a reason *for* buying. In this case, you're turning the full force of the customer's resistance back on itself.

To a time objection, you might reply, "Yes, it does take a few minutes longer each day right now. That's exactly why this is so important to you. In the long run, you're going to save several hours a week at the time when you're most busy.

Quickly, you're back to discussing your product strengths.

Applying the reverse concept to a price objection, you might say, "It is somewhat high at this order size, but if you could increase your order by one-third, you'd cut your per-unit cost to half of what you're paying now."

In the life insurance industry, if a customer says he can't afford the product, the salesperson typically responds, "If it seems expensive now, think what a spot you'd be in if you did have a disaster."

One of the cleverest applications I've heard of the reverse technique is used by a salesperson who attended one of our seminars. He answered the objection, "I don't need it" by saying, "Of course, you don't need it. If you needed more, you would have ordered more. I'm here to find out why you don't need more. Aren't your customers buying the brands you're carrying now?"

Ronald Reagan used this reverse judo selling move in a September, 1982, press conference. When he was asked if he would accept any blame for the recession, Reagan smiled and said, "Yes, because for many years I was a Democrat."

It's important to know several ways to answer objections, since each move is most effective in different situations and you may have to try several methods to answer the same objection.

Some judo selling moves may actually result in a fast close by gaining the customer's commitment to buy if you can answer one objection. For example, you might ask, "If we can do it, do you want it?"

Whatever judo selling move you use, the key to answering objections is to move the discussion toward the strengths of your product. Success builds on success.

Olympian Jesse Owens once described his running style this way: "I let my feet spend as little time on the ground as possible." This same philosophy applies to handling objections. Once you've answered an objection, check for the customer's agreement and move on.

As you try these judo selling moves, focus on what seams to get the best results for you. Soak in the feel of your successes so you can repeat them.

THE TOUGHEST OBJECTIONS IN SELLING

The objection you'll encounter most frequently in selling is, "I'll think it over." When a person tries to delay, he's usually negotiating with you, arguing with himself, looking for reassurance, or trying to escape.

Your first response to a delay objection should be to "enter and blend." Express your understanding and concern for the customer's desire to delay. Regain his trust so you can determine *why* he wants to delay.

When a customer says, "I'll think it over," he's often thinking, "I'll think it over *forever*." Your objective should be to get him to think it over for a few minutes, a day, a week—any *definite* time frame. Anything is better than "forever."

When a customer wants to think things over, try saying, "I know this is an important decision for you, and you'll want some time to think it over." (You can't say "No, don't think it over.") "I have a few things to get done myself. So you don't have to make another trip, why don't you take a few minutes to discuss this alone, and then I'll be here to answer any questions you may have."

Notice the seller gave the customer *good reason* to think it over while he was there. It's important to give the customer a benefit for making his decision *now*.

This is a good time to remind the customer of the losses he's incurring, and how he'll feel enjoying the benefits.

I include price as one of the toughest objections only because salespeople *believe* it is. Many prospects don't know what the price of your product should be, but they believe that questioning it will prompt a discount or a concession. In fact, price is only a difficult issue when you haven't established value, and that's what the whole process of selling is about.

A product is worth what it can *do* for the buyer, not what it costs him.

The real issue in answering price objections is convincing the customer he's concerned about price *one* time, but he loses everything if the product he buys doesn't do what he wants it to do.

Prospects sometimes try to rush you in and out of topics. If a prospect says, "Just tell me the price before we go any further," you could be forced to defend your price before you've had a chance to discuss the benefits of your product. In this instance you should delay in giving him your price information: "I know cost is important to you, Mr. Lawrence. So I can give you a cost figure that reflects your situation and *keeps your costs as low as possible*, could you tell me more about what you're looking for?"

This brief delay buys you time to develop the *value* of your product, build trust, and do some problem solving to identify your customer's objectives.

Delaying your price quotation is particularly difficult on the telephone where customers try hard to sell you the idea that they don't have time to wait. The rule remains the same: avoid quoting price until you've developed a relationship with the caller and established value for your product. While you're selling value, remove your competitors from consideration by convincing the caller you can save him a lot of running around.

If you jump at the temptation to quote a price and be rid of the prospect, he's likely to compare your product "apple to orange" instead of "apple to apple," with no consideration other than price, and you'll be rid of him forever.

What about "No?" "No" is nothing more than an objection, a question about the value of your product at this point in time. It's not a rejection, it's just a wrong turn. Back up and try another path.

When what you're doing isn't working, try something else.

When a customer says "no," give him your assurance that "no" is OK. Then find out *why* he said it, and answer this objections as you would answer any other.

If the customer's reply is still a *firm* "no" show your understanding for his decision, and arrange a follow-up contact at a future date to determine if his circumstances have changed.

Every day, you're going one on one with each of the other salespeople who are competing with you for the time, attention, and dollars of the people you're selling to. To outsell your competition you need a *competitive edge*.

The closer you follow the six steps of selling to *prevent* sales resistance, and the more skilled you become in judo selling, the sharper your competitive edge will be.

Remember, in most sales situations you're selling against only a few competitors. When you're feeling overwhelmed by competition, think of the two hunters trapped in the woods with a grizzly bear. The first hunter asks, "What are we going to do?" The second hunter says "I'm going to run." The first hunter says, "But you can't outrun a bear." And the second hunter replies, "No but I can outrun *you*."

How do you gain a competitive edge? If you *believe* you can handle sales resistance, you've already got that edge. You've got the feel of success.

MAKING LEMONS INTO LEMONADE

In some sales and customer relations jobs, conflict resolution may command as much as 50 percent of a person's time.

For the average seller, complaining customers are *lemons*, leaving them with a sour taste in return for the time they've invested. For peak performance sellers, complaining customers are an opportunity to make those lemons into lemonade.

Complaint situations are some of your best opportunities to strengthen customer relationships and increase your sales.

When customers complain, it's often because they've been using the wrong product, they're not using the product properly, they've been made to feel unimportant by someone in the organization, or they need additional services from you. All of these situations represent *opportunities* to sell the customer something else.

For some sales organizations, service questions and complaints lead to as much as 10 percent of their new business, and they're a significant factor in customer *retention*. You're not making much progress in selling if business is walking out the back door as fast as it's coming in the front door.

Many salespeople try too hard to avoid conflict. By not resolving problems quickly, and by not confronting resistance directly, they lose their customer's trust.

Effective negotiation of conflict requires satisfying *emotional* needs as much as it requires resolving issues.

Anger is a natural reaction all people have when they are frustrated in getting what they want or when they feel unimportant. The customer's anger in a complaint situation is probably not directed at you, but at the *situation*.

An angry customer may have been inconvenienced by an error or policy of your organization; he may not have achieved the results he expected with your product; he may have received misinformation; or he may have been mistreated or had an argument with someone else. He may simply not feel well. And, frankly, some people walk around angry all the time.

Often, the customer is carrying more than one complaint. He may have been understanding about the first problem, or even the first several problems, but this new situation is the last straw.

Whatever the source of his anger, the customer usually has a *good reason* from *his* point of view for feeling the way he does. If you can keep this perspective, you can control your reaction.

Abraham Lincoln once wrote, "You shouldn't become angry with a person who blocks your path any more that you should with a tree which the wind blew across the road."

By not tuning in to the customer's viewpoint, *you* lose, not him. Dr. Denis Waitley, psychiatrist and motivational speaker, writes, "Alarm and resistance as a lifestyle lead to early exhaustion. Emotionally upset individuals literally withdraw all of their energy reserves ahead of schedule and run out of life too soon."

The negative stress you create by losing control of your anger is a drain on your energy, on your concentration, and on your enjoyment of life. It robs you of the very things you need most for your success.

In *Feeling Good*, Dr. David Burns writes,

If you defend yourself from negative feedback in a defensive and vengeful way, you will reduce the prospects for productive interaction in the future. Thus, while your angry outburst momentarily *feels good,*

you may defeat yourself in the long run by burning your bridges...
Your rage... will function as a self-fulfilling prophecy. What you resist
will persist.

Burns adds, "The events of this world don't make you angry, your 'hot
thoughts create your anger." He suggests you ask yourself, "Is my anger useful? Does it help me achieve a desired goal or does it simply defeat me?"

What you *think* about a complaint situation matters. If you can stop your
own anger, if you can control yourself, you can control the situation.

HOW TO DEFUSE A SHORT FUSE

Aroused emotion makes anyone a different person. When a person is red-hot,
"bouncing-off-the-ceiling" angry, the adrenaline flows faster, strength increases by about 20 percent and blood supply to the problem-solving part of the
brain is severely decreased. Do you really want to argue with this person?

New research suggests that expressing anger too freely can actually
make a person *angrier* by giving him an opportunity to *practice* it. As a person
argues, he reviews the situation that originally made him angry. His emotion
builds up again, making him feel as angry as he was when the situation first
happened.

Anger between two people often starts with an issue. But the longer the
anger persists, the more likely it is that the conflict will shift to personality,
general beliefs, and other issues. The original issue becomes secondary as
emotion takes control.

If you lose your perspective, you're going to lose your self-control. You
can never take back what you say in a moment of anger or defensiveness.
That's why you have to stay focused on your goal in complaint situations.

The angry customer in front of you may represent a lifetime revenue of
thousands of dollars to your organization. Do you really want to lose him over
$30, or over protecting your ego?

Training authorities Carl Albrecht and Ron Zemke write,

People do not just buy things, they also buy expectations. One expectation is that the item they buy will produce the benefits the seller
promised. Another is that if it doesn't, the seller will make good on
the promises.

There's only one primary goal in customer complaint situations—to send
the customer away *satisfied*. Sometimes that requires *selling* the customer
something to solve his problem. It *always* requires satisfying his emotional
needs.

What would go through your mind if a customer came up to you and
yelled, "You guys screwed up my account again this month. I'm getting tired
of this."

Your response would probably depend on how long you had been with the company. If you were new, your reaction might be, "What did I do? Will I still have a job in the morning?" If you had been around a while, your response might be, "This customer isn't going to push me around again."

Whatever your response, it would probably be an *emotional* response.

The most frequent mistake salespeople make in trying to calm an angry customer is to try to solve the problem before they've cleared away the customer's emotion.

THE SECRETS OF SELLING:
With angry customers, clear away the emotion *before* you solve the problem.

Salespeople tend to respond first to angry customers by saying something such as, "Could you tell me your name and account number, please." And how does the customer respond? He's likely to scream, "And that's another thing. I've been dealing with you people for five years and no one knows who I am!"

Controlling emotion, yours *and* the customer's, is the key to resolving complaint situations. You can't negotiate at a level of reason until you've cleared away the emotion.

Resolving complaint situations is good training for peak performance sellers because it requires total dedication to understanding the customer's viewpoint. And sometimes it's pretty difficult to be understanding.

One of the most frequent questions I get from women in our seminars is, "What do I say when an angry customer approaches me and barks, 'I need to speak to a *man*,' or 'I want to deal with the boss.'?" These situations are frustrating because it's easy to take these comments *personally*. The seller may either withdraw and lose credibility, or overreact and make the customer angrier.

What customers are really saying in these situations is, "I want to get this resolved," or "I want to feel important." If you can keep your perspective, you can keep your cool.

The most frequent reason for a customer to be angry is feeling *unimportant*, feeling like a blip on a computer screen that has gone haywire. If you think of the customer's comments as *needs* instead of threats, and if you respond with confidence, these people will almost always be satisfied to deal with you.

You might simply say, "I'm sorry you've had a problem. I'm the sales representative for your region, and I'm sure I can help you."

Remember your goal. It's not to *win*. It's to calm the customer and to move him toward agreement so you can meet your objectives. You want the customer to walk away *satisfied*, on matter who was in error.

The issue is *what's* right, not who's right.

Faced with conflict, salespeople too often lose control of their emotions and say something that *inflames* the situation. The first step should always be to clear away emotion. If you can gain control of yourself, you can gain control of the situation.

Most of us are more inflamed by the statements we make to ourselves about difficult situations than by the situations themselves. Changing your interpretation of the situation from "Who does he think he is?" to "Maybe he's having a bad day," or "Maybe he's not feeling well," can give you better control of your own reaction.

Be ready to be friendly at any moment. Don't let your anger make you miss a chance to capitalize on an opportunity for agreement.

Even if your emotions are under control, you won't be able to deal with a customer at the level of reason as long as *he's* blinded by emotion. As long as the customer is angry, as long as there is one more complaint in his mind he hasn't unloaded, the customer isn't going to hear anything you say.

Clearing away the customer's emotion can take a few seconds, or it can take a long time.

To help you take the emotion out of angry customer situations, you're going to learn one technique you can use in *every* complaint situation. The objective of this technique is to help people vent their anger and return their attention to reason and agreement.

This technique has been "scientifically tested" and proven effective through centuries of research in human relations. it's the same technique you learned to respond to objections. *Relax, pause*, and *understand*—the RPU response.

Even before you say a word, your body language will begin to have an impact on your customer. If you look defensive, or if your voice rises, the customer's anger will also rise in self-defense. By talking slowly and softly, so you appear calm and concerned, you'll keep emotion under control.

If you seem *genuinely* concerned, the customer begins to realize that there's no one to fight with. As the Chinese say, "Shaped like water, you can wear away the hardest stone."

First, tell yourself, "I can handle this." Your calm and confident reaction will discourage the customer from trying to overpower you.

Your next response should be to *pause* for three seconds. Three seconds will seem like a lifetime to you, but the customer will feel you're *listening*. This pause also gives the customer time to vent any other complaints that may be on his mind.

If you don't allow an angry person to vent *all* of his issues, you'll never get the person down to the level of reason. He'll be too busy thinking about how to get out those second and third "zingers" he spent the whole evening dreaming up. You won't have a chance to be heard.

The three-second pause also buys you time to think of a response so you won't say anything that makes the customer even angrier. It allows you time for your own emotions to rise and fall again.

AFTER THE CALM

Unfortunately, you can't pause forever. Eventually, you've got to say something, and you want it to be something that *softens* the customer's anger, not intensifies it. But what?

Your first words should send a message you're listening, you understand the customer's feelings, and you're concerned. They should indicate you're taking the customer's concerns seriously.

Calming an angry customer is like reigning a wild horse. You have to ride in the direction he's going in for a while before you can get his attention.

One word will help you think of something to say in every complaint situation. That word is "*understand.*" If you can think of this one word, you'll be able to hang others around it that will calm your customer.

Be sure to say you understand the customer's feelings, not that you agree with his position. You might say, "I can understand why you'd be upset if that happened," or "I can understand why you might feel that way." As you say it, your voice should project confidence, authority, calm, and concern.

By repeating this *relax*, *pause*, and *understand* sequence to each flash of concern from the customer, you'll gradually lower the customer's emotions to the point where you can deal with the *issues.*

If the customer doesn't believe you could understand his feelings, say, "I may not know much about what you're feeling, but if you'd like to tell me about it, I'll try to understand and help you any way I can."

Repeat the RPU response until the customer's emotion has subsided, even if you have to repeat the sequence four or five times. As simple as this technique is, I *guarantee* it will work for you if you don't give up after after the first pause and understand.

Success builds on success. Once the emotion is cleared away, you can deal with the issues.

After you've cleared away the emotion, your first words to the customer should include a stretch benefit such as, "*So this won't happen again,* could you tell me exactly what happened?" Tell him what you *can* do before you tell him what you can't do.

Since most complaints are the result of the customer being made to feel unimportant, tell the customer how *important* he is to you.

Sometimes *humor* can help resolve conflict by changing the customer's expectations for the encounter from the prospect of pending conflict to the prospect of a friendly resolution. One note of caution: be careful that use of humor doesn't come across as belittling, or as indifference to the other person's concerns.

Whenever possible, use the customer's *name*. This helps him regain his sense of importance. He also loses his anonymity, and people behave better when they're known by name to those around them. If I'm identified as Mr. Schneider to those around me, I'm less likely to make a fool of myself than I might be as just another customer.

People also resist less if you can get them to sit down. (They resist least of all if you can get them to *lie* down!) But watch carefully. If the customer won't sit, you need to remain standing so you don't feel overpowered and intimidated. You don't want your body language to appear either threatening or cowering.

In many situations, it's helpful to get an angry customer away from the place where the anger erupted. Often, just the surroundings can set the customer off again. If the potential loss of business is large, or if the customer wants to make a scene in front of other customers, get him away from them.

If you're confronted with an outburst of anger in front of other people, say, "I want to hear everything you have to say. Let's go where we can really talk well so we can get this resolved right for you."

In resolving a complaint, take responsibility for action. Never send an angry customer to someone else as if the problem isn't *your* problem.

To get started, ask questions to make sure you're trying to resolve the right problem. If the problem involves some negotiation, appeal to the customer's fairness, and ask him what *he* would like you to do about the problem. Often the customer will settle for much less than you would think.

While you're with an angry customer, try to avoid "you language" (You claim," You say," etc.). Don't refer to a problem as a complaint. Don't say, "This has never happened before," or promise what you can't deliver.

My mother taught me one of the best human relations principles of all: if you can, take people off the hook and save face for them so they don't have to defend their positions. For years I've watched her get amazing results with upset people simply by saving them from embarrassment by blaming their behavior on situations beyond their control.

People like to know you're trying as hard as you can to resolve the situation. Tell them, "We're doing everything possible to correct this for you," or *show* them by involving a supervisor or making a similar gesture.

If you have to get back to the customer about his problem, tell him why, especially if resolving it will take some time. Stay in communication to let him know you're working on his problem and concerned about it.

These techniques for resolving conflict are taught in most human relations courses because they work. They work in business settings in handling objections and complaints, and they work in personal settings in responding to anger. Some research even suggests these strategies for dealing with anger actually result in less change in your blood pressure than other ways of handling anger.

Dr. David Burns writes, "Although you feel convinced the other guy is acting unfairly, you must realize he is only acting *unfairly* relative to *your* value system. But *he* is operating from *his* value system, not yours."

The feel of success in selling is focused on the *customer's* viewpoint. As a judo seller, that force is always with you.

In the next chapter, you'll learn how to negotiate any sale to your advantage.

10

Negotiating the Sale: Tea Dance at the OK Corral

Salespeople tend to associate negotiation with multi-million dollar sports contracts, shuttle diplomacy, and collective bargaining—with *anything* but their selling.

Selling *is* a negotiation: a negotiation of mutual needs. In negotiation, as in selling, you're a partner in problem-solving.

Every day of your life, you negotiate for time, money, attention, influence, and sales. Deal after deal, issue after issue, comes down to, "If you'll do this, I'll do that."

The choices you make in these negotiations can be the difference between average performance and peak performance. For sellers of big-ticket items like defense contracts or heavy equipment, small differences in the outcome of negotiations can be worth millions of dollars.

When salespeople believe they have less negotiating power than they really do, they often end up losing. They may lose sales by not negotiating effectively, or they may get the sale, but leave their commission on the negotiating table.

You grew up with negotiation; you just didn't call it that. You traded baseball cards, or promised to wash the dishes if you could stay up late. You may have even negotiated with God, hoping the phone would ring for a date on Saturday night.

Now you negotiate issues such as a selling price, your consumer rights, or a two-career marriage.

At work, it is essential to negotiate sales, budgets, performance goals, and complaints. At home, any relationship is a *continuous* negotiation, a series of trade-offs that never ends.

Selling is essentially a negotiation of needs.

Once a salesperson and a customer have agreed on the customer's needs, they negotiate issues such as price, terms, add-on sales, timing of the purchase, delivery, guarantees, freight costs, product features, parts replacement, co-op advertising, support to the customer from other areas of the seller's company, the degree of personal attention or special service that will be offered, and resolution of customer service complaints.

A salesperson may even negotiate with others in his own company for resources, concessions, or back-up to what he has sold. One Forum Group study found peak performance sellers were particularly effective in negotiating with their own support staff for thorough follow-through for their customers on such issues as installation and servicing.

Talking about selling my father used to tell me "We all want the same thing. We all want *more*." However, too many salespeople *assume* their customers and co-workers won't consider any alternatives. Usually they will.

Sales are always in danger of breaking down. As a seller, you have certain needs and see things one way, and your prospects have different needs and see things another way.

Negotiation is a way to resolve these conflicts and reach agreement on mutual goals. It's simply an attempt by two parties to change the terms and conditions of their relationship to better meet the mutual needs of each.

The best negotiators make something out of nothing, creating *possibilities* out of dead ends. The goal of sales negotiation is to increase the options available to *both* parties, giving both more opportunities to meet their needs.

IT'S ALL IN THE MIND

Reaching agreement in negotiation may require a gambler's nerves, an athlete's timing, a geisha's attention, a magician's tricks, and a gentleman's patience.

Think of negotiation as a tea dance at the OK Corral.

Here's what a sales executive in Ohio said to me about his experience in negotiating sales:

> When I started in this business, I was reluctant to negotiate on our contracts. It just didn't seem professional. When buyers told me they needed a lower price I found myself reacting defensively. Now, after twenty years of doing this, I know that by negotiating, I also have opportunities for better deals.

The major obstacles to success in negotiation are fear and embarrassment about the process itself.

Some salespeople are uncomfortable with negotiation because they view it as gaining power at someone else's expense. Some are afraid of angering another person, of *losing*, of feeling incompetent in the negotiating process, or of seeming pushy in asking for money.

What you *feel* affects your ability to negotiate because that feeling is broadcast to your customers. If you withdraw from negotiation because you feel uncomfortable, you won't sell to your potential.

Negotiation is stressful to many salespeople because the process seems to put them in a win/lose situation. They worry that if conflict erupts, they may lose the sale entirely.

It doesn't even occur to many salespeople that their customers might consider more costly alternatives providing extra benefits, or that not taking a firm negotiating stance on price might lower the perceived value of their product.

We're brought up in a world of *seemingly* fixed prices and rules. The truth is, almost *everything* in life is negotiable.

Many salespeople fail to get what they want because they *won't* negotiate, or because they mistakenly believe their customers won't negotiate.

President Lyndon Johnson once said, "I'm a compromiser and a maneuverer. I try to get something. That's the way our system works..."

Negotiation is a process of seeking an agreement "fair" or "unfair"—that *satisfies* both parties. Both parties want something more than they can get without negotiating.

The settlement determines what is fair in each negotiation, based on how much each person values what the other person is offering *at that moment* in time.

Customers *expect* you to negotiate. Some will think less of you if you don't. For example, you could lose a sale by cutting your price too much and too soon. Your soft negotiating stance might raise doubts about the value of your product, or cause the buyer to think you *need* the sale.

WINNERS AND LOSERS

Salespeople *underestimate* their negotiating power. You have all the power you need, if you can help your prospects get what they want. Products are worth what they do, not what they cost.

If a prospect says you have an order if you can come up with the right price, *he's* made the first concession. He wants your product.

Negotiating power doesn't come by *winning*, although one party frequently gains more than the other.

The goal of negotiation is finding the point of balance that results in satisfaction for *both* parties. Publisher Malcom Forbes writes, "It's never a good deal when only one party thinks it is." You don't want to win issues and lose relationships.

Of course, a few negotiations are one-shot, win-at-all-cost affairs. When you're faced with this type of negotiation, you have to take a tougher bargaining stance or be run over. Rewarding tough behavior with easy concessions only encourages more of it. But in selling, one-shot deals are rare.

In most sales, the goal of negotiations is to make the pie *bigger*, not cut it up.

Both parties should feel they've gained something, or the loser will see to it that the settlement doesn't stay settled. In selling, your negotiations are often repeated, and who wants to face someone who's looking for a chance to get even?

So, in addition to considering what you can receive in the negotiation, you should also consider how a loss will affect your customer.

THE PATH TO COMMITMENT

In negotiating, no single action has meaning by itself. Everyone's strategy is dependent on his perception of the rules of the game and on everyone else's strategy and needs, including their *emotional* needs.

Following the six steps of selling described earlier will help you stay in control of the negotiation process. The step-by-step process of feeling successful, developing trust, problem-solving, counseling, advancing the sale, and follow-up keeps you focused on the *customer's* point of view and minimizes resistance to your negotiating positions.

In negotiating, the six steps of selling translate into: believing you can negotiate what you want, developing trust by breaking down the adversary relationship, screening for the customer's viewpoint and for possible options, proposing a settlement, gaining commitment, and seeing that the agreement *stays* settled.

Since emotion and the *perception* of strength are such major factors in negotiations, developing trust may be the most important of these steps.

Research by psychologist Dr. Melvin Kimmel has proven that when two people in a negotiation don't trust each other they tend to

(a) hide their priorities, making it difficult to meet their needs;

(b) hold back key information that could lead to a solution; and

(c) avoid cooperative behavior by settling for compromises that leave both sides unsatisfied.

Trust-busting behavior in the first minutes of a negotiation can poison the negotiating atmosphere for everything that follows. In theses early stages of negotiation, share what you want *for* the customer as well as what you want *from* the customer.

The critical success factors in sales negotiation are:

- The *expectations* of each participant
- The number of *options* you can develop
- *Power,* including advantages in information
- *Communication,* including trust, listening, assertiveness, persuasiveness, and resolution of conflict.

WHAT YOU EXPECT IS WHAT YOU GET

Research has proven that sellers who *expect* to get what they want in a negotiation do get more. That's why kids are such great negotiators: there's no limit to their expectations.

Your job in negotiating sales is to sell the customer out of overvaluing what he'll give up and undervaluing what he's asking for.

The firmness of your belief that you'll get what you want reduces the buyer's expectations. Negotiators assess their probability of success by their *perception* of the relative strength of the other person's position. If that position seems weak, the negotiator drives a harder bargain. For example, if a salesperson gives off signals that he *needs* a sale, the prospect will challenge the salesperson more forcefully on the price.

The more the customer believes you want something, the more you should go out of your way to appear you don't.

THE SECRETS OF SELLING:
If you can't reduce the buyer's expectations, you might as well reduce your own.

Ask for what you want. If the customer doesn't like it, he doesn't have to accept it. And does it really matter if he's a little upset for a while? Chances are, *he's* not afraid to make demands. He's trying to do what's best for him.

Be ready for a strong reaction. The customer's job is to convince you to give him your best price. You may hear, "Hey, I thought we had a deal!" or "That's not even close to your competition!" He may shake his head in disbelief or turn away.

The buyer uses these tactics to provoke an expected response from you, one that *weakens* your position. Like many sellers, you may wind up cutting your price before you're even asked to cut it!

Remove the customer's payoff by not reacting the way he expects, and you'll change his behavior.

It's smart to set maximum/minimum goals for each negotiation. Your commitment to these goals will show in your manner and affect the customer's expectations. Also, without specific goals you may negotiate for the wrong things. You might lose what you really want by taking too firm a stand on a secondary issue.

The opening "feeling out" process is a critical part of the negotiation. You have only *one* opportunity to state your opening position. You don't want to lock yourself into a position you can't live with, or state a position that either inflates the customer's expectations or ends negotiations.

Ask the customer to state *his* interests first. You might say, "Bill, what's most important to you here?" Next, state your interests and your opening position. Get your requirements on the table early so people have time to get used to them. The idea is to get the offers and counter offers under way.

Keep telling yourself, "I know what I need, and I know the *value* of what I have to offer." To be a peak performance seller, you have to *feel* successful.

Start "high" as a seller and "low" as a buyer. Everybody knows this, but not everyone *does* it. If you're going to return on a later sales call with a final proposal, you may be able to "float" a price to gauge the buyer's reaction. If he seems comfortable with your price and wants your product, you can probably hold or increase your price in your final proposal.

If you can, frame the issues and your position in a way that explains how the customer will benefit. Normally, agreement occurs where your position and the customer's position overlap.

As you state your opening position, offer reasons which give it credibility. For example, you might state a precedent such as, "When we sold the property next door, we got $207,000." Use *exact* numbers, not rough numbers, so you sound as though you've given the issue thought.

If you take a particularly firm stand in your opening position, make it clear that you *want* the buyer's business, but your product is *worth* what you're asking.

You can use evidence such as printed policies or prices to support your position: "This is our *published* price." If the buyer tries to use this tactic against you, simply say the policy doesn't apply in this situation.

Give yourself room to negotiate. If the buyer asks, "What's your rock bottom price?," reply, "That depends on what kind of total deal we're able to work out. What did you have in mind?"

When the buyer asks you questions, tell him only what you *want* him to know.

To reduce the buyer's expectations, challenge his opening position. See how serious he really is. Ask him for the reasoning behind his position: "How did you arrive at that figure?" Test his position by asking, "*What if*?" until you learn where he's most flexible.

Now mention some facts that poke holes in his position. You might say, "As you know, I'm limited by the guidelines in our new pricing catalogue."

Sometimes you can use the customer's rationale for his position to support *your* position. For example, you might say, "Tom, is comparable sales price the standard you want to use in these discussions? I agree that it's a fair place to start. Here are three houses that have sold at or near my figure within the past six weeks."

Show concern for the customer's needs by using the "relax, pause, and understand" response to demands. Think of the words "flexible" and "feasible." Your position is *flexible*, and you'll see if what the customer wants is *feasible*.

THE SECRETS OF SELLING:
Make the customer win each concession the old fashioned way. Make him *earn* it.

The outcome of sales negotiations is affected substantially by the *pattern* of concessions. Research has proven you should avoid making the *first* major concession and you should make concessions in small and diminishing increments.

Don't raise the customer's expectations by giving up too much too fast. Make each concession seem as important as possible. When you make a concession, stress your concern for the *customer's* goals.

Watch the *increments* of concession carefully. They're a good indicator of a customer's limits. For your part, keep them *small*. Suppose that as a seller I set my price at $1,500. If your first offer is $1,000 and my first counter offer is $1,200 instead of $1,400, you'll believe I'll go much lower.

It's the customer's *feeling* about the concession that counts. He won't feel he received much if you concede your position right away.

A customer who has to work hard for a small discount may actually be much more satisfied than a customer who gets a bigger discount easily.

When you do make a major concession, be sure to tell the customer he's getting a special deal so he won't expect the same concession automatically the next time.

When you can, use your concessions to close the sale. *"If* we do that, *then* will you buy today?"

As the negotiation progresses, keep increasing your resistance to moving further from your position. Reduce the size of each step toward what the customer wants, to signal that he'll have to work harder to get what he wants.

Make statements that indicate your needs aren't being met. You might say, "That's more than we can afford to discount on an order of this size," or "We need to get to $10,000. You've got to do significantly better than that."

When you concede something, *always* ask for something in return. There's no better time to ask for something than when you're giving something.

For example, you might say, "I can cut the unit price to $3.00 if you take 750 instead of 500," or "We'll accept your figure if you make it for two years instead of one.'

Patience is the key to a good deal. When you hear an offer, don't commit yourself immediately. Wait to see if the customer will go even further.

Silence can be an effective strategy. Without saying a word, you may find the customer *giving* his position away.

If you can find a way to give the buyer only what he really wants, you'll make far fewer concessions. Why make concessions the buyer hasn't asked for or doesn't want?

To keep yourself from giving away too much too fast, work from a checklist of possible concessions by each side and their dollar value. During negotiations, keep track of the concessions that have been made.

Once you've established the expectations for a negotiation, you can begin the creative part of negotiating.

CREATING OPTIONS

Most sellers think of negotiation as a power struggle leading to compromise on conflicting positions. Thinking this way, you're likely to miss opportunities for creative solutions that might work for both parties.

THE SECRETS OF SELLING:
The great sellers keep creating *options* for themselves. The poor sellers run out of options and their negotiations break down.

The more options you create, the more *possibilities* you have for agreement.

If you say, "This is it. Take it or leave it," you're likely to miss the best opportunities for agreement. There's *always* one more option. Instead of saying you can't sell your product for $30,000, you might say, "Sure, you can have it for $30,000, but without some of the features that weren't that important to you."

Creating options is the soul of negotiation, possibility thinking at its best. Make sure the customer knows you're open to a blending of your ideas.

In creative problem-solving, suspend judgment and *build* on the ideas of other people. Say something *positive* about the customer's ideas before you say something negative, so the the good ideas aren't lost simply because one aspect of the idea doesn't work.

In *Getting to Yes*, Roger Fisher and William Ury of the Harvard Negotiation Project argue persuasively that negotiators should focus on the *interests* behind negotiating positions, not on the stands they take on the issues.

They write:

> As more attention is paid to positions, less attention is devoted to meeting the underlying concerns of the parties. Agreement becomes less likely. Any agreement reached may reflect a mechanical splitting of the differences between final positions rather than a solution carefully crafted to meet the legitimate interests of the parties. The result is

frequently an agreement less satisfactory to each side than it could have been.

By focusing on *interests*, the key to negotiating becomes creating as many options as possible that might compensate for differences in interests. The more options you have, the more likely you are to find a way to meet everyone's needs.

For the *right* deal, we're all willing to give a little.

Mark McCormack writes, "If you can take a moment to listen to *why* someone wants to change his mind and then place it in the perspective of the overall relationship, you my find it in your best interest to let him."

To move your negotiations toward "options thinking," state the issues in terms of *needs*, rather than conflicting positions. In a simple analogy, instead of saying, "I have to have the car tonight," to someone at home, you might say, "I need to go shopping and you need to go to the tennis match. How can we work this out?"

Each person understands the problem in his own way, based on his own interests, and that's OK. Focus your problem solving on *how* it could work.

Convert absolute statements such as, "We'll never agree to a delivery schedule like that," into workable issues such as *how often* you deliver, *where* you deliver, *when* you deliver, etc.

To help you think of more possibilities for a settlement, make a list of your interests and your customer's interests as shown below.

At this moment...

I WANT

1. _____
2. _____
3. _____
4. _____
5. _____

HE CAN GIVE

1. _____
2. _____
3. _____
4. _____
5. _____

HE WANTS

1. _____
2. _____
3. _____
4. _____
5. _____

I CAN GIVE

1. _____
2. _____
3. _____
4. _____
5. _____

There's almost always more than one way to get what you want from a sale.

Ask yourself, "What interests of mine do his interests conflict with?" In many cases, the answer will be surprising—*none*. Always leave the door open for options that work for both of you.

NEGOTIATING FROM POWER

The next best thing to having options that enable you to walk away from the negotiation is making the buyer *think* you have them.

Your *perceived* power may give the buyer the impression you can get what you want with or without negotiation.

Power in selling is like a teeter-totter. If one side doesn't get it, the other side will.

Power can be shifted by such factors as deadlines, how much each person needs the other, or what one person knows that the other doesn't. The seller can always increase his power by filling a need.

On a sales call, a salesperson can actually *feel* the power shift as he uncovers a strong need for the prospect to buy from him.

A seller might walk into a prospect's office and discover that because of pressure from the buyer's boss, the prospect *needs* his product by Monday, and he's the only supplier who can meet his deadline. His new power in that situation makes it possible for him to maintain a firm position on his price, or get other concessions.

The more a buyer needs to settle, the less he'll be willing to hold out. The less he needs to settle, the more he'll hold out. You get the worst deal on anything when you *must* have it. Always keep your options in mind.

You can get a feel for your power by asking yourself what both you and the buyer will do if you're *not* able to reach agreement. As promoter Jerry Weintraub writes, "When you have 'go to hell' money it's easy to say "'Go to hell.'"

In negotiation, the key to power is knowing what the buyer *really* wants, what his *real* limits are. What may be worth nothing to one person at a garage sale may be worth $20 to someone else.

I think most salespeople underestimate the value of their products to their customers.

Anything someone else wants is a source of bargaining power. That's why the critical source of power in negotiations is *information.*

If you get a customer to talk about his expectations and demands *before* you talk about yours, you can get a feel for the limits he'll set during negotiations. For example, asking a buyer how much of your product he expects to sell will tell you a lot about how important your product is to him and how far he'll go in price concessions.

THE SECRETS OF SELLING:
Never forget that *information* is power
in negotiations. Get as much information as
you can from your customers, and give
as little as possible.

The key to power negotiation is knowing your customer.

The buyer often wants less than you think. For example, if you're willing to sell for $700, and the buyer speaks first and offers $800, you've saved $100.

Listen carefully for what people want.

Keep a list of the customer's major interests as he talks so you can refer back to them. When a customer states a firm position, ask, "Why is that so important to you?" or "What do you mean?" He's likely to explain it differently the second time, giving you better insight to his thinking.

Power is the result of what people perceive you *could* do to meet their needs or to exercise other options.

Negotiating authority Herb Cohen writes, "All power is based on perception. If you think you've got it, then you've got it. If you think you don't have it, even if you have it, then you don't have it."

Sellers who have *the feel of success* gain negotiating power by influencing expectations. The best defense is a good offense. Cohen adds, "By demonstrating that you don't care 'that much' and that you have other options, you'll have more power."

IN SELF-DEFENSE

In negotiating, you'll be tested by outrageous demands, delaying tactics, attempts to confuse the real issues and suggestions that you "split the difference." In some cases, buyers will even try to reopen negotiations on one issue after you've both agreed to a settlement.

Remember, the customer is only doing what he thinks is best for him. Try not to respond defensively.

What can you do to protect your interests in the face of these tactics?

Start by picking the *right time* to negotiate—not the day the prospect's budget has been cut, for example. Never negotiate a major sale when you feel like "death warmed over," or unexpectedly, when you're not prepared. Simply postpone the discussion until you know what you want and you know your "walk-away" position.

Think through your options *before* you negotiate. Know what you want and what you're willing to give up.

Another key aspect of preparation is determining the right person with whom to negotiate, the person with the power to make the decisions. When a buyer says he's the decision-maker, you've won a concession because he's given up his excuse for deferring a decision to someone else.

Never reduce your power by performing services *before* the negotiation is final. (This is sometimes referred to as "The Call Girl Principle.") The value of services is greater *before* they are performed than after.

Probe for the buyer's sense of urgency. Most concessions occur near a deadline.

If necessary, create an artificial deadline, such as making your price offer good for thirty days, and use it to move negotiations ahead. Sell the benefits of reaching agreement before the deadline.

Don't *assume* the buyer knows your weaknesses. Why give your power away? Conceal your deadlines and reveal as little as possible about your need to settle. And that includes staying in control of your *nonverbal* communication.

If a buyer tries to add a last-minute change to a completed agreement, increase your own demands on some other settled part of the agreement. If possible, stay in control of the information to the end by writing the proposed agreement yourself.

Use your negotiation power. Once you're in a favorable position, *close the sale.*

COMMUNICATING FOR AGREEMENT

For two people to sustain a negotiation, they also have to sustain a *relationship*. Most negotiations break down because of *emotion*, not because of differences on issues. Your ability to control your reactions is a key factor in preventing these breakdowns.

THE SECRETS OF SELLING:
The major obstacle to negotiating a deal is almost always *emotion*, not the issues.

Emotion is an especially powerful force at those delicate moments when the balance of power shifts to your advantage. After all, people want to maintain their self-respect, save face, and give themselves high marks for their negotiating skill.

Try to establish as much common ground for trust as you can. Neutralize the customer's will to "win." Negotiation authority Gerard I. Nierenberg writes, "If the other person sits down, and immediately feels that you are out to beat him, he'll immediately want to beat you ."

Nierenberg suggests that sellers try to build trust by making non-judgmental statements that express "empathy, trust, flexibility, and a willingness to explore alternatives." For example, you might say, "I can see how important it is for you to know you can count on such-and-such happening next year. Can you think of any other ways we might be able to give you that assurance, without our giving up what we need?"

Resolve the easiest issues and the points in which you're in agreement first. Stress the similarities in your position as much or more as the differences.

If it's necessary to take a position that might be damaging to your relationship with the buyer, have a third party explain that position so you're not associated with it directly. This "good guy/bad guy" tactic helps to sustain the trust that's so important to negotiations.

To strengthen trust, listen closely to the buyer so you can piggyback on his ideas whenever possible. Whatever negotiating position he's taken previously, weigh most heavily his *last* response to what you've said. Build a sense of mutual interest with phrases such as, "Let's consider ..." or "How can we resolve this?"

Work around resistance, or *use* it. Instead of defending yourself or your negotiating position, treat the buyer's views as concerns and options. Ask questions about *why* he feels the way he does.

If the buyer steers the conversation into the past or into the future, bring the negotiations back to *now*. Say, "Forget about that. What's the key issue right now?"

Above all, stay in control. Keep thinking of your goal: an agreement that works for you. You never want to walk away from a good deal because of ego.

HOW TO BREAK THE IMPOSSIBLE IMPASSE

In negotiation, everyone fears a deadlock because delays and uncertainty are stressful and sometimes very costly. Most breakdowns in negotiations occur because of emotional obstacles.

Here are some suggestions for breaking an impasse:

- If you're told to "Take it or leave it," ignore the ultimatum and probe for other solutions. Listen to the buyer's *exact* words to see if he really means the words to be as strong as they sound.

- Review the *progress* you've made together toward a deal, and discuss the outcome if you don't negotiate.

President Carter successfully used this tactic when Premier Anwar Sadat of Egypt announced that a stalemate had been reached on the Sinai Settlements. Carter writes,

I was desperate, and quickly outlined the areas of agreement and the adverse consequences to both men if the peace effort floundered at this point. I emphasized the U.S. role in the Middle East and reminded them that a new war in this troubled region under present conditions could easily escalate into World War.

- Agree to disagree until later. Offer to reschedule your meeting, or put difficult issues on the shelf until you have agreement on smaller issues.

- Show your interest in new options. You might say, "There must be some way we can make this work. Do you have any suggestions?" or "What if ...?"

- Instead of challenging a buyer's expertise, use questions to help him see for himself the problems with his negotiating positions. You might say, "I'm having a little trouble seeing how this will work without causing problems in servicing your account. Would you explain it to me again?"

- Take a break or change the negotiating environment. Move to another location, break for lunch, etc.

- Show your concern for the buyer by reminding him how much you think of him or saying things such as, "I know you're tired," before you raise a difficult issue. Look for any signal of reconciliation to build on.

- Find ways for the buyer to *save face* in changing his position— usually "new" information.

- With chronic complainers, indecisive people, and others who try to escape negotiations, force them to refocus on *solutions* instead of problems. Say, "How would you like this to end?"

- Prepare a *written* draft of your suggested plan and ask for criticism. At least, you'll get a reaction that might lead to a breakthrough.

- If you sense that you haven't identified the real obstacle to your negotiations, try a *guess.* "It looks to me as if this is going on...".

- Ask yourself what was said or done that might be causing the person to react defensively, and if you identify something, *try something different.* The impasse may be due to *feelings* rather than issues.

- As a last resort, pull the cord on negotiations. Some business isn't worth having. If negotiations are this difficult in gaining the business, the customer may be so demanding that his business won't be profitable.

AGREEMENTS THAT LAST

Try to resolve negotiating issues so they *stay* resolved. Agreement in the short run usually isn't as important as setting up agreements that will sustain your relationship over the long run.

You have *nothing* if the agreement you negotiate doesn't last.

No matter who seems to have gained the most from negotiation, be sure the buyer leaves feeling like a *winner*, not a loser.

In continuing your relationships with your customers *after* the sale, you'll encounter dozens of issues that have to be negotiated to *sustain* the relationship.

Often, issues remain unsaid and unnegotiated until they result in conflict.

Don't walk on eggs with your customers. Take the initiative to clear up misunderstandings. It's *your* customer, *your* commissions and *your* reputation at stake.

Many salespeople give up on a customer when all they really need to do is negotiate changes in the agreements that define their relationship. Try to renegotiate contracts when the buyer is *happiest*, not at the expiration date of the contract.

Being honest in your dealings is essential in selling. Developing a record of integrity and concern for the customer builds the trust you need to sustain strong relationships.

Still, sometimes telling the truth can *destroy* trust. Some sellers tell *too* much about the deficiencies of their companies or their negotiating position, or express their feelings about the buyer's shortcomings too freely. Honesty should be balanced with common sense and, at times, your "poker face."

Skill in negotiating is one of the great secrets of influence. It can help you close more sales and sustain your relationships with your best customers.

In the next chapter, you'll learn how to focus your time and your energy on the right selling actions, the ones that pay off in more sales.

PART FOUR

Self-Management

CHAPTER 11
The Eye of the Tiger

The fuel that keeps success pumping through your selling is the drive to get what you want.

If you can focus clearly on what you want, you can focus your attention and your energy to get it.

In the movie *Rocky III,* the boxing hero Rocky regains the feel of success by capturing the "eye of the tiger"—a hungry resolve to win back his championship. Salespeople can learn from Rocky's experience. The most important factor in getting to peak sales performance is the *intention* to get there.

Clear goals are more important to your success than knowing how to achieve them.

Your thinking is the one variable in selling you can control. You can create self-fulfilling prophecies of success by directing your full attention to what you want.

Charles Garfield of The Peak Performance Center in Berkeley, California writes, "The single most powerful predictor of success in the long run (is) commitment." He adds, "the ability to stick to it longer than anyone else" is often more important to success than talent.

Top salespeople are *disciplined*, the opposite of their stereotypical image. They have a sense of mission.

Few salespeople make it to the top of their profession without clear goals. After analyzing successful executives in a cooperative study with researchers at Stanford, Yale, Harvard, and the University of California, psychologist Steven DeVore writes,

> These people knew what they wanted out of life. They could see it, taste it, smell it, and imagine the sounds and emotions associated with it. They prelived it before they had it, and that sharp, sensory vision became a powerful driving force in their lives.

183

The peak performance seller focuses his attention, investing his time and thinking where he gets the greatest payoff.

You *choose* how to invest your time and energy. You're responsible for your own success.

You can give your full attention to only one thing or one part of one thing at one moment. You're forced to narrow your field of vision and focus your attention on certain things to the exclusion of others.

Psychologists call this perceptual choice "selective attention."

By focusing their attention, successful sellers learn to *feel* the subtle shifts that take them off track, or lead them down the track at a faster pace. They're able to overpower distractions like self-doubt, sales discomfort and fatigue, and to recognize opportunities other salespeople don't.

Once you've focused your attention on what you want, you're much more likely to find a way to get it. You're more likely to recognize the activities and relationships that will help you achieve success.

Other people also become aware of what you want, and treat you differently.

Salespeople who seem to be "lucky" in life actually attract luck because their minds are focused on well defined opportunities. They've committed their attention to their goal.

Clear goals make you less distracted and more alert to opportunities. Here's what one salesperson with a major retailer in New York told me about focused attention:

> Now that I've committed myself to becoming a store manager, I'm amazed how often I find opportunities to sell merchandise from other departments. Learning new lines and developing a customer following means more to me now. It seems like I know what to do with every second of my time.

Focused attention seems to alert the subconscious to people, factors, and situations that will help you achieve your goals.

Religious philosopher Douglas Steere writes,

> The New Testament records instance after instance of this power of attention achieved in great measure by Jesus. The miserable tax gatherer Zaccheus... sat perched on the limb of the tree when Jesus passed. Jesus seemed to see in this man something no townsman saw, a new man waiting to be born, and the account says that He called out to him to come down and be His host for the day. This power of attention seems to give to those who possess it new eyes...

For the seller, these focused eyes are "the eye of the tiger." And every salesperson can have them.

WHEN YOU'RE HOT, YOU'RE HOT

One word sums up what most researchers think is the prime factor in concentration—*interest*. If you're interested in something, you won't have trouble concentrating on it.

The desire for success stimulates a focused attention on success, which builds the *habit* of success. Actor and champion bodybuilder Arnold Schwarzenegger writes, "The first step is to create the vision, because when you see the vision there—the beautiful vision—that creates the 'want power.' "

This gut feeling of knowing what you want provides the power for your success drive. Your thinking controls the *focus* of that energy.

I'm a confirmed believer in focused attention. I've pictured myself as a consultant, speaker, and author since I was in high school. Even then, I could visualize my satisfaction working with people to solve their problems.

Getting to the point where I could accomplish my goals wasn't easy. It would have been easier to choose jobs that paid more in the short run, but didn't move me toward my goal.

It would have been easier to avoid speeches when I wasn't very good. It would have been easier to have my weekends and evenings free during the years it took me to write this book, while I was traveling from one end of North America to the other.

But in the end, the shortest distance to achieving my goal was sticking to it.

Knowing what I wanted, and focusing my attention, I turned everything I read into an opportunity to research my book. Every seminar I conducted became an opportunity to learn firsthand the problems of salespeople from different industries, and to develop my speaking abilities.

Every day, one step at a time, I strengthened my motivation and my knowledge, and I made my own "luck." It works.

THE SECRETS OF SELLING:
The shortest distance between the way things are and the way you want them to be is *focused attention*. If you have too many goals, you won't have priorities.

The French Chef Julia Child writes, "There are some people who are not hungry enough to be good cooks." There are also thousands of salespeople who aren't hungry enough to be peak performance salespeople.

Not having goals, most salespeople don't have the *desire*, and therefore the *energy*, to pursue peak performance. But anyone can learn to get in touch with what motivates him and use that motivation to drive his selling.

Focused attention to one area of your selling also requires reduced attention to other aspects of your selling. No one can have it all.

Study your goals carefully before you commit to them. Focused attention requires important choices and trade-offs.

Because of these trade-offs, success requires an intense *belief* in the value of what you're focusing on and in your probability of succeeding. This belief becomes a continuous reinforcer to what you're doing.

Management philosopher Peter Drucker writes, "Whenever anything is being accomplished, it is being done, I have learned, by a monomaniac with a mission."

SETTING YOUR GOALS

Goal setting is your first rehearsal for success.

Among salespeople of equal ability, those who set challenging goals for themselves almost always make more sales.

Management researchers and authors Edwin A. Locke and Gary B. Latham write,

> Extensive research based on more than fifty studies has established
> that, within reasonable limits, the harder or more challenging the goal,
> the better the resulting performance. They conclude that challenging
> goals work for the simple reason that people try harder and longer to
> achieve them.

Goal setting *works*. It increases your motivation, forces you to choose priorities and makes you accountable to yourself. Having goals makes it possible for you to succeed more often. And once you've set goals, the *value* of your time is clear.

No one is more interested in your success than you are. Set goals that are consistent with what you want for your life, goals you can get excited about. You'll stay motivated longer if you choose goals that benefit others, too.

Having *written* goals helps. When you write things out, you see what's really important and what isn't because you're forced to make choices.

Most motivation speakers talk about goals in pretty simplistic ways. Goal-setting isn't as simple as it sounds. In fact, it's difficult enough that very few salespeople take the time to set goals for themselves. The process itself reminds them of what they *haven't* done.

Your goals tell you a lot about your self-confidence. A salesperson who lacks confidence can fail either by overreaching or by not reaching high enough.

Some sellers throw away the possibility for success before they even start, by setting limiting or unrealistic goals, or by setting too many.

Every seller needs a good fix on which goals are within his grasp. That's why it's important to examine your past realistically before you set them. Your goals must be believable to you and usually to other people who you need to support you. Don't expect your future performance to be too much different from your past—at least, not right away.

On the other hand, many salespeople don't think big enough. They put an imaginary ceiling on their possibilities.

Even more sellers have big goals and never take action on them. They have no *plan*, no specific steps toward their goals.

If you get the feeling that your goals are *not* really possible to achieve, take another look at them. Ask yourself what you *really* want with each one. Sometimes what you really want is one aspect of a goal, one you can accomplish without accomplishing the whole thing.

As you begin setting goals, start with the longest planning horizon you're comfortable with.

Each of us has our own secret mission. And having a few important long-term goals provides a different perspective on the obstacles and problems along the way. It also assures you that your short term goals are driving you toward a destination you'll be happy with.

Focus your efforts, but not too narrowly. Set *quality* goals for your life as well as quantity goals.

Your long-term goals should be broad enough to be accomplished with a variety of strategies. Peak performers often don't know precisely how they'll meet their long-term goals. They experiment and find their way.

Be specific. If you don't know specifically what you want and by *when*, you may not get enough of what you want, or you may get too much.

Salespeople who want more money, without knowing *how much* more, often trap themselves into losing sight of more important things than money. To be more specific, express your goals as though you have already achieved them: "I'm sales manager for a company with $25,000,000 in sales, and I'm making $100,000 a year."

In *The One Minute Manager*, Kenneth Blanchard and Spencer Johnson write,

> The One Minute Manager feels that a goal, and its performance standard, should take no more than 250 words to express. He insists that anyone be able to read it within a minute... 80% of your really important results will come from 20% of your goals. So we only do One Minute Goal Setting on that 20%.

Limit yourself to three to five major goals at one time.

In my company, we ask every employee to set three to five goals with us each quarter. It's amazing how this focuses energy on the *right* issues.

What opened my eyes was how often I would ask someone to do something, and hear, "I'll get right on it. What priority does it have in relation to the goals I'm working on right now?" The greatest impact of goal setting on the company was forcing me and other managers to constantly reassess our priorities.

State your goals as measurable results, not as activities. They are really descriptions of what things will be like if you succeed.

Your sales goals are more meaningful when you relate them to your personal goals. For example, meeting your sales goals might lead to a promotion you want or to extra money that will buy something special.

Next, translate your goals into the selling actions you need to get those results. For example, a sales representative who works on commission should translate his income goals into sales goals, and his sales goals into goals for the selling activity that will be required.

If possible, get someone to set goals with you so you can encourage each other. Sharing your goals builds in reinforcement, and helps you *lock in* your commitment. But never share your goals with negative people. Their comments only distract you and sap your energy.

You may think your job in goal setting is done after you've set your goals. But that's when it really *begins*. Feedback on your results is what *sustains* your motivation.

At the time you choose your goals, also choose *rewards* for achieving each of them. And always take the reward if you've earned it.

Break each of your major goals into smaller ones that are less overwhelming and easier to achieve. Set a timetable for meeting each of these "step" goals. Without a timetable, a goal isn't a *commitment*. It's a *wish*.

THE SECRETS OF SELLING:
Break your goals into smaller, *"step"* goals, so you focus your attention on immediate action and succeed more often.

With step goals you're saying to yourself, "I'll get X and then I'll go for Y." You're giving yourself an opportunity to reward yourself for *partial* success. And that helps you strengthen your confidence, and make corrections when you get off course.

Don't just resolve to make 200 sales. Resolve to make four sales each week for fifty weeks. Now you've got fifty opportunities to feel good about your progress.

Set specific sales goals each quarter for your top ten customers, your top ten prospects, and your top five referral sources.

Generally, others only reward you for results. You'll make money when you close a major sale, but there are no rewards for the five calls you made to close it. Getting yourself to make those five calls is where your self-motivation needs a boost. Contract with yourself to make those calls and reward yourself.

It's easier to *believe* you can accomplish step goals. Olympic volleyball coach Arie Selinger has his team memorize the names and faces of their opponents prior to key matches:

> Rather than thinking we're playing against, say, Cuba, we think we're playing against this player and that player. This makes it easier to take the pressure. If you think in terms of 'Cuba,' instead of six individuals, it can destroy you.

Always set your working goals slightly higher (but not too much higher) than your actual goals. If a salesperson bases his step goals merely on meeting his quota, he's not likely to make it. Something almost always goes wrong unexpectedly, like your getting sick or the company raising its prices.

Of course, the most important step is the *first* one. It's also the most difficult. When you're not in the mood to get started, it's even more important to set goals.

Review your goals frequently.

Some goals you'll reach; some you won't. Some you'll realize aren't worth the price you're paying to achieve them. And some of your goals will start to conflict with others you've decided are more important.

You may keep your original goals, but have to change the *date* you plan to accomplish them. Most salespeople work on the basis of annual goals, but the only thing special about one year is that the earth travels once around the sun!

Throw out any goal that isn't what you really want any more.

Changing your goals may seem like giving up, or destroying everything you worked so hard to build. It's not. Consider these experiences your stepping stones.

Goals aren't sacred. In fact, you should *expect* them to change. You're always *learning* from your experiences in life, and you may find something you value more. Set goals, and invest yourself in them, so *other* people's priories don't set your course.

As my father used to say, "Don't reinvent the wheel. Just get it moving."

Setting goals begins with *commitment. Almost anything is possible when you really want it.* And believing in something gives you the courage to stay on track.

YOU CAN BELIEVE IN BELIEF

Success isn't achieved suddenly. It requires a commitment every day.

At some point in your selling, the problems of creating start-up energy and momentum give way to the problems of managing the drive for success.

Belief in the probability of your success sustains your motivation and persistence. Belief is an outgrowth of focused attention and *optimism*, the "psychological sweet tooth." The positive attitude that flows from belief is energizing.

The advantage of belief is that whether you're right or you're wrong, you'll have the enjoyment of *thinking* you'll get what you want. And that strengths your motivation.

Belief is important. Merely the suggestion of success can increase the probability of success. The probability of reaching your goals should be so clear to you that you experience almost the same feelings just thinking about them as you will when you actually achieve them. This natural "high" helps you sustain your energy.

To strengthen your belief, replace any thoughts that won't support your goals with thoughts that will. Make any thoughts about what you *lack* a cue for giving yourself positive messages.

Writing for *Esquire,* Keith Thompson explains, "The inner game begins when you come up against what you believe to be your limits."

IS IT POSSIBLE THAT ANYTHING IS POSSIBLE?

The Rev. Robert Schuller writes, "When you've exhausted all possibilities, you haven't. There are almost always more options.

Schuller popularized the term "possibility thinking" as a way to help people recognize their full potential. Possibility thinking can also help you become a better salesperson.

Sales motivation speaker Zig Ziglar says, "Positive thinking won't let you do *anything*, but it will help you do *everything* better than negative thinking will."

No one believed life could exist 2650 meters deep in the ocean at 663'F. But it does. Referring to this discovery in an essay for *Discover Magazine,* Lewis Thomas writes,

> These days we can use all the reasons we can summon for respecting life, lest we fall into the habit of taking it for granted. These bacteria, opening up as they do the possibility that life can take hold in environments quite different from ours, anywhere in the universe, open up as well the possibility that the whole universe may, in a sense, be alive or ready to come alive whenever it feels like it.

The same can be said of your selling. There's untapped possibility in you that can *come alive* at any moment.

Sellers are successful largely because they've developed more options. They ask themselves, "If this isn't possible, what *else* is possible? If I can't make this sale today, what else is possible while I'm here?"

THE SECRETS OF SELLING:
The peak performance seller is both a *possibility* thinker, and a *probability* thinker.

It doesn't take genius to discover new possibilities. The key is to avoid handicapping yourself by *thinking* you're handicapped.

Never reject a sales possibility because you feel handicapped in some way unless you've tried everything to expand your options. Experts in creative problem solving have found it effective to say something positive about an idea before expressing your reservations. The idea is to keep possibilities alive, to *build* on them.

Ask yourself how you'd like things to be, and dream up a plan to make them that way. Build on each idea you have, no matter how abstract or illogical it seems.

Look at your disadvantages and the qualities that make you unique in new ways to see if they might also represent possibilities.

Make a list of the things you say you "can't" do. Then cross out every "can't" that is actually a "won't," or is based on a "should" or a never." Won't simply means you *choose* not to do something, not that it's impossible.

Possibility thinking works best when you take it in *increments*. Some tasks are so big you'd never take them on all at once.

Try making a list of at least three ways to do the impossible. Most goals are attained if you can achieve three more reasonable goals. And just making the list makes the task seem possible. For example, if your sales goal is $500,000, you can make it with ten $50,000 sales, one hundred $5,000 sales, or one thousand $500 sales.

Possibility thinking is finding and creating options for yourself. Thinking of creative strategies to make the sale is one of the great arts of salesmanship.

BE A PROBABILITY THINKER

What could be as intoxicating to a salesperson as possibility? Possibility thinking is the seller's aphrodisiac for success. It's a great help, as long as you recognize the mathematical *chances* of those possibilities and the trade-offs they may require.

The idea you can master *anything* is dead wrong. Any number of choices are possible, but only a limited number are *probable*. We can only do the best we can with what we've got.

Is anyone ever hurt by going for it all and not making it? The answer is *yes*.

Some salespeople waste a lifetime trying to prove the impossible to themselves and to others, selling something they'll never be able to sell. At risk is your self-confidence, your achievement, and your feelings of success.

Newspaper columnist Sydney J. Harris writes, "The person who imagines that 'You can do anything with your life' is just as foolish and futile as the one who believes "you can do nothing with your life...""

Your possibilities are limitless only in the sense that you probably have more choices than you realize.

Explore *all* your possibilities, but choose with realistic expectations or your energies will be drained by your disappointments. Thousands of salespeople have ruined their careers by chasing the big sales that always got away.

Bob Conklin of Personal Dynamics, Inc. writes, "Positive thinking is like driving a race car. In the hands of the skilled, high speeds and exhilarating victories can be achieved. The inexperienced at the wheel, however, can end up smashed against a wall."

In mathematics, regression to the mean usually results in an extraordinary event being followed by a more ordinary one. If you beat the odds once, you're not likely to beat them the next time.

Let's say a salesperson knows that 95 percent of the salespeople in his region require 75 sales calls or more to make quota. If he plans to make only 50 calls and beat the odds, he's playing on the wrong side of the laws of chance.

I'll never tell any salesperson that he can do *anything* he wants. You *can* do more than you've ever dreamed, if you focus your energy on what you do best.

When you're evaluating probability, be sure to factor in what you don't do well, can't stand, and won't do.

Interviewed in *Success Magazine*, author James S. Michener said,

> Discounting the driven man, who might be driven by a wide variety of factors which we sometimes don't understand, it seems to me that the person who succeeds makes some kind of peace with his own capacity, an honest evaluating, and a rigorous analysis—that is, to know what you're good at, to do it, and to hold yourself to very high standards. Self-knowledge, to me, is very, very important.

As you make important choices, ask yourself, "What *else* is possible?" Then add, "Is it probable in *this* situation?" and "Is it worth the trade-offs?" You may be able to make it against the odds, but not without giving up something, usually your time.

YOUR TIME IS YOUR LIFE

Possibility is selective. No one can do *everything*.

How you use your time is one of the critical issues in selling. Too many salespeople start their day late, end their day early, and spend what's left with the wrong prospects. Between two salespeople of equal ability, the one who makes more presentations to the *right* prospects will be more successful.

Most salespeople spend only 5 percent to 15 percent of their time face-to-face with their prospects.

For managers, time management is about *getting* the right things done with people. For salespeople, time management is about getting yourself in front of the right prospects as often as possible.

Sometimes getting better results simply requires investing more time. In selling, that might mean stretching for *one more call*. Joe Gandolfo, who sold over $1 billion of life insurance in one year, says the majority of his sales were made before 9 a.m. Starting early gave him an edge.

Sales motivational speaker Zig Ziglar writes,

> You probably spend the first six or seven hours every day working for everybody *except* yourself... Now wouldn't it be a shame to go top speed all day until that last hour so that you can pay *everybody* else and then run out of steam when you start working for yourself?

THE SECRETS OF SELLING:
Peak performance sellers *make* time for the things that are important to their success. They do the *right* things, not more things.

The average seller looks for better products or for a better territory. The peak performance seller looks for better ways to work with what he's got.

How you spend your time isn't as important as what you *achieve* with your sales time.

There's only one thing a salesperson needs to know about time management: spend your time on the *right* things, the actions that contribute most to achieving your goals. Do what's *important*, what you must do to be successful and feel successful.

Instead of always reacting to what *other* people think is important, use your time to achieve what is important. Ask yourself, "What are my priorities? What will give me the greatest payoff?"

Put everything you do into the context of serving your purpose. To stay on course, occasionally record how you spend your time so you can refocus your attention when necessary.

To free your time for pursuing your most important goals, rank them in order of priority. Give them labels such as A, B, or C, with A representing the highest priority. Ten minutes of your time devoted to an A-priority will bring you more success than 60 minutes spent on something of low priority.

If your time is focused, those ten minutes can be used effectively to move at least one small step closer to completing your A-priority goals. It's the sales-people who get the *right* things done, not more things done, who get ahead.

One study of CEO's shows that one-half of their activities are completed in nine minutes or less. Like CEO's, sales executives have to be focused on their goals to make good use of such fragmented time.

Successful sales executives also learn to say *no* to people who make C priority demands on their time.

Time management is like speed reading. The real key to speed reading is choosing *what* to read, not faster reading of irrelevant material. But, be sure you don't get so wrapped up in being "efficient" that you don't spend time with the *people* you need to be successful.

Above all, make yourself an A priority. It's difficult to stay focused on your goals if you're tired, or if you've forgotten the A priorities in your personal life.

Here are a few timesavers that seem to work well for peak performance sellers.

TIMESAVERS FOR SELLERS
(Do the *right* things, not more things)

1. Sell by appointment, so sales time is *quality* time.

2. Have a pocket-size list of your twenty best prospects with you at all times, so you can use even a few minutes of unexpected free time to strengthen one or more of these relationships.

3. Write a "to do" list each night for the next day, so you're already half-committed to completing it. Do the A-priority items on your list first.

4. When prospects become marginal, change your selling to telephone or mail.

5. Make your sales calls in concentrated, well-planned bursts of selling rather than spreading them out throughout your schedule.

6. Sell to *decision-makers*, and leverage each sales contact by meeting other buying influences or gaining referrals.

7. Do what *needs* to be done, not what you like.

8. Always make *one more call*.

9. Continually refer to your goals and ask yourself, "What's the best use of my sales time right now?"

10. Stay away from other salespeople who *don't* use their time well.

11. Whatever sales actions you choose to take, give them your *full* attention so you get results in less time.

12. Break time consuming sales activities into smaller projects, so you can make progress on completing them without waiting for a large block of time.

13. Give highest priority to closing your best few prospects, developing your key accounts, and adding new, qualified prospects.

14. Don't *over*schedule. You want *quality* time with your prospects, and you want time available to react to key people, inquiries, and other A opportunities.

15. Build a network of referral sources who will sell for you.

16. Respond *immediately* to inquiries.

17. Delegate as many aspects of your selling as you can such as scheduling, follow-up, prospect identification, proposal writing, etc.

18. Qualify ruthlessly the prospects you invest multiple calls on, and do whatever it takes to move your best few prospects from prospect to customer.

19. Say yes to success by saying no to distractions from your goals.

20. Think small—narrow your focus of attention.

Sales time is worth gold. Yet there are times when two sellers calling on the same prospect are better than one. If this selling tactic closes a sale faster, it *saves* you time.

The "double team" pays off best when you're neck and neck with a competitor for a sale, and a senior executive's presence will show your commitment to the account.

This tactic is also useful when you're selling to a buyer with a difficult personal style who might relate better to someone else, or when a technical specialist is necessary to define the customer's needs.

It's essential for you and your partner to *plan* your sales strategy together, and to define the exact role each of you will play on the call.

As you meet the customer, the person who will take the lead should initiate conversation by introducing his partner, and take the seat directly across from the buyer. While the seller is speaking, his partner should face the seller, not the customer, so there is no doubt who is in control.

The seller's partner should take notes, signal the seller regarding subtleties in the buyer's style or objections, reinforce key selling points and provide technical, closing, or negotiating support when necessary.

SETTING LIMITS AND SAYING NO

Instead of saying "no," many salespeople allow their time to be wasted. These salespeople open themselves to painful negotiation, stress, and lost time.

Saying "no" confidently requires being able to say to yourself, "I have another, *higher* priority."

Don't give other people a lot of reasons why you've set your limits where you have. You'll only get arguments why they should be set differently. As you explain your position, stick with your feelings—they can't be argued.

Saying "no" can sometimes be an opportunity to *strengthen* a relationship, but many salespeople lose these opportunities by giving people the impression they've said "no" to them as a person.

How can you say "no" to a customer without weakening or losing a relationship?

Say "yes" to the person before you say "no" to his request.

Start your conversation by saying something positive. Let the customer know you believe he's important to you as a *person*.

Express your concern for the customer's needs by repeating his request: "I can understand why you'd like to spread this over twenty-four months, Tom."

Say what you *can* do before you say what you can't do. If you can say "yes" to some part of the customer's request, start with that.

State your decision firmly but supportively, without long explanation or apology. Be honest and direct.

Try to find something good to say about the customer's request, even if it's only, "Thank you for asking." If possible, suggest some alternatives, and offer to help him pursue those alternatives.

End each conversation with something positive. If you can't do anything for him, at least soften the "no" by indicating you wish you could.

The key in all of this is to say "no" without giving the customer the feeling you're rejecting *him*.

SOME PROSPECTS ARE BETTER THAN OTHERS

To become a peak performance seller, you need a constant pipeline of new prospects. Getting in front of the right prospects is the hard work of selling. There's no simple formula that works for sellers in every industry.

No matter how good you are face-to-face with prospects, you won't get the results you want if you spend your time with the *wrong* prospects—the 80 percent of your prospects who give you 20 percent of your business, or those who can't make a decision to buy.

One McGraw Hill study found that 65 percent of sales calls are made on the wrong person.

Even if you close 100 percent of the time with $500 prospects, your results will only be one-fourth as good as they would be closing 20 percent of the time with $10,000 prospects.

The *right* prospects are usually your current key accounts, your best few prospects by expected value analysis (see below), prospects who pre-screen themselves for you by inquiring, referral prospects, and the centers of influence who give you most of your referrals.

Key account sales authority Mack Hanan writes, "There are three rules for increasing profits on sales. Rule one is to concentrate on penetrating your key accounts. Rule two is to concentrate more. Rule three is to concentrate even more again."

With a little planning, you can replace "cold calls" with hot prospect calls. The objective of your prospecting strategy is to get you in front of the right prospects at the right time.

THE SECRETS OF SELLING:
In prospecting, the *probability* of closing
is as important as sales potential.

One of the most widely used methods of evaluating prospect potential is *expected value analysis*. It's a method for establishing sales priority which combines your estimate of the prospect's *immediate* potential sales volume with your estimate of the *probability* that you can close that business over the next ninety days.

To determine the expected value of a particular prospect, multiply your expected maximum share of the prospect's *dollar potential* times the *probability* that you'll get the business. Once you have an expected value assigned to each prospect, assign an A, B, or C priority to each prospect, and determine how many calls you're willing to invest to get his business.

For example, let's say you have one prospect with an estimated $100,000 potential, of which you can reasonably expect to get a maximum share of $80,000. You also estimate you have a 10% probability of closing. This prospect's expected *value* as a return on your investment in sales time is $8,000. (Remember, these are only ball park figures. The better you know a prospect, the more precise these numbers become.)

If you have a second prospect whose estimated sales potential is $50,000 with a 100% maximum expected share, and whose probability of closing is 50%, this second prospect's expected value is $25,000.

In most cases, you'll do better to call on the second prospect ahead of the first.

One of the side benefits of analyzing your prospects this way is that many prospects who look good in terms of potential don't look so good when you factor in their probability of being a good prospect *at this moment*. And *this moment* is when your selling is taking place!

To assess your probability of closing a sale, ask yourself the questions below. Every "yes" raises the estimated probability of closing the sale.

HOW *PROBABLE* IS THIS SALE?

Is the prospect, or has the prospect ever been, your customer?

Is the time and expense required to obtain the business likely to be minimal?

Is the prospect currently a user of your product, so the sale will only require selection of a supplier, not sale of the concept itself?

Do you know the buyer well, or do you have a third party referral?

Are there any dollar incentives, or immediate problems to be solved, that provide good reasons for the prospect to buy your product now?

Are you selling against light or nonentrenched competition?

Have you met with the prospect to qualify his interest, or has the prospect inquired recently about your product?

Is the timing right regarding the prospect's budgeting process, buying cycle, and availability of money?

Do you have any strong advantages of convenience or price over your competition?

Is the prospect free of distractions such as a merger, a reorganization, or a major company or family event?

Do you have access to all the people who will influence this particular sale, including the *signer*.

Is your track record with this type of prospect good?

Is your unique selling advantage highly valued by this type of prospect?

Is the prospect ready to act to solve his problem?

Will you have access to the information you need to make the sale, including the data to calculate the *financial* impact of your product on the prospect?

The objective in selling is to find *qualified* prospects and move them to a sale in the least amount of time possible. Once in the pipeline, a prospect moves from "C" status to "B" to "A," and, finally to status as one of the seller's *best few* prospects.

Your selling cycle is the *average* length of time it takes to move a qualified "C" prospect to the point of releasing dollars for the sale.

Of the prospects that enter this pipeline, most will not make it all the way through.

Which group of prospects do you think most salespeople make their highest priority? If you guessed their best few prospects, you're right. And that's what they should do.

But which group do most sellers make their next highest priority? They invest too much time trying to move "A," "B" and "C" prospects already in the pipeline on through, causing the pipeline to run dry.

Many of the prospects in the pipeline will move themselves through because of their immediate needs. Others will drop out no matter what you do, because your product isn't right for them at *this* point in time. Only you can put *new*, qualified prospects into the pipeline.

THE SECRETS OF SELLING:
The moment a salesperson stops filling his prospect pipeline, he's no longer pumping success.

Let's assume your sales cycle is three months. If you sell only to prospects already in the pipeline, once you've closed whatever sales you're going to get from them, it will take you three months to make another sale.

If you're experiencing recurring peaks and valleys in your sales, they aren't the result of changes in your luck. They're the result of inconsistent prospecting.

At the same time you're closing sales, you should *always* keep adding prospects to the pipeline.

Most peak performance sellers sell on a schedule. They keep careful records, and know exactly how many completed calls they have to make per week to add the right number of qualified prospects to the pipeline to meet their sales objectives.

Peak performance seller Frank Bettger found he was spending 50 percent of his time in the life insurance business making third, fourth, and fifth calls on prospects already in the sales pipeline, yet only 7 percent of his business was coming from these calls. He decided he was using his time to add new prospects to his pipeline. For other types of selling, the magic number may be five, or even ten calls.

Peak performance sellers are disciplined in their approach. By organizing himself well for prospecting, Metropolitan Life salesman Harvey A. Cook sells $1.5 million worth of insurance each month—*only* on Mondays and Tuesdays!

One of the signs of your maturity in selling is learning to adjust your timetable to the timetable of your prospects.

If the buyer doesn't have the money, if he's overconfident about the success of what he's doing now, or if the politics within his organization or within his family make the timing wrong, the buyer won't buy. On the other hand, if the prospect has a pressing problem to solve, you can sometimes close a sale with very little selling.

The heart of prospecting is knowing which prospects are which, and having enough *new* prospects coming into your pipeline that timing works *for* you, not against you.

For prospecting, you need "the eye of the tiger."

RELATIONSHIP SELLING: DEVELOPING YOUR KEY ACCOUNTS

For every seller, some customers are worth more than others. Their orders, or their influence with other prospects in referring business to you, merit more of your discretionary sales time.

A seller's best customers are almost always his best prospects for additional business—for many sellers, potentially as much as 100 percent more. And they represent potential for high profit margins because of low sales expense, and because the seller's knowledge of the customer's business justifies a higher profit.

I'm continually amazed at how little time most salespeople devote to development of their key accounts. Most salespeople in my seminars can't even *name* their key accounts, so I know they don't have a *strategy* for developing them.

Very few salespeople can estimate the potential *additional* business their key customers represent, or cite any significant difference in their selling to these customers than in their selling to others.

If you consistently do something *extra* for your key accounts, you'll *save* selling time because many of the other 80 percent of your customers will come on referrals.

The relationship seller should be interested in increasing his importance to his customer, in becoming the *lead* supplier. He should also be interested in selling deeper into the organization or family to strengthen his ties for *retention.*

If you don't stay on top of the needs of your key accounts and ask them for more business, your competitors will. And you may lose *all* their business.

The key account has to be viewed in the context of a *continuing* relationship. Over time, you'll probably have to sell many buying influences, and respond to many changes in your buyers' objectives and the way they make decisions. You'll need to know what these buyers depend on most for profits, and how they talk about the financial impact of their problems.

The key to relationship selling is *knowing your customer*. The peak performance seller is a problem *preventer* who knows his customer's problems and objectives.

Salespeople tend to build key account relationships around the people they're comfortable with. That's not enough.

To sustain a key customer relationship over time, you'll need a relationship with *all* the buying influences. This will protect you on sales controlled by different buyers, and keep your position secure even if your key contact leaves.

To reach other buying influences without upsetting your primary contact, ask your primary contact to introduce you to the other buying influences, or try to arrange a group presentation involving everyone concerned.

For each key account ask yourself frequently, "What have we *not* done lately?" and "Am I talking to the right people about the right issues?"

Every seller should have a penetration plan for developing the full potential of each key account including *prearranged* meetings to review the results of the relationship.

Make yourself so valuable as a problem solver that the buyer can't afford to lose his relationship with you.

By focusing your attention on the *right* goals, the *right* use of time, and the *right* prospects and customers, you'll have *the eye of the tiger* in your selling. You'll always know where to invest your sales time, and you'll recognize sales opportunities that other salespeople won't.

In the next chapter, you'll learn how to use "invisible" sales strategies to multiply the impact of your selling.

12

The Invisible Sellers

There's more to selling than face-to-face persuasion. Peak performance sellers also build their sales with *invisible* sales strategies such as orchestrating the environment for sales, developing a network of people who sell for them, and using sales letters and phone calls to expand their sales time.

These invisible sellers can help you close sales and increase *use* of your product.

Selling doesn't take place in a vacuum. Getting things to happen your way almost always requires a little *orchestration*, a little attention to *timing*, and awareness of the *environment* for change.

Other people won't always want to move at your pace. They won't see the same need for change you do. Even if they'd like to change, they may face constraints that make it difficult.

There are times when pushing for a sale only creates more resistance. This is when to *orchestrate*, to use your imagination to influence the environment for change.

The secret to orchestration is meeting the needs of the people affected by change. Describing Secretary of State George Schultz in *Esquire*, Jerome Schector writes,

The key to Schultz is the 'incremental approach'—no forcing of issues or bold strokes. Progression depends on adding one small piece at a time to an existing policy structure... Schultz defuses the most pressing and dangerous issues by trying to remove them from the limelight, depoliticizing them and returning them to the desks of political bureaucracy.

Like most successful people, Schultz knows how to orchestrate, how to use his influence to meet the needs of other people so things get done.

THE SECRETS OF SELLING:
Peak performance sellers get things in order *before* they push for change. There's a right time and a wrong time for every sale.

I've found that my greatest contribution to a client is frequently helping management get a sense of how much change its organization can absorb at one time and what support has to be in place before it can pull off substantial change. Salesmanship requires sensitivity.

Instead of trying to change the buyer's environment, adapt to it and use it. Ask yourself, "What does this organization want *now*?"

Sometimes buyers need your help in developing support for change.

Change has to take shape from what buyers want for themselves, what they're ready for, and what can be supported by the environment.

Any seller who doesn't take the *culture* of the buyer's organization into account is destined for failure. Every organization has its own definition of what's important and merits reward, as well as common beliefs as to *how* things should be done.

Orchestrating a sale may simply require adjusting to the *buyer's* way of doing business, knowing *how* and *when* you and your buyer can operate most successfully.

Eventually, every seller has to develop "maze skill." He has to learn the idiosyncrasies of his buyers, how the buyer makes money, the possible barriers to buying, and how to get around the organization's psychological barriers.

Orchestrating the sale requires knowing the right *timing* for change.

HOW'S YOUR TIMING?

If you ask a successful athlete, salesperson, or actor what separates him from others, he's likely to tell you it's his sense of *timing*: knowing not only the right response, but the right moment to give it. Successful sellers seem to know when to back down and when to move ahead. They know when to invest their energy and resources to the maximum.

Lee Iacoca, chairman of Chrysler Corporation, writes,

> I guess if I had to say one thing about management, it would be that the key is decisiveness... I know people who want to have 100 percent of the facts in... by the time they get all that put together, their decision isn't timely. It may be right, but it's too late, and they get clobbered in the marketplace.

All issues are *not* equally important. Save your time and energy for those situations that really do make a difference.

Selling is like sports. There are only four to five big plays in any game. The decisive moment in any sport is when you *let go*, the moment of explosiveness. As boxer Muhammad Ali used to say, "Float like a butterfly; sting like a bee."

If you press your point in a meeting when you're clearly outvoted, you may lose your leverage for the next big play. Yet some salespeople just won't let go of *any* aspect of the prospective sale.

In *Leaders*, President Richard Nixon writes,

> It is easy for the armchair strategist to conclude breathlessly that the leader must fight and win on this battle or that one, without taking in to account the other battles he must fight. There are times when the one who has responsibility will conclude that the cost of winning a particular battle is too great if he is going to succeed in winning the war.

People can't handle too many changes at one time. The number and timing of changes introduced into a relationship or organization substantially effects the amount of resistance.

You can orchestrate change best by beginning with proposals to which your subject will be receptive. For example, if a woman wanted to move to another home and her husband wasn't quite ready, she would be better off beginning this dialogue by saying, "Let's look at some houses this weekend for *fun*," instead of saying, "Let's buy a new house." In the long run, she would have a better chance of getting her way.

Give buyers time to think about the change you're asking for and become comfortable with it.

You wouldn't ask your boss for a raise the day your company reported record losses. Why would you want to force a buyer into a similar defensive response?

In addition to learning *how* to sell, learn to recognize the cues that tell you *when*.

You'll encounter maximum resistance if you try to sell when buyers are most likely to be resistant—when they're tired or rushed, for example. In selling, you always have to think of the *buyer's* needs.

It's either a good time to talk, or it isn't.

Peak performance sellers back off when the sale isn't there, and make the most of their time with their customers when the timing is right.

If it isn't the right time, is the issue so urgent it's worth losing this sale or, even worse, losing a customer? The smart bet is to orchestrate better timing for your sale.

Some sellers confront their customers over many little things. They're consistently demanding, with no concern for the needs of other people.

When a sale you want badly is being delayed, think of your *goal,* not your emotions. Push too hard, and the defensiveness you might create could block you from what you really want.

The best time to ask for change is when you have a third party in your corner. Building a solid network of support is a key aspect of orchestrating sales.

HOW TO STRETCH YOUR NETWORK
OF INFLUENCE

Orchestrating sales includes building a network of people who will sell for you.

In many areas of the world, you *have* to have a friend to make things happen.

E.T. Hall writes,

They say, 'How could you do business by having a friend? What's that got to do with the bottom line?' As it turns out, it has everything to do with it... all over the world, if you have a friend, you can do anything. That's how the system works.

THE SECRETS OF SELLING:
Who you know will always be as important as what you know. Build a network of people who will sell for you.

Knowledge alone won't get you ahead in selling. Customers also make decisions based on *trust. Who* you know is still an important success force. Personal relationships and business relationships are intertwined. Instead of resisting this idea, accept it, and *use* it to your advantage.

The system *works* because trust and compatibility are important in relationships. People tend to build closer relationships with people who think like they do. And if you disappoint your contacts, or don't live up to your recommendations, you'll soon discover your contacts are gone.

Some salespeople believe there's something degrading about cultivating and using connections. You've probably heard someone say, "I *couldn't* ask a friend to help me make a sale. " Some sellers believe this so strongly that, as they move from position to position or from territory to territory, they leave behind people who could have helped them for the rest of their lives.

Few successful attorneys, salespeople, brokers, or politicians could have achieved as much as they did without building a network of trusting contacts.

Every seller, no matter how high his position, needs a support system.

There are people all around you who can influence your success. They can coach you, and give you access to important resources, contacts, and information.

The salesperson who makes a major sale may be the one who spent several hours getting to know the buyer's friend in another company. One seller's servicing work may run smoother than another's because he has developed relationships in other departments that make it possible to borrow resources or to rearrange priorities to handle his customers.

National sales research has consistently found that one of the key factors that separate top sales performers from average performers is the ability of top performers to gain the cooperation of their own support staff on behalf of their customers.

There's no use being run over while you pretend this isn't the way the world works. Learn how to make this success force work for you.

For every seller, there are people in positions to refer substantial numbers of prospects.

Salespeople in most industries find that 60-80% of referred leads buy, and in fewer calls. Referred leads are also four times more likely than other prospects to refer you to someone else.

In many sales situations, just mentioning someone's name can get you in the door. Even within a specific organization, you can often find a champion for your product who will sell it to the other people involved in the decision, introduce you to the signer, or coach you in how to make the sale.

Your network among these influence centers can have the impact of a sales force working for you free. Yet few salespeople really have a referral sales strategy.

In some industries, with a little imagination, you should almost never have to make a sales call without a referral.

The top retail car salesman in history, Joe Girard, sold more cars than many dealerships—an average of 18 cars a week over 14 years. He attributes at least part of his success to following his "Law of 250," which he believes leveraged his time with each customer into influence with 250 other prospects.

The first step in developing a referral sales strategy is to identify both the people who are giving you referrals now and your best prospects for future referral. As in any form of selling, 10 percent to 20 percent of your referral sources will give you 80 percent of your referrals.

To get started, identify the referral sources who have immediate potential. For example, whom will you be seeing *this* week who might have potential as a referral source?

To help you select the right people for your network, think of a good contact as someone who can do something for you and someone for whom you can do something. You want to invest in relationships you can sustain.

Ask people directly for their referrals. Tell them you need their help. They won't think of it if you don't ask. About 90 percent will say yes, and about 50 percent will actually help.

You have to close the sale for a referral just as you have to close any other sale. If you were calling on a CPA, you might say, "Is there anyone you're working with right now who could use our product?" If your contact thinks of someone right away, ask him if he would mention to his friend that you'll be calling, and ask him why he selected that person and what he thinks the prospect needs.

Be specific about what type of referrals you want; it's easier for people to think of a specific name. For example, you might say, "I'm looking for more prospects like you—people with large homes who enjoy contemporary art," or "I'm looking for mid-size corporations that are having cash flow problems."

THE SECRETS OF SELLING:
The most difficult sale of all is persuading people to do what it takes to sell your product to others. Give your network sales team the information it needs to do a good job of selling.

To do a good job of selling for you, your referral sales team will need good information about what your product does for the customer. Be specific in telling your referral source what you would like him to tell his friends.

Most important, give these people something *they* want in return. Do favors for them, support them in their work, and listen to their problems. Try to give them referrals, information, access to higher-level managers in their own organizations, extra service, whatever seems important to them. In most cases, what they want will be something as simple as your time and friendship. They need someone they can rely on, too.

Whenever you're helped by a referral, make a special effort to acknowledge the referral with a thank you, and tell the referral party how your sales contact went. I think you'll be surprised by how often you'll get another referral at the time you make the thank you call.

Who is in *your* sales network? Take a few moments right now to write down the names of ten people who can expand your possibilities for sales by influencing other people in your behalf.

COACH ME IF YOU CAN

Every peak performance seller is also a *coach*. Once you've identified the key buying influences for a given sale, you may have to focus your attention on coaching one person to help you move your product through the organization.

Coaching is salesmanship, using your relationship to help another person learn something or reach a goal that one or both of you want to achieve.

To make a sale, you may need to coach your customer in *how* to sell your product to other people. To increase his use of your product, you may have to coach your customer in *how* to use it. And every seller has to coach other people in his own organization how to support his selling to his customers.

To succeed, your coaching has to move people from interest in your success to an *investment* in your success.

The customer may have to stick his neck out for you, and persist in championing your product through his organization against strong resistance. To do so he needs both strong belief in your product and *confidence* that he knows how to sell it. Confidence increases motivation.

Coaching is about *learning*, but you coach the person, not the subject.

As Blanchard and Spencer write in *The One Minute Manager*, "People who feel good about themselves produce good results." Coaching the customer requires as much attention to overcoming his fears about his ability to sell, as to helping him learn the benefits of your product.

The major responsibility of a coach is to help the people he coaches believe they *can* be successful. The best coaches work hard to develop a person's *courage* to face difficult tasks.

The seller's role as coach is to sell the customer on himself, to set motivating goals based on what the product means for the customer, to keep the buyer excited about those goals, and to catch him doing something *right* in selling it.

Motivation to learn is the key to learning. You can do an adequate job of coaching your buyer just by providing *encouragement*. Encouragement creates a climate that leads to *trying*.

To get a customer to persist in championing your product, you have to find him reasons for buying that drive him to action. A super seller tries to get others to say, 'Come on, self, let's go.'

Motivation isn't something you do to someone. You can build a motivational fire with *reasons* to act, and you can poke the fire a little to keep it going, but you can't light the fire.

As a coach, you're a learner, too. Your goal is to learn which obstacles might block the customer from championing your product, and overcome them.

If the customer is worried that taking the lead in recommending your product will risk his position with senior management, coach him in how to get other buying influences to champion the product. If he's worried that he won't be able to answer senior management's objections or prove the value of your product, coach him in the sales techniques which have worked for you, particularly calculating the *financial* impact of your product. Better yet, offer to write his proposal for him, or coach him in how to arrange a meeting for you to sell your product firsthand.

HOW TO WRITE SALES LETTERS THAT SELL

Putting your sales story in writing for a prospect clears away confusion and focuses his thinking on your key sales points. Persuasive letter writing is indispensable in making strong first impressions, in following up sales contacts, and helping customers sell your product to other buying influences. It's a cost - effective way to prospect or to sell additional business to your customers.

There's one secret to writing good sales letters, and only one. You have to *work* at selling from the customer's viewpoint.

Very few salespeople invest the time necessary to analyze each situation so their letters are individualized. Even fewer write and rewrite their letters until they're *clear* and *concise*, and *sell*. And almost none invest the time it takes to turn a routine letter into a mini-proposal that might be circulated to other buying influences.

THE SECRETS OF SELLING:
Most salespeople don't write good sales letters so writing sales letters is one of your best opportunities to be *clearly different* and *better* than other salespeople.

The only way you can know if your sale letters are good is to *test* them. For each selling situation you're likely to encounter, develop several versions of your letter and keep track of what works and what doesn't. Over time, you'll compile a resource book of sales letters with a consistently high success rate.

The most important rule of letter writing is *write like you talk*, conversational and to the point with a low "fog index" of reading difficulty. Pretend your reader is sitting across from you and you're talking to him!

Use a simple first sentence to state the purpose of the letter in terms of the *customer's* objectives, and underline the key stretch benefit phrases throughout your letter. If there's nothing to underline, rewrite the letter.

How long should a sales letter be? Long enough to get the job done. If you can make your point "pop" in one paragraph, do it. If you can sustain a strong benefit story for five pages without losing the customer's interest, do it. The final measure is what *works*.

I always apply one final test to my sales letters. For each paragraph, I ask myself, "So what?" from the customer's point of view. If I don't have a good answer, I strike the paragraph from the letter

If you do mass mailings of your sales letters, be sure you stagger them so you'll be able to follow up by phone.

If you're in a business which requires proposal selling, fit the proposal to the buyer. For example, if the buyer is analytical, include a lot of supporting information.

Proposals to senior management should begin with a brief executive summary of the *financial* impact of your product. Keep the meat of your proposal brief so senior executives will read the essentials, at least.

The next time you write a sales letter, write one that *sells*.

DIALING FOR DOLLARS

For many salespeople, their first impression with customers isn't face-to-face. It's by telephone.

Selling by phone, you can increase your *number* of sales contacts.

In telephone selling you rely on the enthusiasm, confidence, and concern in your voice, on quickly identifying the potential and key selling points for each customer, and on customer participation.

Smile, even gesture, to sound "up" in projecting your personality over the phone. (Your coworkers may look at you a little strangely, but so what? It's *your* effectiveness at stake.)

On inquiries, screen for the prospect's name and objectives *before* you talk about your product. Your objective on these calls is to sell an *appointment*, not your product.

Postpone quoting price or rate. You'll lose a high percentage of inquires to your competition if you just quote a price without first screening the customer's objectives and establishing the *value* of your product.

Follow up *immediately*. You have to work harder to make an impression by phone. In selling, a cold lead is a dead lead.

On out-going prospect calls, your objective is to *qualify* which prospects are worth your time. Work from a script for the first moments of the conversation.

Think of yourself as the rejector, not as the rejected. When a prospect tells you he's not interested, *believe him*, and move on to another prospect, but gain permission to call again when the prospects needs may have changed. If you have negative feelings about scripts, those feelings probably have nothing to do with the use of scripts. They probably have to do with *how* you've seen other salespeople *use* scripts to lock their customers out of the sale. Remember, the customer has his script, too—"Not interested," "I don't talk to salespeople by phone," etc.

Most major direct marketing firms in the U.S. ask their salespeople to use scripts so they can consistently repeat the approaches that work.

The script is only your take-off point for creative selling. It has to be *flexible* and it has to be written so it feels natural to say.

Plan not to talk more than fifteen seconds before pausing to ask the customer a question. You'll cut sales resistance dramatically.

As you begin, introduce yourself and gain the customer's consent to explore a benefit-producing idea before you "sell." Start slowly so the prospect can focus easily on what you're saying, then pick up your pace to match his, or to increase his interest.

Signal the prospect you'll use his time wisely be referring to his objectives. Back these benefits up with evidence, such as the experience of someone else who has used your products successfully.

Talk for a few moments, then ask a question—almost any question. Show the prospect you're willing to let him participate in this conversation, that you can be *trusted*.

This demonstrates your interest in the prospect as a *person* and instantly separates you from other telephone salespeople.

If you're like me, what really turns you off is the telephone seller who talks nonstop, who tries to *push* or to manipulate you into seeing him. That's *hard-sell,* not soft-sell.

Since telephone calls are interruptions for the prospect, get to the point *fast* by focusing attention on a few key stretch benefits. "Feature dumping" is especially ineffective in telephone selling.

Record the actual words the prospect uses to describe his objectives and problems, and use them throughout your conversation.

Ask for a specific commitment for follow-up action.

In making appointments, begin by introducing yourself, your reason for calling (his objectives) and your credentials. Mention a third party referral if you have one.

A referral is especially effective in gaining the cooperation of a secretary, a spouse, or other gatekeepers in getting through to the person you want to talk to.

Suggest a *specific* appointment time, such as 10 a.m. on Tuesday, and have another specific time in mind as a back-up.

With a specific time in mind, the prospect usually looks at his calendar and says he's available or he's not available.

Always have a reason for not telling your full story on the phone. Prospects frequently ask, "Can't you tell me what this is about?" This is a way of screening out suppliers or finding an easy way to say "no." Don't play this game. You're likely to mention something the prospect doesn't like about your product before you know his objectives, and before he's sold on the benefits.

I've found that prospects will usually accept valid reasons for not explaining your product such as, "I'll need to know more about your situation," "It would take more time than we have right now," "I have some figures that will help you understand it in less time," or "I'd really like to meet you."

Selling by phone, orchestrating sales, developing a sales network, writing effective sales letters, and other invisible sales strategies *expand your sales time* and *extend your influence*. They enable you to continue selling with impact even when you're not able to be face-to-face with your prospects and customers.

In the next chapter, you'll learn how to overcome your fears and discomfort in selling, so you can do with *confidence* what you've learned *how* to do.

CHAPTER 13

Selling Without Fear

In parts of Asia, elephants are tethered to trees in the early weeks of their captivity.

Pulling and straining, the elephants can't escape. Then their trainers tie them to pegs in the ground, and they don't even try to escape. The elephants learn to be helpless.

It happens to salespeople, too.

When a salesperson has the talent for peak performance selling, but he's not willing to do what it takes to be successful, he's either not motivated or he has learned to feel helpless because he expects only the worst.

Thousands of salespeople have fears about such issues as approaching new prospects, making group presentations, closing sales, or negotiating. Because they see these actions as likely to fail or as intruding on other people, they aren't able to sell assertively.

I've known salespeople who are peak performance sellers in the comfort of their own offices, but who fall apart at the thought of holding the same sales conversation with the same prospect at the prospect's office. This call reluctance is a career-threatening condition which limits what they can achieve by limiting the number of sales calls they are able to make.

Sales research suggests that as many as 80% of the salespeople who fail within the first year do so because their fears keep them from doing enough prospecting.

FEAR AND THE ASSERTIVE SELLER

Fear holds salespeople back, making them feel and act helpless in situations when they're not. As a result, it places an imaginary ceiling on their success.

When a salesperson's fears prevent him from acting assertively in his selling, he also feels more stress.

Fear is the most frequent source of sales and human relations problems. Salespeople allow it to freeze their feelings of success, forcing them to look for those feelings by acting in self-defeating ways.

THE SECRETS OF SELLING:
Ultimately, your fears and discomfort in selling affect the way you're treated by other people. The best way to regain control of your feelings is to refocus your thinking outward to how you can *help* your customer more *right now.*

Think of something you wish you could get yourself to do more often in selling situations, or something you don't try in your selling that you'd like to try. What fears are keeping you from doing what needs to be done in your selling?

The most foolish thing you can say to yourself about your fear is, "It's only in my head!" Hey, that's headquarters for the whole body! Real or imagined, fear affects your performance the same way.

Although fear can spur you to extraordinary achievements and protect you from real threats, for the most part, fear is self-defeating. It can destroy your relationships, and it can cause you to run—at the worst possible moments—from people and from the selling actions you want to make.

Salespeople often learn their fears and discomfort watching ineffective salespeople, or suffering thorough traumatic early experiences in selling or "hard sell" sales training.

Fortunately, since fears are learned, they can also be unlearned. At the least, you can learn to cope with fear so you avoid reacting to every imagined threat.

HOW FEAR TAKES CONTROL

Fear takes control of your selling the moment it blocks your relaxation, weakens your self-confidence, or inhibits you from doing what you know needs to be done.

Most fear is concerned with losing something, such as losing self-respect. Fear eventually leads salespeople to self-defeating behaviors that "protect" them from these imagined threats.

For example, an excessive concern over "looking bad" could lead a salesperson into calling on the wrong prospects, the ones he feels comfortable with, but who have minimal potential for closing.

The negative thinking associated with fear also affects salespeople physically. Anxiety makes it difficult for them to relax, and the body sensations it stimulates are distracting.

You can't focus your mind fully on two things at once. If you're worried about selling to someone who knows more about your product than you do, you're more likely to focus on your anxiety than on the customer and the sale.

The net result of fear is a condition in which the body takes control of the mind. Your heart beats faster. Your mouth gets dry. Your breathing picks up. Your voice and hands tremble. You sweat. You become light-headed. Your thoughts jumble.

Does this sound like a peak performance seller?

The physical response may lead to self-doubt: "I'm no good... What's wrong?" ... "Why am I doing this?" A salesperson may even begin to believe, "If I fail at his, I'll fail at anything I try in selling."

These physical and mental reactions are warning signals to stop what you're doing, and ask yourself what's going on.

You may have learned to believe something that really isn't true.

STAMPING YOURSELF: REJECTED

Even the greatest achievers in selling sometimes confuse rejection of their ideas by others with rejection of them.

Yet all rejection usually means is, "I don't see that the benefits of your idea outweigh the costs for me at this point in time."

One customer likes strawberry while another likes vanilla.

When someone reacts negatively to you or to your sales efforts, it may be *his* thinking that's wrong. And who says his negative thinking is going to *stay* negative?

It's not necessary that you be liked and approved by every customer. If you tried to please everyone, you probably wouldn't please anyone. The desire to be likable can be a liability in selling if you depend on being liked for your feelings of success.

Salespeople who aren't prepared for rejection aren't prepared for success.

Success and failure run along the same circle. Failure is a necessary part of stretching for success.

Even the best salespeople don't make sales half the time!

If you're afraid to fail, you won't have the self-confidence to go all out and give it everything you've got.

Sales motivation speaker Zig Ziglar tells his audiences, "Anything worth doing is worth doing poorly until you can do it well.

Only losers expect instant success. Peak performers understand success comes step by step by learning from their partial successes. If you're not making any mistakes in your selling, you're probably not doing anything!

The same numbers game that leads to rejection also leads to sales.

If you normally make three sales for each ten sales calls, and you've just been rejected seven times in a row, your next three sales calls are likely to result in sales. If you happen to reach another prospect who won't buy, find another one.

Many salespeople worry that if they sell aggressively they won't be liked, and they'll be left alone.

Psychologist Frieda Fromm-Reichman writes, "People are more frightened of being lonely than of being hungry, or being deprived of sleep, or of having their sexual needs unfulfilled."

Actually, peak performance sellers have *more* people in their lives, not fewer. Their ability to solve problems and develop strong relationships constantly expands their network.

Some fears of rejection stem from the belief that salespeople have to be "perfect."

The need to be perfect puts you in a self-defeating double bind. If you don't meet your unrealistic expectations, you'll feel as if you failed. If you do meet them, you won't "feel" your success because you'll have only done what you expected of yourself.

Olympic track champion Jesse Owens once said, "Rejection is only correction."

That's the way peak performers think. They use labels such as "false start" and "learning" in place of "failure." If you're not getting the response you want, make some adjustments.

Successful salespeople view their failures as steppingstones, not as defeats.

The real excitement in selling is *not* knowing what's going to happen. Whenever two or more people interact, you can never be certain of the outcome. That's what makes selling so much fun.

It may *seem* less risky and less stressful to withdraw from the situations you fear, but that reaction usually leads to less self-confidence and to worse sales results.

Science philosopher Julian Jaynes writes,

> There is an awkward moment at the top of a ferris wheel when, having come up the inside curvature, whenever we are facing into a firm structure of confident girders, suddenly that structure disappears, and we are thrust out into the sky for the outward curve down.

At that moment of transition in your selling, you're likely to feel both uncertainty and exhilaration. That's when you have to believe in yourself and do what has to be done.

There's no place in peak performance selling for hesitation or second thoughts. It's when your thoughts get "stuck" that you lose the feel of success.

WHEN WINNERS DON'T WANT TO WIN

Many salespeople make it to the very edge of success—to the point where they can almost touch it—and turn back.

For these salespeople, something always seems to go wrong just when success is within their grasp. Inches from their goal, they begin to feel anxious, and they self-destruct.

Some salespeople won't admit they *want* success. They worry that if they're successful, they'll be *expected* to repeat their successes.

Salespeople also worry that success will cut them off from other people. These salespeople may neatly avoid success by *wishing* their life away and setting unrealistic goals for themselves. Since they don't believe in their goals, they don't *prepare* themselves to achieve them.

Once they fail, they program themselves for failure in the future by saying to themselves, "See, I tried and there's no way I could ever be a peak performance seller."

Most tragic of all, some salespeople back away from success because they believe they don't *deserve* it. Psychologically, it's almost impossible to accept something you feel doesn't belong to you. The feel of success requires feeling good about yourself, believing you *deserve* success.

Together, these reactions to the prospect of success are so common that psychiatrists refer to them as "success syndrome."

Here is how some of the salespeople in our seminars have expressed these feelings:

> I'm afraid if I exceed my quota consistently, my sales manager may start to *depend* on me.

> Even though the bonuses could mean an extra $15,000 for me, I'm really not shooting for district manager. I'm not sure I want my life to change *that* much.

> I honestly think my husband would feel threatened if I brought home too much more in commissions.

These are the *real* concerns of real people.

The greatest danger in allowing these fears of success to control your actions is *indifference*, settling for much less than what you really want for yourself.

Say yes to success. Yes is better than no.

Real success, success based on *your* standards, never hurt anyone. It's *less* lonely and less stressful at the top. Even if more *is* expected of you because of your success, *you have more choices.*

You can choose to return to lower levels of accomplishment, or you can choose to continue your peak performance selling. You can choose from the hundreds of new people and new options that come with success.

HOW TO COPE WITH FEAR

Whatever fears you've learned in selling, now is the time to unlearn them.

Most of your fears will disappear the moment you begin selling for the *customer*, instead of for yourself.

In *The One Minute Sales Person,* Spencer Johnson and Larry Wilson remind salespeople that their "...selling purpose is to help people get the good feelings they want about what they bought and about themselves."

They ask sellers to tell themselves, "I *quickly reduce my stress* because I no longer try to get people to do what they don't want to do." Knowing that what you're doing is *helping*, not intruding, gives purpose to your selling, and relaxes you.

To understand your fears, *explore* them a little. Ask yourself what worries you most. When does your fear occur? Where does it occur? What type of people are involved when it occurs? How does fear get in the way of your success in this situation?

Ask yourself what your *usual* response is in this situations. What do you *tell* yourself that makes the situation seem more difficult than it is?

Recognize your fears for what they are—*feelings*. When you do that, you'll begin to sense you can *do* something about them. You'll probably find you're more afraid of your feelings than of the situations that cause them.

The more you dwell on your fears, the stronger they become.

The key to overcoming almost all fears in human relations is to *stop watching yourself*. Refocus your attention outward to the customer and *his* responses. That's where you'll find the real show.

Speaking about the accident that killed famed aerialist Karl Wallenda, Wallenda's wife recalls,

> All Karl thought about for three straight months prior to it was *falling*. It was the first time he'd ever thought about that, and it seemed to me that he put all his energies into *not falling* rather than walking the tightrope.

When you're experiencing fear, do *something*, anything, that will push your fear outward and overcome your feelings of helplessness. *Act* unafraid, and you'll feel unafraid.

If you're in a sales presentation, and you're feeling tense, take the lead in the discussion. Ask some questions to put your focus back on the *customer*. You're more likely to feel unafraid because you're exerting control over the situation.

You can actually *condition* yourself to cope well with sales situations that frighten you.

By confronting difficult situations in small steps, you can develop confidence and test strategies for coping with these situations. The ability to properly handle small, manageable situations gives you a sense of greater control over more threatening situations.

The way to self-confidence in selling is to *do* the thing you're afraid to do so you get a record of successful experiences behind you. Do it even if you need to have someone along for support the first time you try it.

Our fears tend to be arranged in a hierarchy ranging from the least threatening aspects of our fears to the most threatening aspects. Work your way up that hierarchy, building success on success.

One of the best ways to desensitize yourself to a sales situation that makes you nervous is to rehearse it in your mind over and over again until you're able to imagine yourself acting successfully in that situation.

Fear is a creation of your mind. It's a *learned* response. To stop your fears, psychologists recommend substituting *positive* thoughts for negative thoughts as soon as a negative image enters your mind.

The negative thoughts, "I can't do this," or "He knows I don't know this product well," might be replaced by, "I'm starting slowly today, but I'll get the feel of this sale pretty soon." The negative thought, "I'm not good with people," might be replaced by, "I haven't got the feel for this person yet, but I will."

Thought-stopping will keep you from focusing unnecessarily on what you can't control or what you lack.

I know one therapist who drives a car with a license plate that reads, "So what if?" She teaches her patients that the key to handling most fears is forcing yourself to ask, "How important is this to me, *really? So what,* if it happens?

The next time you find yourself nervously asking, "What if?" when you're selling, add one more word— "*So* what, if?"

So what if your idea isn't right for one particular customer at this time?

You may have met someone who can help you in the future. You may have learned something that will help you make an even *bigger sale.*

Think again of something you want to do in your selling that you're not doing because your fear is holding you back. What's the *worst* thing that is likely to happen if your fear came true?

Probably 99% of what salespeople worry about in selling *never* happens, and the consequences of those things that do happen seldom amount to much.

Some worries are needless because the consequences are small, some because they can be easily resolved if they do happen, and some because you can't do anything about them anyway. Once you put aside those worries, you're free to be an assertive seller.

THE ASSERTIVE SELLER

At one time I didn't believe in assertiveness training. It seemed "soft," unrelated to the hard-nosed financial issues of selling.

I was wrong. In my consulting experience with thousands of salespeople and managers, I've found sales and negotiation problems frequently stem in some way from nonassertive behavior.

Industrial psychologists rate assertiveness as one of the several most important personality traits of peak performance sellers.

Your sales assertiveness is the degree to which you try to *influence* the people and events around you, and the degree to which you can cope with your fears in a selling relationship. Everyone experiences some discomfort from time to time in their selling relationships with customers. The top performers in selling have simply made a personal decision to "jump in the water" and sell despite those feelings.

A salesperson has to be assertive enough to speak confidently and positively about himself and his product, to control his time and the momentum of the sale, to state his intentions directly, to ask the questions necessary to uncover information important to the sale, to set limits and say "no" when necessary, and to cope comfortably with conflict.

If you become more assertive in selling, you'll cut your stress, communicate better, save time, and make more sales.

You'll also feel better about yourself. Since assertiveness makes you more comfortable with yourself, other people also find it more comfortable to be with you.

Acting assertively helps customers get what *they* want, too. The assertive seller solves customer problems faster and helps customers enjoy the benefits of his product sooner.

The *passive* seller loses control of his time. He never gains customer trust or the cooperation he needs from people in his own company to support his sales efforts. His tension, indecision, and changing nature *frustrate* his customers and raise doubts about his credibility.

Worst of all, nothing happens. He never gets *action* on his ideas. The passive seller floats like a jellyfish, responding to the motions of the waves, without moving in a direction of his own.

A salesperson needs concern for making a sale just as he needs concern for the customer.

At the other extreme, the negative stereotype most people hold of salespeople as "pushy" is based on their experience with the *aggressive* seller.

When an *aggressive* seller enters a room, you know right away. You feel pushed, and that's death for a sale.

Aggressive sellers leave their customers feeling as though someone had squeezed their juices dry and thrown away the pulp. They *create* resistance to themselves by pressuring customers, overselling them, overpromising, and selling customers what they don't need.

In the long run, salespeople who don't meet the needs of their customers don't get their own needs met.

Everyone is sometimes passive, sometimes aggressive, and sometimes assertive, depending on the situation. You may be assertive in one aspect of your selling and not in others.

One way to know how assertive you are in selling is to observe the responses you're getting from your customers. Another way is to analyze your comfort with various selling actions and the frequency with which you're able to repeat them.

SCORE YOURSELF ON SALES ASSERTIVENESS

Are you holding back from doing or saying something that's important to your success in selling?

To help you identify the selling situations in which you have the most difficulty acting assertively, take a few minutes to complete the Sales Assertiveness Quiz below.

Reviewing the questions on the quiz will help you understand the impact of your assertiveness on your sales behavior and on your *results*.

THE SALES ASSERTIVENESS QUIZ

Thinking of your selling behavior, indicate how comfortable you felt with each of the selling actions below as they occurred by marking a score for that situation in the box beside it, using the following scale:

> 1 = I felt *very uncomfortable* when this happened.
>
> 2 = I felt *somewhat uncomfortable* when this happened.
>
> 3 = I felt *fairly comfortable* when this happened.
>
> 4 = I felt *very comfortable* when this happened.

If a particular selling action has not happened during the past month, rate it according to how you think you would feel if it happened. If a particular selling action happened more than once in the past month, rate how you felt about it on the average.

After you've rated your comfort with each selling action, write Y for yes next to each selling action you take frequently or N for no next to each selling action you take seldom or never.

1. Ask directly for a customer's business ☐

2. Tell a customer you personally will give him outstanding service ☐

3. Defend your product in the face of a customer's strong sales resistance ☐

4. Ask a customer for sensitive information you need to make a sale ☐

5. Ask a customer to refer a friend to you ☐

6. Ask a customer to buy your product *now* ☐

7. Ask a customer for his name, phone number, and commitment to a follow-up step on an incoming call ☐

8. Tell a talkative customer you can't spend more time with him ☐

9. Tell a customer your product is *worth* the difference in price when your price is higher than your competition's price ☐

10. Negotiate a price with a customer ☐

11. Initiate contact with a customer who you don't know and who hasn't approached you ☐

12. Call a customer after a sale to develop an ongoing relationship ☐

13. Ask for clarification when you're confused about what a customer said ☐

14. Ask a customer the names of your competitors for his business ☐

15. Ask a customer who has given you a lot of business to give you *more* ☐

16. Ask to talk to the person who will release the dollars to buy ☐

17. Turn down a customer's request in negotiating ☐

18. Stay in touch with a prospect persistently on a pending sale ☐

19. Ask a customer to buy your product after he has said no at least once ☐

20. Tell a coworker he does something that inhibits your sales performance ☐

21. Ask your boss for something you need in order to sell at peak performance ☐

22. Control a sales conversation so it stays focused on the customer's objectives and your product ☐

23. Calm angry customer situations and resolve conflict ☐

24. Make positive comparisons between your products and those of your competitors ☐

25. Mention products you're not totally familiar with to your customers ☐

26. Discuss the limitations of your product openly with a customer ☐

27. Ask a customer what concerns him when you sense his resistance ☐

28. Contact other people who will influence a sale in addition to your primary contact ☐

29. Make a definite recommendation to a customer on a difficult buying decision ☐

30. Strongly defend your product to a group of three or more people ☐

31. Display your enthusiasm to customers ☐

32. Delay answering a customer's questions about price until you've determined his objectives ☐

TOTAL SCORE ☐

To find your sales assertiveness comfort score, add up the numbers you've placed in the boxes. Enter that number in the box marked *Total Score.*

The higher your score is above 80, the more comfortable you are in being assertive in selling. The lower your score is below 80, the less comfortable and more stressed you are in being assertive. The highest possible score is 128.

The selling actions for which you rated yourself low in comfort, or marked N for not taking them frequently, are *red flags* for your attention. You should think more about how *frequently* you do these things. If you're not able to act assertively in these situations despite your discomfort, your lack of assertiveness will be the source of continuing sales problems for you, blocking you from peak performance.

If you scored *very* high on the quiz, you might want to ask yourself if you're being too aggressive in your selling.

If you're assertive when you need to be and want to be, you're on the right track.

Think of a situation in which you want to act assertively, but are holding back—maybe one of the selling actions on The Sales Assertiveness Quiz on which you rated yourself low.

Write what you would like to do in that situation in one sentence. Write beside it what you tell yourself that makes that action seem so difficult.

Now, *talk back.*

If you're worried your actions will lead to conflict that will be difficult to handle, tell yourself you can handle it. You *can.*

If you're worried that you might look bad or you'll feel uncomfortable, ask yourself, "So what?"

FIGHTING BACK

In our sales management seminars I frequently ask salespeople to describe one of their most difficult sales or sales coaching problems. After everyone has described his problem, I ask each person one question, "Have you ever directly asked the person to do what you want done?" About 75% of the participants answer, "No."

Many salespeople try so hard to be *liked*, they don't do the one thing their customers and employees like most. They don't tell them what they want.

Don't let this happen to you.

In those selling situations in which you're uncomfortable and you're not acting assertively, *fight back*. Attack your fears step by step.

You'll be a better salesperson, and a better person.

Theodore Roosevelt wrote,

> Far better is it to dare mighty things, to win glorious triumphs, even though checkered by failure, than to take rank with those poor spirits who neither enjoy much nor suffer much, because they live in the gray twilight that knows not victory or defeat.

So what are you afraid of? *Do* what you need to do to become a peak performance seller.

In the next chapter, you'll learn how to make sales with group presentations: how to *speak without fear*.

CHAPTER 14

Selling to Groups: How to Speak Without Fear

I was standing alone in a television studio completely dark except for the lights focused on me. For the first time in my life, I was staring at a cold teleprompter and a full production crew. After years of speaking to warm, friendly, live audiences, this was my first time on camera.

When the floor director said "Five seconds," my heart seemed to take over my brain. In just five seconds, I had to *speak without fear.*

You may never have to speak before a television camera, but you may be asked to speak before a group the *one* time it makes a real difference in your career. Your ability to speak may be the edge that closes your most important sale, or lands you the promotion you really want.

You're likely to find yourself trying to persuade a group many times in your life. As a seller, you have to expect that any sales presentation could become a *group* sales presentation.

Whether you're making complex sales to large buying committees, developing referral sales by public speaking, or selling to a family of retail shoppers, much of your selling will be group selling. To sell in today's world you need the confidence to speak without fear. Fortunately, you can use your success in one-on-one selling to become successful in group selling.

This chapter is about *persuasive* speaking, the type of speaking you do in selling your coworkers, selling your customers, and occasionally, selling an audience.

The ability to speak effectively will set you apart from other salespeople. Businessman Philip D. Armour writes, "There is no other accomplishment which any person can have which will so quickly make a career and secure recognition as the ability to speak."

THE SECRETS OF SELLING:
The power to make people listen to you
is one of the great secrets of influence.
For starters, be yourself.

Think about your use of group presentations in your selling. Can you stand in front of a group and persuade them to take the action you want?

Very few salespeople even *try* group presentation selling, much less become skilled at it. As a result, sellers often miss opportunities to increase the payoff on their sales time, to move a sale involving group decision-making to consensus, or to strengthen their credibility.

Every so often, I unexpectedly ask the participants in our sales seminars to prepare a two-minute presentation to the group. After a few minutes, I let them off the hook and ask them instead to report on how they *felt* when they received the assignment.

Universally, salespeople unload an outpouring of true terror at the thought of speaking to a group. Ironically, once they feel free to be themselves, they speak eloquently about why they can't speak in front of a group.

When you speak, people only want you to be you. They like to feel as if you're talking to them one-to-one. Otherwise, they might as well *read* your presentation or listen to someone else.

The more natural you are, the more believable and interesting you are. And if you can be yourself, you can *relax*.

OH, THOSE BUTTERFLIES!

When you know you have to speak to a group, do you find yourself worrying for hours, even *days*, ahead?

You're not alone. Very few speakers, even the great ones, escape the "butterflies." In fact, you wouldn't be as good without them.

Television news legend Edward R. Murrow called stage fright "the sweat of perfection." The adrenaline that accompanies those butterflies helps you think faster, speak with greater intensity, and release the energy and movement that attracts audiences.

Fear is a healthy response to taking risks such as sharing your ideas with a group. The secret of coping successfully with this fear is to use the accompanying surge of adrenaline in *positive* ways.

Audience research has proven that a speaker's nervousness usually doesn't show to other people. No one knows the difference; no one, that is, except *you*. You're the problem, and you're the solution.

As you speak, your fear tends to run in a self-defeating and continuing cycle.

In your mind, you may actually *see* yourself forgetting what you have to say. By the time you speak, you've programmed yourself to do just that. You feel your heart pound so you say to yourself, "I'm *nervous!*" and you begin to perspire. You say, "I'm *sweating!*"—and your voice begins to waiver. You think, "*They* can tell I'm nervous,"—and your mind draws a blank. You think, "I've failed." And you do.

It's probably not the audience, but your own self-criticism you fear most.

Cary Grant says he felt the same fear almost every night as an actor. "I studied the problem and realized what I had to learn. The audience wasn't making me nervous; I was making myself nervous."

What else would you be afraid of? Forgetting something you wanted to say? The audience doesn't know what you intended to say. Finishing early? They'll love you forever. You can't answer their questions? Simply say you don't know, or throw the question back to the group.

I learned my most important lesson about speaking without fear at my high school graduation from Wirt High School in Gary, Indiana. As student council president, it was my responsibility to give the benediction at the graduation ceremony.

I *knew* I was going to forget the words. Fortunately, my father knew that if I *knew* I was going to forget the words, I would. He suggested that I type the words on a card inside my mortar board.

Sure enough, I forgot the words. I'm sure I was an angelic—looking figure as I took off my mortar board to read the benediction with my head bowed in prayer!

I learned three lessons about group selling from that experience. First, if you *think* you're going to fail, you will. You can't do well what you can't imagine yourself doing well. Second, if things go wrong, the consequences aren't earth shattering. Third, be prepared.

As with all fears, the way to use your butterflies to your advantage is to get a record of successful experiences behind you. Success builds on success.

Volunteer to speak. Ask a prospect to invite someone else to your next presentation. Attend meetings or join an organization where you get a chance to participate in some way in front of a group.

What do people learn when they attend public speaking programs such as those offered by Dale Carnegie, Toastmasters, or Schneider Sales Management, Inc.? They overcome their fear of the unexpected; they discover they have something of interest to say; and they get a taste of success. Of everything they learn, that's what *lasts*, and that's enough to change a career.

Good speakers *practice*, and by practicing, they break down their fear step by step.

Any time you speak to a group, you're likely to have a physical reaction to your anxiety. With practice, you learn to expect it and to control it.

As you're preparing to speak, scan your body for the physical reactions you're expecting. Tell your body to relax any tight muscles. Close your eyes and repeat a soft-sounding word such as "calm" or "relax."

One of the first symptoms of stage fright is short, shallow breathing, which cuts your oxygen flow and weakens your voice. To prevent this reaction, fill up your lungs by taking several deep, slow breaths from your abdomen just before you speak. Focus on *exhaling*. This gives you a sense of letting go.

Think about your *breathing*, or about your *audience*, not about what you're going to say. This is how many athletes and actors stay relaxed before a performance.

Many experienced speakers also go through a short relaxation workout in the few moments before they speak. They may have a success cue that helps them recall their previous successes and relaxes them, something as simple as picturing themselves or another outstanding speaker addressing an audience with great energy and confidence.

Since your hands, arms, shoulders, and the rest of your body are connected, tightness in one area may cause tightness in others. Relax your shoulders and arms by bending at the waist, stretching, and shaking your arms in a rotating pattern until they seem loose. Alternately grip something tightly and relax your hands.

To relax your facial muscles and your voice, yawn, or hum quietly with your lips pushed outward until you can feel vibration in your lips.

THE SECRETS OF SELLING:
Let tension out; don't hold it in. Use it to your advantage in making yourself animated and interesting.

Stand correctly, with your body centered and a slight forward lean. This position will relax you, give you a sense of control, help you breathe properly, and add to your authority.

Stand with your feet apart, in line with your shoulders. Balance your weight evenly from side to side and from front to back, and hold your arms comfortably at your side or in front of you, so it's easy to gesture naturally.

As simple as it is to stand comfortably, most speakers don't do it. Instead, they create unnecessary pockets of tension in their body by distributing their weight unevenly in awkward positions.

TRICKS OF THE TRADE

Experienced speakers *practice* success.

Give your talk in front of a mirror or video recorder, or simply give it in your mind again and again. Using as much detail as possible, visualize yourself as uninhibited, exciting, and effective.

As you practice, imagine yourself talking to one person at a time in different areas of your imaginary audience. Exaggerate your gestures and your voice range. Pause for what seems too long. Hear the applause.

Comedian Milton Berle commented on his preparation for a performance, "Even now, when I play a night club, before I go on stage I will go over everything in my mind. I stand alone in my dressing room, in front of the mirror, and rehearse, rehearse, rehearse what I'm going to say. It's not going to come out that way. I'm going to play the audience, play it glibly, improv, ad-lib. Every show is not the same..."

No sales presentation should go exactly as you plan it. Your selling should always change with the response of your customers. Still, rehearsing your success in speaking works.

Get to the site of your presentation early to get the feel of the surroundings and lose your fears of the unexpected. Introduce yourself to as many participants as possible before you speak. You'll relax immediately as soon as you realize you're talking to real *people*, not to an "audience."

Watch the audience as they gather. Try to guess what their problems might be. To become a good speaker, you first have to become a good observer and a good listener.

Watching the audience gets your mind off yourself and on the *group* where it belongs.

In his book *Winging It: Everybody's Guide to Making Speeches Fly Without Notes,* Keith Spicer describes Hitler's efforts to know what a crowd wanted from him by mixing with the crowd prior to a speech.

> This practice, he found, allowed him to take his audience's "temperature"—to get a feel for its mood, its needs, its expectations. Even with a mainly written speech, he would then adapt his pitch, his rhythm, sometimes even his phrasing, to what he read in those eyes or heard in snatches of talk.

THE SECRETS OF SELLING:
The secret to overcoming the fear of speaking is converting self-concern to *audience* concern.

The more you focus on your audience, the less you'll feed on your own nervousness. Pick out several people in different areas of the room to focus your eyes on. Select people who seem to be enjoying themselves.

Look from person to person, staring straight into their eyes for about four seconds. Don't let your eyes ricochet around.

The most frequent compliment I receive on my speaking is that I give the feeling I'm speaking to each person in the audience, one person at a time. I listen so well with my eyes, after years of training and selling, that occasionally I'll surprise someone in a group by knowing they have a question before they ask it.

You can give people this same one-to-one feeling by holding your eye contact with different people in the group until you've completed a thought (at least four seconds), and then moving on to another person.

Never be afraid to see the group's reaction to what you're saying. Their response tells you how to adjust your presentation so they *will* like it.

Eye contact reduces your nervousness by taking your attention away from yourself and letting you feel as if you're talking to someone one-to-one. It also enables you to see and respond to the audience's reactions, slows down your speaking speed, and gives your listeners a sense of direct communication with you.

To feel brave, *act* brave. The feelings will follow.

Move around and *use* that energy. Be on the attack. Get out and interact with the group rather than stand in one place. Minimize the distance between yourself and the audience.

Think of group presentations as *fun*, as a chance to "do your thing."

THE EYES OF THE GROUP

Actor Jimmy Stewart once said, "I never think of my audiences as customers. I think of them as partners." He'd make a good salesman.

Like everyone, audiences are most interested in themselves. The more you can get them thinking or talking about themselves, the more interested they'll be. And the less you'll feel you're on stage.

Selling to groups is not much different than selling to people one on one. You have to relate your ideas to your prospects' problems, objectives, and feelings. People want to know you have a feel for their problems, even if they don't care for your solution.

THE SECRETS OF SELLING:
Most speaking courses teach you how to get *your* point across to the audience. The real secret in persuasive speaking is to link your ideas to the *audience's* point of view.

I've been involved in many sales presentations and sales meetings where a senior executive turned off his audience by delivering an "economics lecture" to a group that was more interested in knowing, "What's in it for *me*?"

Read the faces in the group for their responses as you talk. You can tailor your message to their needs as you go. Use their words if you can. If you talk to people in *their* language, they'll say, "He really *understands* us. He knew exactly what I was thinking."

If you're working with a small group, relate your ideas to each person or each department represented.

When you don't know what a group wants from your remarks, *ask.* When I make a sales presentation to a small group, I usually begin by asking the group what *their* objectives are before I get into the substance of my presentation. I get them talking.

If possible, I write their goals on a flip chart. And then I look carefully at that flip chart. On that chart is a *new* outline for my presentation—the presentation my *customers* want. I may make the same sales points I planned to make, but you can be sure I'll change my presentation to relate my product to the objectives that are most important to the group at that moment.

Look at your presentation through the eyes of your audience. What's *their* point of view? What's on their minds *today?* What are their problems, their expectations? Do they have any reason to resist your ideas?

Now target the single most important message you want to make to *their* viewpoint.

Here's what a district sales manager said about group selling at one of our seminars:

> I used to make a group presentation and ask if there were any questions. It didn't take long for me to find out there weren't any questions because no one was listening. Now I get people involved all the way through my presentations so they *have* to think about my ideas. This builds their trust in me, too, because I can adjust my presentation to what they've said is important to them.

It's difficult to find time for audience participation in a group sales presentation when you're presenting under tight time restrictions. There's only one way to do it. *Cut the time you talk!*

People don't care, unless they *share.* To sell, you have to get your prospects involved!

WHAT DO I SAY NOW THAT I'M UP HERE?

Now that you're in front of the group, what do you say?

If you haven't thought out what you want to say *today* to *this* group, you're wasting your time.

Well, what do you want to *happen?* What *impression* do you want to leave? You're speaking because you want something from this group.

Ask yourself where the group is now in their thinking, and where you want them to be when you're done. Ask yourself what you want them to *do*.

Whenever you speak, have an *objective*.

The first step in preparing your presentation is to define a single-sentence objective for what you want the audience to *do* when you're done, and a single-sentence message, the central point you want the audience to remember. In other words, build your remarks around the *results* you want.

THE SECRETS OF SELLING:
Never forget *why* you're speaking. You want to walk away with the *result* you want.

To make a persuasive presentation, follow the *six steps of selling* and sell the benefits of your point of view. Group selling is still selling.

Advertising executive David Ogilvy writes,

> When I write an advertisement, I don't want you to tell me that you found it 'creative.' I want you to find it so interesting that you *buy the product*. When Aeschines spoke, they said, 'How well he speaks.' But when Demosthenes spoke, they said, 'Let us march against Philip.'

Choosing the right topic is crucial. Don't speak on a subject you don't know well or can't get enthusiastic about, or one which doesn't meet your objectives. Your time is too valuable. Be assertive enough to shape the subject to what you can do well.

What do you know best? The answer is almost always *your own personal experience*. And that's what people really want to hear anyway.

Talk from your own experience, but organize your talk around your listener's interests. Talk about *them*—their goals, their concerns, and the experiences you've had which relate to them.

The best speaker makes the audience believe that his comments were freshly created just for them. Sell what people want to buy.

To keep your audience from being confused about your objective or message, organize your talk around a few big ideas they can easily remember. A thirty-minute presentation shouldn't have any more major ideas than a five minute presentation, only more supporting information.

Tell the group what you're going to tell them, tell them, and then tell them what you told them. Your key points will come across loud and clear.

TO READ, OR NOT TO READ

Beginning speakers harbor a fear of going blank, of experiencing mental paralysis. To compensate, they tend to either memorize their remarks word for word, or to read them. In the process, they lose their spontaneity and their credibility. Ironically, they also *increase* their chances for drawing a sudden blank.

If you speak without a script, you're more likely to be seen as confident and knowledgeable on your topic. And you're more likely to be yourself. The audience will remember *you* long after they've forgotten your words.

Learn your talk *point by point*, not word for word. Speaking from a mental outline, or even from a wallet size written outline, you won't panic if you skip a line or forget a phrase.

When you memorize or read a presentation word for word, you're likely to concentrate too much on content. The 8 to 10 hours longer it will take you to prepare a written presentation would be better spent thinking about the audience's viewpoint, and practicing your delivery.

Professional actors take years to develop the skill of reading a script so it sounds conversational. Without these years of experience, you're likely to drift into a boring monotone.

To break the habit of reading your speeches, try reducing the theme of your presentation and its major parts to a simple verbal or written outline. Then use a visual image or an easy-to-remember phrase for each part of your outline to trigger your memory. If you're using slides, they can serve this function for you.

As you talk, use this visual outline in your mind as a teleprompter.

Concentrate your preparation for your presentation on associating the key points of your talk with each "trigger" phrase or image. You'll be amazed at how easily the other words will follow for you if you've practiced your presentation.

If you absolutely *have* to read your remarks, mark your notes for emphasis and for frequent pause. As you speak, pause and look at your audience as frequently as possible. If you lose eye contact, you'll lose your audience.

Alternately stress the first and last part of your sentences as you talk. This will avoid a monotone, and add punch to your presentation.

So your reading is less obvious, slide your written pages or index cards from one side of the lectern to the other, rather than turning pages or shuffling notes. And *number* them in case you drop them!

Sometimes you won't have time to prepare what you're going to say. You may be asked to "say a few words" on the spot.

In these situations, your first concern may be that you won't be able to think of anything to say. Fortunately, the audience is with you. They know you didn't have time to prepare, and they want you to succeed.

When you're asked to say something without time to prepare ahead, use your relaxation techniques and follow three simple steps as you walk to the front of the group.

First, choose your own subject, one aspect of the topic you've been given that you feel comfortable with. Second, build a mental outline around the *one* point you want to develop. Finally, buy time to get your thoughts together by talking about the group until you can think of something else.

A memorable speaking style doesn't just happen. You have to *work* at getting the feel of success in speaking.

Before his campaign for election in 1960, even the already persuasive John F. Kennedy listened to recordings of Winston Churchill to learn from the rhythm of his speeches. To become a successful speaker like Kennedy, you have to *practice* projecting confidence, naturalness, authority, energy, and concern for the audience.

HOW TO PUT STYLE INTO SUBSTANCE

In group presentation, you make your point with words, but you make your impact with *style*.

The Rev. Billy Graham tells the story of someone asking Evangelist George Whitefield if he could print one of Whitefield's sermons. Whitefield replied, "You may print it if you put in the thunder, the fire, and the lightning."

Take a risk with your speaking style. Exaggerate what you're feeling with your gestures and voice. Experiment with talking without notes, with adapting more to your audience. You're not going to be loved every minute of your talk, anyway, no matter what you do.

For real impact, get out in *front* of the podium with your audience. *Challenge* the group. This will set you apart from 95 percent of other speakers, and get across the message you're confident in what you're doing.

You won't embarrass yourself. Your natural self-restraints are so strong that the behavior you think of as totally uninhibited will be seen by others as simply more *life* in your presentation.

Let yourself out of your cage. Inside you there's a confident, uninhibited speaker.

The turning point in my speaking came when a friend of mine told me to spend less time preparing the content of my speeches and more time *imagining* myself as an uninhibited speaker, free of scripts and restraints on my natural enthusiasm. She told me I could use my experience better by calling on it naturally to adjust my presentation to what the audience wanted from me.

For my next series of speeches, half of my preparation was spent in mental rehearsal using this new, uninhibited speaking style. The audience reaction was so good that I've never considered returning to my former style.

Your style is what sets off the sparks between you and your audience. Let your warmth and excitement come through. If you're yourself, you'll be *more* persuasive, not less.

Advertising executive David Ogilvy writes,

> Very often, the decisive element in a new-business presentation is personality. I suspect that my own personality has won some contests and lost others, but I believe in letting prospects see who you are, warts and all. If you admit your shortcomings, you're more credible when you

give your strong points. And if someone doesn't like you as you are, chances are it won't be a good relationship anyway.

To put more style in your speaking, mimic the speakers who seem to get good audience response. If what you're doing isn't working, *try something else.*

A common trait of effective speakers is *pacing*, alternating the tempo of their words. The top speakers go at a crisp pace to match their listener's thinking speed, and occasionally slow down for effect.

Top speakers also raise and lower their voices, and speak more slowly over key points and more quickly over minor points.

Watch the responses you're eliciting. If some people are squirming or falling asleep, try something different.

Begin your talk in a low-key manner and build momentum, so you can give emphasis or excitement to your presentation as it progresses.

Pause for effect. A pause makes what you've just said seem more important and better timed. It gives the audience a sense you're speaking with authority. It also gives your audience time to think about what you've said, and helps you gather your breath and your energy to project your voice.

Your audience will remember you best if they think of you as a storyteller.

Help people "see" your talk with stories, analogies, and visual images. Audiences identify their own lives with the speaker's stories. The also like to think they might retell the story later.

Don't be afraid to reuse stories that have worked for you before. Audiences return again and again to hear entertainers, motivational speakers, politicians, and clergy who give the same basic performance or message again and again. They like the *way* it's said.

But don't be *too* slick. If you talk is too perfect, it won't seem customized or believable.

Visual aids can add impact to your presentation, but they work against you if they draw attention away from *you*, or reduce your interaction with the group. Use visual aids to reinforce or "prove" your message, or to save you time in making a point.

Here are some tips on using visual aids to increase the impact of your presentations:

- Talk to the *group*, not to the visual aid.

- *Rehearse* your use of visual aids to minimize distractions and the possibility of errors.

- Never pass an exhibit among your listeners *while* you're speaking.

- Leave visuals hidden until you refer to them. Reveal your point step by step, or uncover the visual after you have created interest.

- Remove your visuals as soon as you're finished with them.

- Express one idea with each visual.

- Make visuals large enough to be seen from the farthest point away in the audience.

FAST STARTS AND BIG FINISHES

The critical moments of any presentation are your *opening* and your *close*. Make them attention-grabbers.

Always have a well-rehearsed opening that will capture attention and get your confidence flowing, and a strong close the group will remember.

Your *first 90 seconds*, and your *last 90 seconds* are so important that they're worth memorizing until you can deliver them word for word, naturally and forcefully. This one step will move your selling from the ordinary to the memorable.

THE SECRETS OF SELLING:
For 90 seconds, *anyone* can be a great speaker. Use your opening and your close to connect with the customer's viewpoint.

Your first impressions begin when you leave your chair to speak. As you walk to the front, show your energy and confidence. Look people in the eye, and act as if you can't wait to share what you know.

In these early moments, follow the Rev. Jesse Jackson's advice on speaking: "You have to struggle to capture the moment. Every preacher does it every Sunday." Use what you've learned about the group's current interests to capture the moment.

Listen carefully to what is said in the few moments before you speak. There's almost always something that will give you a bridge to your audience.

As you begin, pause for several moments to get "the feel of the group" and to get their full attention. Now, get them *involved*. Get right to their self-interest.

Stress the benefits of listening to you. Talk about their objectives and problems. Promise to tell them an inside story of how they can get something they want. Dive right into an interesting story, a personal experience. Ask them a question or force them to react to a startling statement. But get them *involved*. Whatever you do, be different from other speakers. Be yourself.

Unless you're especially good with humor, don't open with jokes. Very few people can tell jokes with the right timing and without stumbling over the punch line.

The best humor is *spontaneous* humor, the kind that comes naturally from what other people have said. Most groups respond well to speakers when they tell jokes on *themselves.*

If you expect a lot of resistance, talk about that resistance in your early remarks. Defuse it. It won't seem like such a big deal if you're willing to talk about it.

Build toward your close throughout your presentation. Then stop at the *height* of audience interest, not at the bottom, particularly if you want action at the end of your presentation.

As speech writer Jack Valenti says, "It's very difficult to make a bad speech out of a short speech."

As you move into the final moments of your remarks, summarize your major points by relating them to the group's objectives. This is the time to speak to the *emotions* of the group. More than what you said, your audience will remember how you *understood* them, how you *moved* them.

Rest your case on *one* key point, one strong line that people can focus their memory on. *Burn* it into their minds.

Your final words should be clear-cut in asking the group exactly what you want from them. What is it you want them to *do.*

TAKING CARE OF BUSINESS

Have you ever talked just a little longer than you were supposed to, just so you wouldn't have to answer any tough questions? C'mon. Admit it. Almost all of the salespeople in our seminars admit they've done it before they learned what they were missing.

If you haven't left time for questions, you haven't left time to *close the sale.*

Questions are symbolic of the major fear of most speakers, the *unexpected.* Yet handling questions is your *second opportunity* to make your sales points.

THE SECRETS OF SELLING:
When the presentation stops, the real *selling* begins.

The question and answer period is your one chance to smoke out group resistance to your ideas so you can answer it firsthand. If you can get the group involved, they'll think more fully about your ideas.

As you answer questions, relate your answers to the central message you want your audience to remember, or the action you want them to take.

To get participation started, look at the person most likely to say something *positive* and say, "There may be some questions, " or ask, "What else would you like to know?" and wait.

Normally, there will be a long period of silence, followed by an almost popcorn-like series of questions. Keep your answers short so you'll have time to get as many people involved as possible.

If there aren't any questions, ask the group questions about their reaction to specific points you made in your presentation, or summarize your major points again. You might say, "The question I get most often with a group like this is ..." and make your point.

While you're being asked a question, think only of the *question*, not of the answer.

Repeat each question to the entire group and direct your answer to the full group. This buys you time to think about your answer.

Show *concern* for the questioner's viewpoint, but rephrase each question the way *you* want to answer it. For example, if you're asked why your price is so high, rephrase the question this way, "The question is: 'What *more* do you get for the small difference in price?" Don't ask for approval of your rephrasing of a question, or of your answer, or you'll never get past the first few questions. Answer, and look away to the next questioner.

If you don't know the answer to a question, don't bluff. Admit it. No one expects you to know everything. But before you do that, try a technique used by most professional trainers. Throw the question back to the group to answer. You might say, "That's a good question. What do the rest of you think about this."

To move a group toward consensus and action, look at the decision-maker (the one everyone else looks at), and ask, "What do you think? Will this work for you?" Now you've got a dialogue that can lead to action.

In a group presentation, the mix of participants can result in sales resistance, due to the opposing agendas of those in attendance. Their internal conflicts may be a barrier to group consensus. To break these obstacles down, focus discussion on the points on which they all *agree*, and look for the one person who can get the decision made without total consensus.

One of the keys to group selling is getting the *right* people to attend your presentation—your allies and the person who can approve the release of dollars for your product.

If you're speaking to a large group, but still want to get people to take action by signing up for something, bring someone with you to handle that step. Otherwise, you're likely to get tied up with prospects and many of the people who are interested in a next step will leave out of frustration.

After the group has left, focus on your *successes*. What did you do that got the responses you wanted? How did you feel as you did those things?

The more you explore your successes, the faster you'll build your confidence and the more likely it is you'll repeat them.

Selling isn't easy. That's why you can never lose sight of your *goals* and your *possibilities*.

Rev. Schuller tells the story of the jogger's hill in his community. As he's pushing himself to make it up the hill he tells himself, "that hill is a toughie. *But it can't get any tougher—I can.*" So can you.

By practicing the skills in this book until you have *the feel of success in selling*, and setting goals so you *want* to excel, you can make success happen.

Parting Thoughts

The feel of success in selling is simple.

Sell with *purpose*. Center your selling around the *customer's* objectives.

Spend your time with the *right* prospects, then build those contacts into problem-solving *relationships*. Repeat what works, and try something different when what you're doing isn't working.

Help people understand the losses they're incurring now, and the *benefits* of changing. Ask for customer action.

Selling is so simple that most sellers know how to sell intuitively. But selling isn't *easy*. Most sellers just aren't *willing* to do what it takes to be successful. Out of lack of confidence or motivation, they hold back from effective selling.

Although the issues in selling will always be the same, *you* can be different. You can change your thinking so you consistently operate in the ways which work best for you. This will strengthen your relationships and increase your sales.

Whether you're selling for dollars or selling your ideas, *you* make the choice of what you achieve in selling.

You already know may of the ways you operate most successfully with people in selling. Your challenge is to avoid the tension and self-defeating thoughts that block your *use* of those successful selling tactics.

If you're relaxed enough to recognize your *successes*, you can repeat them. If you can recognize what isn't working, you can *try something else*.

The feel of success in selling begins with confidence in your potential success. You can't lead a calvary charge if you think you look funny sitting on a horse.

You won't build a track record of successes until you have the confidence to *try*. They key factor in selling is the *desire* to excel.

Day by day, the story of your selling and your effectiveness with people is unfolding. No matter how your story plays out, it will have a happy ending if you can *feel* your success along the way so you can sustain your energy and your selling drive.

The people you sell to are the building blocks for your success. If you can meet *their* needs, you can meet your own.

In the next few weeks, your selling may actually get worse as you try to use the selling skills you've just read about. There's no one "right" way to sell that works for everyone. You'll have to experiment and decide what works best for you. You may feel awkward and strange. But the more you *believe* you can be successful using these sales strategies, and the more you keep your eye on your *successes*, the sooner you'll become a peak performance seller.

As you try new ways of selling, find the success in *every* selling situation, even if it's only that you've *tried* a new approach, or learned something.

These small successes will give you the energy and confidence to *sustain* your success and take you higher, one step at a time.

There's a dimension to selling beyond the sale that many sellers never seem to find: the sheer *joy* of meeting people and developing relationships, of solving problems and being of genuine *help*, of pushing your limits and discovering your potential. Selling is *fun*.

I wish you the feel of success.

                                                    Jim Schneider

INDEX